THE MIRACLE CODE

Elevate Your Mind to Heal Your Body

HOLLY STOKES
Master NLP Coach, Hypnosis Trainer

The Miracle Code
Elevate Your Mind to Heal Your Body

Copyright ©2024 HOLLY STOKES. All rights reserved.

No part of this book may be reproduced in any form or by any mechanical means, including information storage and retrieval systems without permission in writing from the publisher/author, except by a reviewer who may quote passages in a review. All images, logos, quotes, and trademarks included in this book are subject to use according to trademark and copyright laws of the United States of America.

Published by:
Wisdom Within
Publishing Salt Lake City, UT 84044

In Association with:
Elite Online Publishing
63 East 11400 South #230
Sandy, UT 84070
EliteOnlinePublishing.com

ISBN: 978-0-9847663-2-1 (eBook)
ISBN: 978-0-9847663-1-4 (Paperback)

QUANTITY PURCHASES: Schools, companies, professional groups, clubs, and other organizations may qualify for special terms when ordering quantities of this title. For information, email info@eliteonlinepublishing.com.

All rights reserved by Holly Stokes and Wisdom Within Publishing.
This book is printed in the United States of America.

Disclaimer:

The content contained in this book is not meant to diagnose, treat, or cure illness or disease. You are advised to continue following the advice of your qualified mental health and medical care practitioners. You are advised to continue taking your medications and see that they are properly supervised by your prescribing medical personnel as reducing or stopping medications can have severe and life-threatening consequences.

The health information presented in this book is intended only as an informative resource guide to help you make informed decisions; it is not meant to replace the advice of a physician or to serve as a guide to self-treatment. Always seek competent medical help for any health condition or if there is any question about the appropriateness of a procedure or health-related recommendation, consult your qualified health practitioner.

Readers are responsible for adopting any strategies illustrated here at their own risk and are encouraged to take responsibility for their well-being and health outcomes. Each person is unique, and each person's mind-body-spirit system is also unique. The strategies that worked for one person may not work for every body. You are encouraged to take responsibility for your own healing journey by creating awareness with your mind-body-spirit system, developing respect and understanding of your own body, and finding your own intuitive answers.

While this work is the authentic experience of the author, the names have been changed or partially represented to protect privacy, and permissions granted to include their stories.

Bonuses

For more information and free resources visit
TheBrainTrainerllc.com/book

Contents

Chapter 1: Life of Adventure 1

Chapter 2: Life Crashes In 8

Chapter 3: The Mind-Body & The Placebo Effect 17

Chapter 4: My Message: We Can Heal 25

Chapter 5: Armed with Optimism 35

Chapter 6: I Love Prednisone or Do I?. 44

Chapter 7: Dare to Believe in More. 58

Chapter 8: Meditation as Medicine. 69

Chapter 9: Disappointment Asks Us to Refocus 75

Chapter 10: Wisdom Through Multiple Perspectives . . 83

Chapter 11: Elimination Diet When Body Says No. 90

Chapter 12: Rheumatologist & What Should I Eat? 94

Chapter 13: Listening to Your Body & Intuition 106

Chapter 14: Connecting with Your Intuition 120

Chapter 15: Journaling: Ask the Questions 126

Chapter 16: Synchronicities Show Up: Gluten-Free Living. 132

Chapter 17: Healthy Lifestyle Classes. 140

Chapter 18: Self-Reflection to Notice Patterns.........151

Chapter 19: Recoding Stress Triggers & Fears........156

Chapter 20: The Body Responds to What You Think . 166

Chapter 21: Food Sensitivities as Stress Patterns.......174

Chapter 22: Positive Intentions of Cravings..........183

Chapter 23: Irritable Bowel Syndrome:
           Mind-Body Stress..................... 193

Chapter 24: Acupuncture As Energetic Modality 201

Chapter 25: Healing the Heart......................206

Chapter 26: Fibromyalgia as Stress & Pain Habits 215

Update Mental Blocks through ART to Love Process . 232

Chapter 27: Transforming: I Don't Want to Be Here .. 238

Chapter 28: Every Life Has Rapids.................. 248

Chapter 29: Surprise, Full Body Hives!.............. 253

Chapter 30: Support Groups - Battle of Beliefs....... 262

Chapter 31: Life Upturned Again.................... 273

Chapter 32: Healing Beliefs Encoded in Spirit 279

Chapter 33: Sabotage with Sunlight................. 286

Chapter 34: Back to the Hospital....................296

Chapter 35: Gratitude: A Forgotten Medicine....... 303

Chapter 36: Awakening to Joy 311

Chapter 37: Remaking a Life 315

Chapter 38: Kidney Transplant List 319

Chapter 39: Asking the Mind-Body for More Answers . . 324

Chapter 40: I Hate You Tango 331

Chapter 41: Process: The Wishing Well Meditation . . . 346

Chapter 42: Recovery Meditations 350

Chapter 43: Resolving Sabotage of the Mind 355

Chapter 44: The Grand Intelligence of
              Mind-Body-Spirit. 367

Chapter 45: Full Circle at The River's Edge 377

About the Author Holly Stokes 385

Summary of Mind-Body-Spirit Resources: 387

References & Resources 390

CHAPTER 1

Life of Adventure

I opened my eyes to the blue sky of the early morning hours and the sunlight, hearing the birds and the rush of Oregon's lush green Umpqua River. The majestic pines stretched up to the sky encircling our small camp on the river's edge. The emerald green waters whispered hints of the day's upcoming adventures, bidding us to anxiously hustle our morning.

"Coffee's on!" yelled a fellow guide from the kitchen area, waking the guides so we could get on the river early. This was training week before the whitewater rafting season would start where we were honing our Swiftwater rescue and river guiding skills.

I unwrapped myself from the sleeping bag and stretched to greet the sun, feeling my lean muscles tight from the day before, breathing in the fresh air and ready for the adventure of the day. Today we would take on "Pinball" and "African Queen," some of my favorite rapids of the Umpqua River. This was my life, May through September as a whitewater river guide in the Northwest.

I made my way to the kitchen; it was still the early morning hours and dawn was breaking. Martin stood by the camp stove, setting out the cups and plates, the coffee was hot and the two other guides were relaxing for the moment with cups of coffee before the bustle of packing up camp. Martin started adding bacon to the griddle for the morning fare.

"Good morning Martin," I said cheerily as I reached for a cup and adjusted the spout of the coffee pot to fill it with the liquid sunshine. "How are you doin' today?"

"Just another day in paradise," Martin smiled. "No job can compete with this," he waived his hand at the scenery, the boisterous river lined with cottonwoods. Martin, our trip leader, had short brown hair, glasses, and a pleasant face that lit up with his smile. His glasses had that hue of dirty smudges in the morning sunlight as he tended the sizzling bacon on the griddle.

I reached for some creamer to add a little bit of heaven to the dark coffee in my cup and sipped. "Ooohh the coffee is strong today."

"Of course, want to know a secret? If you want your camp to pack up quickly, double the strength of the coffee," he smiled.

"Well it tastes amazing, but maybe it just tastes better out here," I said.

"Coffee definitely tastes better out here," he winked.

"Oh, what's that on your arm?" Martin asked, pointing to my left upper arm.

"Huh?" I turned my arm to look. A purple and blue mottled mass wrapped around my bicep. It was bright and emphatic, an angry bruise.

"I have no idea," I breathed out.

"Didn't you have a big bruise on your leg last week too?" Martin asked while scraping the eggs out of the pan.

"Yes, I did. I still have traces of it," I looked down at the green fading mark on my thigh.

"You might want to get that checked out," Martin said. "We need you in top shape for the summer. Promise me you'll get that checked out."

My mouth twisted, "I'm an herbalist, I don't need no stinking doctors." I hated going to the doctor and I rarely needed to.

"Promise me," said Martin as he looked at me sternly.

"Fine, I'll get it checked," I said as a twinge of concern started to twist in my gut. I had been feeling unreasonably exhausted lately during my morning jogging, it was probably nothing.

The whitewater season would start soon. The days would fill with waking up to blue skies and morning coffee, then ushering clients into the big blue rafts filled with the sounds and splashes of whitewater as we conquered the rapids. I felt so lucky to be on the Northwest's emerald green rivers and summer camping at the river's edge.

The outdoor life was not new to me. Sleeping under the stars was a way of life, my way of life. Before white water guiding, I was a wilderness counselor with at-risk-teen therapy programs. I loved sleeping out under a blanket of stars and waking up to the baby blue sky in the morning. And yep, sometimes there was a mosquito or two that would find the small breathing hole of my mummy bag and buzz me awake, but it was totally worth it. I loved those morning hours, waking up to nothing but fresh air and the expansiveness of the whole world right outside my sleeping bag.

We busied ourselves with coffee and breakfast before breaking down camp. *This was the life,* I thought. *Everything was finally coming together. I had just moved in with my boyfriend of three years, John, who had 5 beautiful acres outside of Vancouver, Washington in the wild Northwest woods. He was so sweet, he too was an outdoorsy adventure guy. I had the best job in the world. Every day I invited clients into my blue rubber boat, an open-air office with 360 views that city skyscrapers couldn't touch.*

Life was good. Damn good.

After breakfast, we loaded up our boats with all the gear for the trip, and we pushed out into the water. The morning was clear and fresh, a thin layer of dew and the water was glass, so calm and quiet. But the quiet wouldn't last because I knew what was ahead.

Just downriver was the biggest rapid of this stretch of the river. Watching the horizon line of water, it all appears calm as glass, but you can hear the impending roar of the waterfall that turns into chaos and then the bottom drops out from underneath. *It's so interesting how quickly the river can change.*

As I pushed my paddle into the water, I thought, *I need to be in top shape to run these rapids. I had noticed feeling more tired than normal. Perhaps I should double my morning running routine or maybe Martin was right, perhaps I should go see a doctor.* The day of sunlight, whitewater, and splashes took over.

It felt like my life was really coming together. Before whitewater guiding, I had worked in wilderness therapy programs for ten years. As wilderness guides and counselors, we led small groups of teens into the backcountry of Utah, with only the gear in our backpacks. Life is much simpler living out of a backpack, each day we packed up our campsite and hiked to new destinations.

Every week, psychologists came in for therapy sessions with the students and then the psychologists would tell us guides what each student should be focusing on during the week, so we could help them through their psychology homework. But even though the youth knew what their issues were, I saw them continue to struggle. Even though they knew their patterns, they still couldn't change them.

I was fascinated with psychology. I recognized the choices we make are not just about the present moment, but really influenced by our past history. There is more going on in the mind than just the present moment. I got to see first-hand how the patterns of the mind affect how we see ourselves and how this affects the choices we make even on a daily basis.

I watched some kids make changes in their attitude and elevate their confidence and communication while others really struggled. I got to see first-hand how the psychology of what we think and feel determines our choices and behaviors.

For ten years, I walked the trails with the kids. I loved the outdoor life, hiking to places off the beaten path, turning a corner to find rock art of ages past etched into canyon walls. Over time, however, the week-on-week off schedule of the wilderness programs became wearing. I found it hard to build a life outside of 'the trail' and so I decided to go back to school to finish my degree in Psychology.

I started back to school at a local college in Bend, Oregon. This would be my fourth attempt at school, yep. It wasn't because I was a bad student, in fact, I got all A's in high school, except for one C which still irked me. I think I just didn't have the patience for taking a bunch of classes that didn't seem applicable to life, I didn't really see the point. And my love for the outdoors gave me itchy feet, whereas being cooped up in a classroom all day sounded too dull and routine.

But this time going back to school was different because I could see what I wanted out of it. I could see the light at the end of the tunnel. I knew I wanted to help people and the road to psychology was the map. During the winters, I was studying, reading books, and working through college classes. And to keep my hunger for wilderness fed, in the summers I was a whitewater rafting guide on Oregon's amazing rivers.

Once I had finished my coursework at the local college, I transferred to Portland State University in Oregon. Living in Portland was an easy fit, I was closer to John's place and the Deschutes River where I guided was about a 90-minute drive away.

Yes, life was really coming together. I was finally finishing my degree in psychology and graduating in a few months. I had just moved in with John to his land of pine trees, meadow, and sunlight. And I had the perfect job of sunshine, splashing water, and excitement every day while being outdoors on the scenic Oregon rivers.

I really didn't have a clue about the rapids of life ahead that proved to be my fate and my future. It is so interesting how quickly the river can change.

CHAPTER 2

Life Crashes In

John brought the black truck to a stop in the parking lot of the wellness clinic. He looked over at me in the passenger's seat with his blue eyes and short dark curls at his temples.

"At least you'll get the results of the tests today so we'll know what's going on," he said.

"It's probably nothing and everyone is just worrying," I replied. Still, it felt good to have him there with me.

"Well, we will get the results and then we'll get a plan, and we'll figure it out. We'll figure it out together," he said very practically. He took my hand and gave it a reassuring squeeze.

John and I had met when we both worked in the wilderness therapy programs, hiking out on the desert of Bend, Oregon with a small band of troubled teens. We shared a love of the outdoors, the simplicity of nature, and we both loved working with the youth. It was so satisfying to watch them develop emotional awareness and resilience, improve communication skills, and grow their self-esteem.

As wilderness backpackers and counselors, each day we hiked to new places, finding the earth's hidden treasures: an iced-over pond at the top of a red rock desert or petroglyphs, the traces of a people long ago calling out from the sandstone. It was a time filled with adventure, blue skies, and heartfelt campfires where we as guides and the teens shared life's challenges in therapy circles under the stars.

John and I had started dating then and we found an easy connection with each other. Over the past few years, he had become my confidante, my rock, my best friend and we just finally decided to cohabitate. It felt comforting that he had wanted to come with me to my doctor's appointment.

We sat across the doctor, in her white lab coat and sparse office. She peered over her silver-rimmed glasses, her lips in a downward turn of concern, "I got the test results back," she said. "Holly, I'm afraid the lab work shows you have the markers for an autoimmune disease."

My brow furrowed with confusion, "What is that? What does that mean?" I asked. John and I sat across the large metal desk on the edge of our seats. His hand wrapped around mine tightly.

"Lupus is an autoimmune disease," she said. "It's why you've been having the skin rashes on your face, the low energy and exhaustion. Autoimmune is where the immune system gets confused and it doesn't recognize the self, so it starts attacking your body's own tissues. There are about a hundred autoimmune disorders, and each type of autoimmune condition is defined by the symptoms and how it affects the body. For example, in Chrone's disease, the immune system attacks the colon: in Hashimoto's, it attacks the thyroid: in Lupus, it attacks the body's soft tissues, skin, and organs."

"You have Lupus. This is why you've been getting that rash across your face and why exercise has been exhausting," she said.

"So what does this mean? I stammered. "Do I just take antibiotics or something?"

"No, it's not like that. Lupus is a chronic illness, an autoimmune condition. We don't know what causes it and there is no cure. It is a degenerative disease."

"What do you mean there's no cure?" My mind went foggy with confusion. "And what do you mean degenerative?"

"Well there is no definitive cure and it's expected to get worse over time," she said.

The doctor continued, "The suggested treatment is to suppress the immune system with medications and hopefully keep the immune system from attacking your tissues. But there are also natural treatments we can try."

Could this really be happening? I thought. *I had always been super healthy. I was a backpacker and whitewater guide for crying out loud.* The fog swirled around my head at the surreal situation.

The doctor continued, "You also need to know there are things that can make it worse, causing your immune system to flare up and attack your body. Twenty years ago Lupus was terminal, but now most people with Lupus can live a full life if they manage the illness. It can however be life threatening if you have a flare-up, so it is important to manage it."

I could feel my mind pushing back, *'Well I'm not most people'* came an inner voice in the back of my mind, like an arrogance switching on. I was certified as an herbalist, I knew the body could heal "incurable" diseases. I heard the words the doctor was saying, but it all seemed so unreal, like a daydream or someone else's movie.

The doctor continued, "Exercise can aggravate your immune system and so can sunlight, even to the point that it's life-threatening. An overexposure can cause a flare-up, aggravating your immune system which could then attack your organs."

My stomach twisted in a knot. "What does this all mean?" I stammered as my world began to spin. My hand attached itself to the corner of the desk as if I could somehow stabilize my reality. John's hand covered mine with a gentle squeeze, it felt good to know he was here with me.

Dr. Nelson continued, "You shouldn't be a river guide anymore, you can't be out in the sunlight and when you go running, you are aggravating your immune system causing the condition to flare up. That's why you feel exhausted when you run because it excites your immune system which overreacts and then attacks your skin. This is also why you've been breaking out in a rash. I recommend you stop running too, any overexcitement could cause a flare, causing your immune system to attack your organs and even kill you."

I was stunned and speechless. Her voice had a distant tinny quality as if it was a recording. "Only mild exercise is recommended, like walking, don't exhaust yourself," she said. "Also stress can cause a flare up, so minimize your stress and don't push yourself too hard."

"Let's talk about treatments," she continued. "Prednisone is the recommended treatment to get the immune system under control and reduce inflammation, there are also natural treatments that we can try."

"Well of course let's try the natural treatments." I could hear my voice shake as I stumbled over the words as I saw my future cloud over with no rivers, no running, no sunshine. *The river season would be starting in just a few weeks maybe we'd get it figured out by then.*

The doctor continued, "Firstly, I recommend doing more thorough testing." She made a few recommendations and scribbled some notes, we wrapped up the visit and left the office.

The heaviness of the conversation followed John and I back to the parking lot. Dark thoughts of a future without sunshine started to creep in. True I lived in the Northwest where it's cloudy more often than not, so cloudy days were not foreign to me, but a life without sunshine, rivers, and running?

It was as if I was an actor in someone else's movie.

"We'll get through this," John said as we walked to the truck, he wrapped me up in a warm hug of reassurance and we climbed in and buckled up.

Seeing John beside me, I was reminded of the countless days on the trail, hiking 5-10 miles a day, seeing new destinations in the backcountry, and leading our small band of teenagers across the desert. I had always been super active and healthy, a degenerative diagnosis didn't make sense.

Although we had kept the love of nature alive between us, life certainly changed when I decided to leave the trail life and head back to college. During the winters, I attended college, and then during the summers I continued whitewater guiding on the Oregon rivers. *I was living my idyllic life and the river season was just about ready to start, but now this?*

How could this diagnosis be real? How could this be my life?

John's presence was comforting as we drove on the familiar road framed by the lush green of spring growth and the brightness of sunlight filtering through the leaves. As we drove home, confusion swarmed as my mind tried to contemplate what was happening. *What did this diagnosis mean about my life and would I be* able to work the rivers this season? And if I couldn't, how would it affect my future?

How could this be? How could I live without sunlight and rivers? Adventuring in nature was more than therapeutic, it was nourishing to my soul. *The outdoor life was more than a job, it was my passion. I lived it, I breathed it, it was who I WAS. And now I had to hide from the sunlight?*

I couldn't imagine a future with no sun, no backpacking, no hiking, no fun. It felt like a cruel twist of fate. *I'd always been a nature girl, a wilderness guide, and outdoor lover. How could this be the end of all that?*

The doctor's words echoed in my mind on repeat, 'An overexposure could cause a flare, causing your immune system to attack your organs and even kill you.'

John took my hand in his as we drove, lending me reassurance and support, which shifted my mind out of the heavy swirl of thoughts. *Maybe John was right, maybe we could figure this out.*

There is no cure, echoed in Dr. Nelson's words.

Well, they just don't know where to look, I thought. *They don't know what I know. Western Medicine is only one opinion, but there are other valid natural health approaches.*

I had certified several years before as a Nutritional Vitalogist and Herbalist. I understood the therapeutic benefits of herbs, natural foods, and the synergy of nature. I had studied in-depth nutrition information and learned to use food and plants as medicine, I had experienced first-hand the magic of natural cures. I had collected and dried wild herbs, mixed up formulas, and made ointments. I had made plant extracts and even created a Herbal First Aid Kit when I worked at a health food store in Eugene, Oregon.

My passion for natural health practices was also fueled by the psychology courses. In my Health Psychology class, we talked about a new holistic model of health, recognizing the multiple factors influencing our health and well-being, it's called the Bio-Psycho-Social model of health. This integrative model recognizes that our biology, even our biochemistry is affected by our psychology. Psychology is simply the study of what we think, feel, and do. So even the thoughts we think and the feelings we feel affect our biology. Then too, even our social relationships can affect both our biology and psychology, they are all interrelated and affect each other.

I was also recently certified as a Clinical Hypnotherapist and Neuro Linguistic Programming Practitioner Coach, which looked at deeper layers of our thoughts, habits, and patterns of the mind and how they affect our choices. By peering into and understanding our inner meanings, we can shift our inner world to create change in our lives. I learned the tools to help people create new habits, change cravings, and even transform the brain habits causing addictions and sabotage, there must be things from NLP and hypnosis I could implement as well.

Somebody must have figured out how to work with health and healing. I wasn't willing to give up so easily, at least not without trying everything I already knew I thought. I had seen first-hand amazing results using herbal remedies, I had heard of remarkable recoveries with NLP and hypnosis, and I could be my own experiment.

Armed with optimism and determination, I set my mind to smug. *I got this. I can figure it out.* With John's support and reassurance, maybe something more was possible than a future of debilitating illness and pain.

CHAPTER 3

The Mind-Body & The Placebo Effect

I wasn't always a believer in Hypnosis. In fact, I have a healthy inner skeptic, my mind asks, *"Is this true and does it apply to me?"* I had thought hypnosis was fascinating, but was it really real?

I remember one Health psychology class where I learned just how much the mind can affect the body through the placebo effect. I watched spellbound as the documentary highlighted the research explaining that a consistent percentage of people taking a fake pill (a placebo with no chemical compound), will show an improvement in symptoms just by the power of belief.

The modern world has known about the placebo effect for almost 300 years. In fact, because of this phenomenon, just thinking you are taking medicine even though it's a placebo or sugar pill can affect 50% or more of research results just by this power of belief.

Other factors and even small details can influence this placebo effect as well. For example, if the administrator wore a white lab coat, the placebo effect results would rank higher for participants. Or if the person giving the pills had a clipboard, the effect would be even higher still. Even the color of the placebo pill can affect the results. Red placebo pills often have a stimulant effect, whereas blue pills have a sedating effect. Research also found that if the administrator knew which participants in the study were getting a sugar pill or the real medicine, it would skew the results of the study even further.

Because of this phenomenon, science now uses the double-blind testing method, where none of the participants of the experiment know if they are getting the placebo or the real medicine. Even the person giving the pills doesn't know who is getting the placebo or the medication until the unveiling the results at the end of the study.

Since 1962, for drugs to be proven effective, they need to be scientifically tested and show results above the placebo effect to prove they work. The placebo effect can account for 50% or more of research results. But if the pharmaceutical being tested passes the results of the comparative placebo group, the drug is deemed effective. Some drugs are getting approvals on very slim margins, even at 3% above the placebo group, which could actually be margins of error.

As we continued to watch the documentary, one segment even showed a double-blind study of knee surgery treatments. In this study, Dr. Bruce Mosely, a surgeon in Texas was performing a two-part arthroscopic surgery for addressing crippling knee pain and wanted to know which part of the surgery was more effective. The first part entailed rinsing out debris of the joint and the second part was a process of smoothing out rough cartilage in the joint. He enlisted the help of his colleagues to set up the study to compare the two processes of the surgery.

He was informed that in order for the study to meet scientific research guidelines, he would also need a placebo group. The placebo group participants in the trial would receive no surgery, but be treated as if they were getting the procedure. They then set up the clinical trial with three groups, the first group included participants getting the surgery where they rinsed the knee of debris, and the second group had the procedure of smoothing out the cartilage. The third group of participants was the placebo surgery group, with no physical intervention, however, they went through the same steps of the procedure as if they were getting the physical surgery like the other two groups.

The results were shocking. The mock surgery participants had the same recovery rates and benefits as the participants who got the real surgery, even though no surgery was actually done for the placebo group. Researchers even followed up with the participants up to 2 and 5 years later, and the mock surgery patients' results were just as good as the actual surgeries. My mind was blown.

I had heard of the placebo effect before, but it was always used somewhat dismissively, "Oh that's just the placebo." But wait placebo surgeries fared just as well as the actual surgery? And they followed up with the participants two years later, showing the patients walking with no pain. They still had the same recovery results as the other two groups who got the surgery.

How could our belief about taking a pill or our belief about surgery cause the body to heal and overcome an illness or health issue? It wasn't just a trick of the mind, something very real was happening. This knee surgery study especially showed that the body was actually creating real healing, it wasn't just a trick or short-term results.

I was fascinated.

Near the end of the film, it showed a man undergoing brain surgery with no anesthesia using only hypnosis. The man undergoing surgery was aware and awake, talking with the surgeons while they operated on his brain. He didn't report any discomfort or pain. Hypnosis had 'turned off' the pain response.

At the end of the movie, our psychology professor said, "Well class that's The Placebo Effect and that's why we do double-blind studies," as if to finalize class.

I was dumbfounded, how could she skip over watching the part about the man using Hypnosis instead of anesthesia during brain surgery? No one was asking, so my arm shot up in the air. A benefit of being a thirty-year-old back in college, I was no longer shy in classes.

"So what about Hypnosis?" I asked.

"What do you mean?" She asked.

"We just saw a man undergoing brain surgery using only Hypnosis, are we going to talk about how that works?" I asked.

"We aren't going to talk about Hypnosis in this class. There's a lot of controversy around it, mostly psychologists believe that people are just playing along and it's not real."

"Well someone undergoing brain surgery with no anesthesia, isn't that more than someone just playing along?" I asked wanting more answers.

"I really don't know," she said, turning to the class, "Okay for next week read chapter four and have a good weekend."

I gathered up my papers, piling them into my backpack and hurried afterwards to catch her. "Ms. Thomson, I'm really interested in hypnosis. Do you have any resources that you'd recommend?"

"We don't cover hypnosis in the course materials, in fact not really at all. You'd just have to do your own research," Ms. Thomson said. "I've heard the National Institute of Health is doing some interesting research including alternative modalities, you might want to start there."

I was floored by the information, my mind kept spinning over and over, *'How is it possible that you could turn off pain by using your mind? How is it that the body could physically recover just by thinking you are taking medicine when it's only a placebo? And what about the knee surgeries?*

I wanted more answers. I'd heard of the placebo effect before, it was mostly dismissive, but this research was showing that something very real was going on. *What is the mind doing that it can control the body to the point of no pain? How is the mind overriding the body into full recovery even though no reparative knee surgery was actually done?*

And if the mind can do that – what else is it capable of? And how can we tap into the power of the mind to heal the body? This was totally mind-over-body magic. I wanted in.

I ran home, looked up online, and researched case studies from the National Institute of Health. Most of the information available through the NIH site said, "In conclusion, more research is needed." It was inconclusive, but of course, researchers would want more funding for more research. I knew there had to be more going on.

As I continued to research, I found Hypnosis had a whole range of applications: stop smoking, weight loss, changing habits and behaviors. I read review after review about people who had used hypnosis to change cravings, addictions, anxiety, insomnia, and various other conditions where they had struggled to make changes prior to using Hypnotherapy.

As I did my research, it seemed that Hypnosis was an avenue to change the problematic habits of the mind at a profound level. In the time I worked with the teens in the wilderness programs, I had become well-versed in understanding that we humans operate largely by default and have automatic habits and motivations. It appeared that Hypnosis was actually shifting these deeper patterns and inner motivations to create different patterns and better results in so many areas of life.

One exciting study in particular, Alfred Barrios in 1970, brought hypnosis into mainstream acceptance as a valid and effective form of therapy and personal improvement. Barrios compared 1,018 studies and articles on hypnosis, 899 articles on psychoanalytic therapy, and 355 studies on behavioral therapy. He compared the overall success rates found in these therapies and his results found:

- Hypnotherapy had a massive 93% success rate after only 6 sessions.
- Behavioral therapy had a 72% success rate after 22 sessions.
- Psychotherapy had only a 38% success rate after an average of 600 sessions.

From his compiling, he concluded that, "Hypnosis was not only the most effective method, but that it needed less time and fewer sessions than any other type of therapy." I was intrigued and fascinated. What are they doing in hypnosis that gets results so much faster than other methodologies? Can they really access the power of the mind to create change and heal the body?

And when I googled "Hypnosis" in Portland, Oregon, a local Hypnosis Training and Certification school popped up. They were accepting new students with joint certifications in Hypnosis and NLP, Neuro-Linguistic Programming. I had no idea what NLP was, but I was sold on the power of Hypnosis, so I applied immediately.

From day one of the training, I was hooked. I took all the trainings I could on Hypnosis, NLP and Coaching. The thing that fascinated me was these modalities focused on our inward experience, whereas so much of the course work of psychology was on 'observable behaviors.' To me, it seemed the world of psychology wasn't paying much attention to the inner thoughts and feelings that actually were creating the behavioral patterns to begin with. These were exactly the tools I wanted to help people create deep-level change and transformation.

CHAPTER 4

My Message: We Can Heal

The year 2006 was a storm of big life changes, I was diagnosed with Lupus, a debilitating and degenerative Autoimmune condition. At about this same time, I graduated from Portland State University with a Bachelor's in Science degree as well as completed certification as a Neuro-Linguistic Programming (NLP) Practitioner and Clinical Hypnotherapist. I had just moved in with John to his home surrounded by the beauty of northwest 60-foot pine trees. I also opened my private practice in Vancouver, Washington where I started seeing clients for NLP Coaching and Hypnotherapy to change habits, patterns, and programs of the mind.

 Since 2006, starting my own practice and helping clients 'rewire' the automatic thought and feeling patterns of the mind, I've watched thousands of men and women overcome deeply stuck habits like smoking addiction, overeating, and procrastination. In changing the brain habits behind our behaviors, NLP and Hypnosis can address and rewire the problematic thought patterns causing emotional habits like anxiety and depression. We have obvious habits in what we do, but we also have internal habits of what we think and how we feel.

It's these inner habits of what we think that create our emotions, our emotional habits, and even our cravings and addictions like smoking or alcohol. All these are wired into the unconscious mind and they are not logical and rational, which is why they feel so hard to change with logic.

Hypnosis and NLP offer a new model of change. The mainstream model of change is to recognize what we want to change in ourselves and then we try to control our inner urges using willpower. But willpower doesn't last and this old model of change creates a cycle of struggle. It's almost as if part of the mind wants to eat healthy, but part of the mind still wants the sugary soda or candy bar. So then we end up fighting between these parts of ourselves and it may even take us down that spiral of self-blame and shame that leaves us feeling defeated. We recognize that we want to make a change, but we end up feeling disappointed and discouraged with our lack of 'willpower' when in truth the deeper mind is running a different program.

If we look at the bigger picture of how our brain-body system interacts, then we recognize if we want lasting change, we must look at our internal system of what we think and how we feel that are actually behind the bad behavior, causing the impulse.

When we add understanding these layers of the mind, it becomes even more obvious as to how the brain and body are interacting. It's within the deeper layers of the mind, by applying healing perspectives, we can create fast and even lasting change.

What are the deeper layers of the mind? In understanding how the mind works, a useful model is an iceberg. There's the top of the iceberg above the water, this is what we see and what we are aware of, this represents our conscious mind, but it's a much smaller portion of the iceberg about 10%. At the conscious level of our mind, we are logical and rational, we choose our goals and what we want to change in our lives, but there's a deeper story.

The larger part of the iceberg is below the surface, it's the other 90% of the mind. It's underneath our conscious awareness and it represents the unconscious mind. I like to call it the Automatic mind because it's in charge of whatever habits or patterns are running automatically.

Most people notice a disconnect between the change we say we want at the Conscious level, versus our automatic habits and patterns. We make resolutions like, "I want to eat healthy or I want to work out more," but then we find ourselves falling off the wagon.

It's the automatic mind that encodes our thought and feeling habits that are running in the background of our minds. Our thoughts and feelings have everything to do with our motivations and choices. So, if we want to create profound and lasting change and end the struggle of fighting against ourselves, we need to address the unconscious mind and the automatic habits and patterns that are encoded there.

Utilizing this model from the field of Hypnosis, we recognize that it's the unconscious mind that runs the automatic habits and patterns of our thoughts, feelings, and ultimately behaviors. And we can apply this same model to the patterns of the mind that affect the body. We know for example that the body physically responds to stress. As we think of stressful thoughts or worries, the body responds physically through the fight or flight response which creates a cascade of effects such as releasing stress hormones, affecting heart rate, blood sugar levels, and more. We'll cover this more in-depth in later chapters. From this we can recognize that the mind-body connection is very real, the body physically responds to what we think.

This book is my story of applying the skills of Neuro-Linguistic Programming (NLP) and Hypnosis to my own body and the autoimmune condition I was diagnosed with. By recognizing and changing the automatic habits and patterns of the mind that cause interference in the body, we can create the inner space of healing so the mind-body can rebalance. As we use deeper awareness to identify and change the inner habits and patterns of the mind, we can curtail messages the mind sends to the body and thus change the body's habits and how it operates.

The negative thoughts and emotions of our minds particularly the stress habits, directly impact how well the body performs and even how the immune system itself operates. We can recognize negative thoughts and emotions as interference. It's these inner stressors, the mental blocks, that create stress and interference in the body's operating systems, which over time can even create patterns of illness.

In the course of this book, I outline how our inner world of brain habits, meanings, and perceptions then directly impact our body's functioning. Our minds are either adding to our health and well-being or detracting from health and well-being. It's more than positive thinking, and the underlying mental blocks that interfere with our body's operating systems are rooted in the automatic mind or unconscious level and so they can be quite elusive.

My journey of addressing these inner blocks to affect the body's outer healing encompassed many areas of mind-body-spirit interactions. It actually took me several years to figure out and identify the layers involved so I could work through and resolve them. By addressing the inner brain habits, traumas, and perceptions, we can upgrade our inner world into clarity and inner harmony. In creating the inner environment of well-being, clarity, and harmony, the mind can send the body new messages to rebalance, heal, and essentially overcome the patterns of illness and transform its expression into well-being, health, and vitality.

In sharing my journey with you, I hope you are inspired to recognize your own path of changing the habits of your mind to create healing in the body. As you create your own recipe of inner harmony, engaging your brain and body to rebalance and heal, you can embrace your body's higher potential of health, vitality, and more aliveness in every day. I share the tools and principles to simplify and clarify your own healing journey, shortening the learning curve as you move through your own process. I hope you are empowered and inspired to recognize what your own mind-body system wants and needs, so you can navigate health issues and move into wellness.

In this book, I share tools for harnessing your unconscious mind to create the changes you want in your life and even the changes you want in your body. There is a path, even a formula to getting to where you want to be. As you are empowered with tools and keep your focus on your positive future, you can follow those synchronicities, those little ah-ha's along the way that guide you. By adopting the curious explorer, you can uncover your own path and even enjoy the revelations along the way to living with more inner harmony and aliveness.

Every body is unique. My path may not be your path, but healing is possible to whatever degree your mind-body-spirit system will allow. It's useful to think of it as a process or journey, that each step builds up to the next. My healing journey didn't happen overnight, it took dedication to the process and patience in working through the many layers. I did however feel better by degrees along the way. As each piece of the puzzle fell into place, I felt more clear within myself and more connected with my inner truth.

As you move through your own process of directing your mind and body toward health, healing and vitality, may you have the inner drive, intuition, and tenacity for decoding illness and transforming your inner patterns into the inner peace that creates alignment, harmony and healing.

Since 2006, I have worked as a Consulting Hypnotist, Master NLP Practitioner and Life Coach, helping people change habits and behaviors of both the mind and body. I saw remarkable results both with my clients as well as with my own situation. As I applied the healing tools and principles to myself, I found relief by degrees. As I continued to work with clients in their healing journeys, I also found important levels of the mind-body-spirit system to address for deep healing and profound change.

I learned to look for the inner habits and the deeper patterns that could be updated and leveraged through each stage. I worked through the underlying belief systems that my mind had taken on years ago from past traumas that had been running in the background. I worked through clearing out old ideas about myself, the cultural programs that I had picked up from my parents, from religion, from culture, and the experiences of life along the way. As I continued to apply the principles of what I knew, spurred on by my clients and their results, I was inspired to continue moving forward with each small adjustment in untangling the bad ideas and untruths lodged in my mind.

This book is my healing journey as I unraveled the many factors of mind-body-spirit interactions and found my path to increased well-being and inner harmony. By clearing my mind of stress habits, clearing out unconscious mental blocks, creating inner peace, I was able to resolve the conditions of the mind that created the autoimmune disorder in the first place. By resolving the multiple layers and causes of the condition, I was then able to retrain mind and body to work together for harmony, re-educate the immune system to better balance, and create new expressions of health and vitality within the mind the body. I utilized these skills with my own brain-body system, to teach the mind to learn its way out of the patterns causing the autoimmune condition and create new inner habits that allowed for inner harmony, rebalancing, and healing.

Where-ever you are in your health journey, be patient with yourself as it's a process and every body is unique. It's the automatic brain habits of your mind determining how your mind-body system is operating for you. Every person's healing journey is unique as we each have unique families, cultural systems, beliefs, stress habits and triggers, attitudes, and environments where we grew up.

With these tools and skills, may you find a greater understanding of your own brain habits and patterns that you can leverage for your healing path to health and vitality. As I share the "ah-ha" moments that I've had through the process, I hope that you will find the pieces of the puzzle for your own healing journey. Keep in mind there can be many layers of the mind-body-spirit system that need to be addressed to resolving the underlying patterns causing a health condition. Read as a curious explorer, applying the principles, tools, and exercises in creating your path. As you focus on what works for you, you can do more of what's working and empower your journey to find your code for a miracle.

A miracle is simply something we don't understand, but as we recognize the bigger picture of the puzzle, we have more ways to leverage the mind-body-spirit system and unlock our fullest human and health potential. We are more than a biological package of materials, we are thinking, feeling, and aspiring human beings. And we have choices in our inner world about what we think, how we feel, and what we choose in life. We are aspiring and inspired, we are spiritual and we can see new possibilities that haven't been invented yet. The human spirit is creative and innovative and we can receive inspiration and higher wisdom. May you be inspired to reach for new possibilities in mind-body healing and find the inner clarity, peace, and well-being that creates the foundations to recognize and embrace even the smallest of miracles in your own life.

"There are only two ways to live your life. One is as though nothing is a miracle, the other is as though everything is a miracle." — Albert Einstein

As we open to new perspectives and possibilities, we create the space for miracles.

CHAPTER 5

Armed with Optimism

After hearing the autoimmune diagnosis from the doctor, I was shaken from the news, but I was also hopeful. I had after all certified as an herbalist in my twenties. I had heard of remarkable cases of recovery. I believed miraculous recoveries were possible. I had heard first-hand accounts of the body's ability to heal and recover from many conditions using the power of herbs. I refused to believe that an illness is incurable, I refused to believe I was powerless in this equation. I was committed to my own recovery. I had also seen the placebo documentaries in classes, showing the unexplained remissions and healing of the body through the power of the mind.

I also knew that you find what you look for. If you don't believe you can recover, you will dismiss the people and resources that can help you. If you believe that healing isn't possible, you will miss the clues that point you in the right direction. But if you keep an open mind, your brain becomes primed to recognize the answers when they show up for you.

So I had on my "I can do this" hat and I dug into research. I looked online at the approved sites first.

What was Lupus and autoimmune disease? Lupus is classified as an autoimmune disorder where the body's own immune system attacks the body's skin, organs, and soft tissues. The immune system's job is to recognize foreign invaders and protect the body from intruding bacteria and viruses. The body has a system of coding the immune cells to recognize what is a foreign invader and what is the body's cells. In Lupus, somehow the immune cells don't distinguish the body's own tissues and the immune cells attack the body. In this condition, the immune system is on overdrive which also creates flu-like symptoms of exhaustion, fatigue, inflammation, and skin rashes.

There are hundreds of different kinds of autoimmune disorders categorized mostly by the symptoms they create. In type 1 diabetes, the body doesn't make insulin because the immune system targets the pancreas. In Crohn's disease, the immune system attacks the colon. In Hashimoto's, the immune system attacks the thyroid. In Lupus, the immune system targets the body's soft tissues as in organs and skin and the list goes on.

Autoimmune disorders affect more than 32 million people in the United States and according to statistics, the numbers are on the rise. As I researched, I was shocked to find out how common chronic illness actually is. The Center for Disease Control says that as of 2012, half of American adults, that's one in two people have some form of chronic illness. I didn't realize how big this problem was, that's half of the American population. One in five people have an autoimmune condition and the numbers of autoimmune diagnoses are on the rise.

Autoimmune is the third most common category of disease in the United States after cancer and heart disease. Chronic illness also accounts for 86% of U.S. healthcare costs. If chronic illness and autoimmune disorders are this rampant in our culture, what is it that we are doing that is creating this level of epidemic? Why was this so widespread? I wanted to find out what factors were creating such widespread illness.

I remembered from my nutrition studies in college, we looked at the areas of disease and diet around the world. The nutrition course recognized that Americans had higher cases of diabetes, heart disease, and cancer than other areas of the world. The research showed that as other areas of the world adopted the "American diet," these other countries not only gained more weight but also showed an increase in American diseases like heart disease, diabetes, and chronic illnesses.

Cases of autoimmune are higher in the United States and England than in any other country. What are we doing as Americans that are creating this statistic? The diet seemed like a likely suspect. What are we doing in our culture, in our food, and in our society that was causing and contributing to this epidemic of chronic illness and autoimmune disorders?

I remembered from my studies as an herbalist in my twenties, the foundation of natural health is to eat whole foods and minimize processed foods to create a base foundation of health. One quote from the founder, Dr. John R Christopher of the School of Natural Healing echoed in my mind, *"Let food be your medicine."* In working with herbal remedies, your foundation of health comes from what you eat consistently, and a healthy diet is an essential foundation for natural remedies and herbal cures to work effectively. It wasn't enough to have a junk food diet and then throw some herbal remedies on top.

In my training as a Herbalist and Nutritional Vitalogist, it emphasized that the foods you eat are the building blocks of your body. Food is foundational to how the body operates. Your body takes in food and then secretes saliva, digestive juices, and enzymes to break down the food into nutrient particles. The body then absorbs these nutrients and uses them as building blocks to create new cells, repair damages, and grow new tissues, so you literally are what you eat. I had heard countless stories of people healing the body through eating a "regenerative diet" which was largely plant-based with whole foods and limiting processed foods like grains, sugar, and dairy.

In the words of Dr. Christopher, "If you plant your food in the yard and it won't grow, it's not food. Only eat what will grow: whole foods, fruits, vegetables, nuts, grains, and seeds." Want better health? Eat better food - right?

I got this, I'd done the regenerative diet before, so it shouldn't be a problem. I thought to myself.

I started by making the changes I knew how to do first. I changed my diet. I cut out the processed foods that had crept into my busy life of school and studying. I cleaned out the freezer of the microwaveable instant foods. I cleaned my cupboards of the sugar and bakery items. Yes, sugar was my weakness. Oh, yes I liked my cookies. But if I wanted to improve my situation, I had to make the changes. I could commit to returning to whole foods eating, I knew it was important.

And I thought humans are resourceful. We're intelligent, we're smart - we figure things out. Somewhere, someone had surely faced an autoimmune and overcame it through natural methods, so I continued to research.

And I found it! A woman diagnosed with Lupus was cured. I saw the newspaper article, she had been interviewed by a television station in Arkansas. There was a picture of her in the newspaper standing next to her wheelchair. Ok, this is great. I dove into digesting the article. Come to find out, she had stopped eating potatoes. Great that was it - no potatoes!

Wait - I wasn't eating any potatoes.

A family member sent me more articles; someone else stopped drinking artificial sweeteners and their symptoms improved. But I was already not drinking any artificial sweeteners! I wasn't drinking soda pop, diet products, or sugar-free foods, my diet was fairly healthy already. My spirits fell, it was disappointing that I wasn't finding good answers.

My boyfriend, John was so supportive. He joined the search online and found a woman who had been cured of Lupus, she had an online downloadable book about it. *This is exactly what I'm looking for,* I thought. I dove in to read her story. As it turned out, she had gone to Canada to work with a faith healer and she was cured overnight in a single session. Again, disappointment clouded over hope. Her story gave me nothing. Healing through faith sounded like a pipe dream, I felt even more frustrated.

I had heard of faith healers, I believed it was possible, but it also seemed so random. Why are some people healed and others are not? Why does God grant wishes for some and shun the prayers of others? And if you didn't heal, then that meant you just didn't have enough faith? It was like an ironic twist, faith healers could charge money, and say it's all up to your own faith, it didn't sit right with me.

The rest of her book contained a bunch of healthy food recipes, but I already knew all of that. She was promoting a healthy diet, ironically something she hadn't tried because she was healed by 'faith'. But she would toss me a crumb as if to say, "Here eat healthy,

I've heard that it works." As I did more research, I felt more disappointed and disillusioned.

I dug into my herbal books, videos, and research papers. Scanning back through my notes, there had to be something for Lupus. Leafing through my notes and binders, I finally found it, an herbal formula for autoimmune diseases.

I was saved!

I added the two herbs to my smoothie everyday and took it religiously morning and night. I was certain this would do it. All my body needed was a little extra support and herbs were the ticket.

I had seen first-hand the amazing power of herbs to heal. I learned to use herbs to stop flus, colds, rashes, and more. I had created salves to pull out infections that worked quicker than the commercial ointments. I'd used herbs for skincare, healing ulcers, clearing sinus infections, and stopping strep throat in less than 24 hours. Ever since my herbal training, herbs were my first go-to. I could do this.

This was my ticket, this I could believe in. Faithfully every morning I made my smoothie with the two herbs and set off to work. But the results I expected didn't come. In fact, as the week progressed, I felt worse and worse. The aches in my joints that were manageable at the beginning of the week became so bad within just a few days that by the weekend, I could barely walk.

By the end of the week, every joint of my body ached with any movement. Getting out of bed became a chore. I felt creaky, exhausted, and even hopeless. *I'm too young to feel this old I thought, I'm only 33* as I limped through my house to the phone. I had clients to see, I had just opened my practice as an NLP Coach & Hypnotherapist and I couldn't hardly function.

With my tail tucked between my legs, I hobbled over to the phone and dialed Doctor Nelson.

"Hello?"

"Hi Doctor Nelson, I just can't take the natural route anymore, I can't live like this. The herbs aren't working. I want to try the medical treatment."

"Okay, I'll get that prescription for prednisone to you," she said and we wrapped up the call.

Within 24 hours of getting the prescription and taking prednisone, the achiness started to subside. It was like the prednisone was unlocking my energy and I started to feel better. By day three, I could move easier, my joints were working again and the pain was gone! I could move. I could walk. I was feeling better and better.

And energy, oh the energy!

As the days passed, I had even more energy, I started waking up early at 5 am. I used the time to clean and organize my office. I still had boxes at John's that I hadn't unpacked yet. We had set up a desk for my computer and an office space. John's acreage was lush and green and wild and the deer wandered across the lawn every morning.

Then 5 am became 4 am. It was exciting to have so much energy, I could get so much more done. Although I was waking up earlier, it was remarkable that I just wasn't feeling tired or groggy. By the end of the week of prednisone, I felt terrific, I loved prednisone! Waking up early was an extra bonus, *I was going to be okay. I could do this.*

CHAPTER 6

I Love Prednisone or Do I?

The weeks passed by in a flurry of activity with all the extra energy. I was waking up early to attend local business networking meetings. In building my practice I had a never-ending string of activities to do such as putting together business cards, creating a website, and more. Life was moving fast and now I had the energy to make it all happen.

Yay, prednisone! I was on a high, a prednisone drug-induced high, but hey it was working.

Maybe I could go back out on the rivers after all, I thought.

A few more weeks went by in this flurry of energy and activity, and then the spaciness started.

At first, it was just little things, like *'Where did I leave that business card?'* or forgetting to check my voicemails and call people back. Brain fog would settle in on me and then sometime later it would clear.

Okay, I'm just getting busy, so I need to keep lists, I thought. *In running a business, there was just a lot to track* I thought. And then I started finding lists half written, where the text trailed off into scrawl I couldn't read, thoughts unfinished trailing off the page in scribbles. *Oh, this is curious, what was I thinking?*

I dismissed it, *I just need to be more focused,* I thought.

The spaciness started to interlace with waves of bliss. Bliss as if all was well with the world as if seeing life through the eyes of love and perfection. After a few weeks of riding the waves of bliss, I was feeling great. I had so much energy. I was only sleeping five hours a night, but feeling supercharged, energized, and rested. The energy continued to build and the waves of bliss were lovely, but they also became distracting.

A time or two, the thought passed through my mind, *Dang I should get off prednisone*. But the thought was soon lost in a flurry of busy to-doing. I had a flight to schedule and accommodations to plan. I was really excited about an upcoming training using NLP Skills for Health and Healing, maybe that would give me the answers I needed.

And then, bouts of disorientation set in, like I was floating above everything. It flowed in waves. I felt my mind wandering off into little corners of confusion. At first, it wasn't so bad, because it felt as if I was tapping into higher states of consciousness. I had learned long ago to meditate and tap into higher states of bliss and well-being, so that was not new. I felt really good, love and bliss aren't a bad thing, right?

And then the love and bliss started to alternate into fears and fits of crying. Out of the blue, I would be struck with deep sobbing as if my heart was broken and I was completely inconsolable. Fortunately, I would cry it out, the fit would pass and then I felt fine again.

It was making me nervous. What's going on with my mind?

However, I would get caught up in the busyness of life again, planning and preparing to travel for training in San Francisco. I was super excited to learn more about health and healing through the mind-body connection. I was hoping to find some skills and tools that could help me in overcoming this autoimmune condition.

The day I was to leave, I woke early with a start from a nightmare that seemed all too real. I was in a forest, being chased by men with knives. They were in the shadows, tracking me, hunting me. I awoke trembling and my heart pounding. My pajamas soaked with sweat clung to my skin. *Where was I?* As I stared at the white textured ceiling, *how did I get here?*

As I looked around the room, the French doors ahead of me, the velvety green duvet cover, it seemed familiar. My body jumped as I saw a man sleeping next to me. *Oh yes, I'm with John, I am okay.* I told myself, I was at home in my bed, our German Shepherd Riley sprawled out at my feet. The clock said 4:00 am, *time to get going, I had a plane to catch.*

I shook off the fear and rolled out of bed, I could still feel the whisps of fear in my veins, coursing through my body as I got in the shower to wash off the feeling.

As John drove me to the airport, I could feel myself going in and out of confusion. We were quiet on the way to the airport, my mind was looping in and out of strange stories. *What if we crashed right here? What if that car veered out of its lane and into ours? What if my plane went down?*

That's weird, I don't usually think like this, I thought.

I brought myself back to the truck and John's face as he listened to the music. I acted as normally as possible. I knew that if John thought something was wrong, he wouldn't let me get on the plane.

John pulled up to the curbside, unloaded my bags, and looked into my eyes. "Are you sure you are feeling okay? It's been a tough month and if you're not feeling up to it, maybe you shouldn't go."

"I'm fine," I assured him and gave him my best smile.

He brushed my hair back from my cheek and held my head as he kissed me gently. "I'll miss you, call me when you get in okay?"

"Of course," I said, "I'll be fine."

I collected my bags and wheeled them through the airport eventually finding my gate and I sat down to wait. I waited and waited. The time for my plane to board came and went, yet no one came to the gate. I finally asked the attendant what the matter was. The matter was me, I was at the wrong gate! I made my way across the airport to another gate and I was too late, they had already closed boarding.

Okay, calm down Holly. Let's see if we I can get another flight. I found an attendant and she set me up to board in a little over an hour. I went to the gate and sat down against the wall. Suddenly, I startled awake, *where was I?* I felt my hands on my legs, saw the green speckled carpet, the airport, I was at the airport. I checked my watch, it was 2 hours later, I had missed the flight!

Again, I hunted down another attendant. *How could I have missed a second flight? This was unbelievable.* Talking to the ticket counter lady, I explained that I was on medications that made me sleepy and I just slept through the whole boarding process. She looked at me for a second with a flash of *'Who sleeps through the whole boarding of their flight?'* but she assigned me a new flight. I said thank you and hurried to the gate.

This time I made it on the plane. I could feel the spaciness and the confusion and the embarrassment, *how could I have missed two flights?* Still, I shook it off. Refocus. Refocus.

Hazily, I took my seat and felt the strange spaciness creep in as the plane accelerated into the air, I knew I was climbing higher and higher, you could see Earth down below through the window. *All those people living their little lives down below and never really seeing the reality of who we are and what we are capable of. I thought about so many people caught up in their emotions, believing their emotions are real or justified.* So many different ways of living life. So many different belief systems that we buy into and then over time they become a part of us that we don't even recognize that they are only ideas. Ideas about life, ideas about ourselves, and reality. What is reality anyway, only the perceptions we've chosen to believe?

The entire flight, I traveled in and out of the waves of spaciness, detachment, and disorientation. As we arrived at San Francisco airport, I hurriedly departed the plane to find the train. I found my connection, taking the train through the city and connecting to my bus which would take me to the hotel for the training.

Finally, I arrived at the hotel. I was sharing a room with another student in the training. It was around dinner time. I was only eating raw foods now and I felt so spacey and so tired and so cold, like I couldn't get warm. I ate an apple and then tucked myself into bed and felt my mind swirling in a collection of thoughts. Thoughts drifted by like green clouds and whisperings of something at the edges of my mind, something dark and haunting.

I felt so cold, like the cold if I was dead. A line of a song brushed by, and I thought that *perhaps I was dead, the cursed undead, walking in the world of shadows.*

Fear gripped me. Shelly, the other student sharing my room would come in soon and see me for who I was, part of the undead. She would know I was cursed! *I needed to run and hide. I could run out on the street, into the shadows. ...and then what? I was unsure.*

I could die, but I couldn't die. After all, I was the undead, masquerading as a human. I could take the bottle of pills and die. And then I would not be the undead, then I could go to God.

Rushing into the bathroom, I poured the tiny pills into my hand, mounding up a pile in my palm. Then washed them down with a couple of swigs of water. *Okay, it's done. In dying, I would leave the undead and the curse behind. I could move on into spirit, I'd give my life up to God, and God would come for me. I had solved the problem, nothing to do now...just wait.*

Suicides don't go back to God my mind thought. *Oh no, what do I do now? Well, maybe I'll just have one life away from God. Contented with the twisted logic,* I tucked myself back into bed to wait it out and let sleep take me away from this world. Just as I snuggled into the sheets, my cell phone rang.

"What's going on Holly?" John asked, his voice had an edge of urgency. "I keep feeling like there's something wrong and I need to call you. Are you okay?"

"I did it!" I blurted out. "I took the pills."

"What do you mean, you took the pills?" John demanded. "Holly, tell me exactly what you did."

"I took the whole bottle so I could go to God. I won't be the undead anymore and I'll be okay," I said matter of factly.

"Okay, where are you staying?" John asked, I hadn't given him the name of the hotel.

"San Francisco," I replied.

"I know you're in San Francisco," John replied, "but what hotel?"

"I'm not sure," I said, it was a sparse hotel room like any other hotel, my eyes wandered in confusion.

"Look by the phone, is there a paper what does it say?" John asked.

"There is... it says The Hilton," I said.

"Okay stay with me, hold on," John said gently but firmly. "Keep talking to me. Tell me again what your training is about?"

I rambled on talking about how you could train the mind out of old habits and patterns and how I wanted to make a difference in the world by helping people live better lives. Five minutes later, there was a knock on my hotel door. When I opened it, two police officers stood imposingly, their badges glinting in the dim lighting of the hotel hallway.

"Are you Holly Stokes?" one of them asked.

"No," I said, *I didn't want to incriminate myself to the police.* Confused at their appearance and not wanting to be in trouble and also because denying who you are when the police ask just made sense, especially if you were in trouble for something. *Could they tell I was one of the undead?*

One officer was talking on a cell phone, "Does she have short light brown hair and blue eyes?" he asked into the phone. He nodded and looked back at the other officer. "That's her," he said. "Show me what pills you took," he directed at me.

I led him to the bathroom and gave him the nearly empty bottle of prednisone.

"You are very lucky that your boyfriend called us," the officer said. "I need you to put your hands behind your back." He put cuffs on me, they found my coat which I put on over my pajamas, got my shoes, and they led me down the stairs to their patrol car.

Sitting in the cop car looking out the window, I wondered about the undead. *I was grateful I didn't have to be out there, hiding among the shadows with them.* The streets looked dark with creepy corners and things that moved between the shadows. *I didn't know where they were taking me, but at least I didn't have to wander the street. I wonder when the pills would kick in?...... Would I make it to the policemen's lair? Wasn't I supposed to just go to sleep or something?* My mind continued to wander in and out of reality.

They checked me into the hospital where people with scrubs took me to a small room, a cell in the hospital and I could feel the darkness after me. And so I began singing, singing church songs and hymns to keep the darkness at bay.

"Shut up!" I heard people yell from the hallway.

But they didn't understand, I had to sing, I had to sing to keep the shadows from creeping out of the corners. I drifted in and out in a haze of hymns from my childhood.

Several people came and went, poking me with needles, like I deserved it like I was despised, like I was wrong and being punished for something, but I didn't know what.

Then someone was praying over me, one of the nurses I suspect. And the darkness seemed to clear a little. And then I was moved up the floors of the hospital into my own room. I remember waves of sorrow, deep sorrow, and fits of inconsolable crying that would grip me and shake me. At one point I had a roommate, but with the crying fits, the hospital workers moved her to a separate room.

I sat in the art room, the kind lady had given me some watercolor paints. I started to draw flowers and a meadow, and then I felt this deep, dark, and twisted feeling take me and I scribbled black all across the picture. I looked at the strange contrasting image.

I heard my mind say, *'rift of consciousness.'*

The world was in trouble, in a rift. Sorrow for the world fell upon me like a cloud, it wrapped around my heart and again I sank into waves of despair that shook my body as the tears flowed and the hopelessness enveloped me.

The coloring and painting felt empty, I felt listless and couldn't hold a focus.

I remember in one hazy episode, I saw a sea of clouds, and all the earth was covered with islands of clouds and each cloud represented a belief systems. The beliefs are the paradigms that we've accepted and agreed to whether in culture, religion, families, or by the self, they make up the filter in how we see the world. So many ways to believe.

As I looked out across the sea of clouds, I could see that as souls we chose the different islands of belief because each offers a different experience. One culture is not better than another, they are just different, a different experience. And it was as if each paradigm, each culture, each religion, and each life situation has something to learn and overcome and that's why we choose them, we choose them for the experience. We choose them for the learning, even for the puzzle of it. Being born a Christian is a different experience than being born a Jew, which is also a different experience than being born a Hindu, Buddhist, or Muslim.

Religious cultures create a backdrop in our experience, like a filter coloring the meanings and purposes in our lives. Every soul's journey is unique, every soul's journey is special. It's a little like each culture or religion, or life experience is a puzzle box for the soul. We choose one and jump in to figure it out to understand its workings and eventually climb back out.

I woke, my mouth felt parched and cracking, my lips stuck together.

"Water, I need some water." My voice cracked and I could feel my swollen tongue.

A familiar face was at the foot of my bed. He offered me a swab with water on it, brushing it across my lips.

I soaked up the moisture as the liquid spread relief across my tongue, but I wanted more.

"You gave me a real scare, pumpkin," he said through a warm smile. His dark hair curled at the temples, his blue eyes glowed.

"What do you mean? What day is it? What time is it? Where am I? And who are you?" I queried.

"You're okay, we're in San Francisco. I am John, your boyfriend. You took a bottle of pills, do you remember that?"

"No, I would never do that." I said with confusion. "What are you talking about? I was at the hotel."

"It's been five days now since the hotel," he said.

The familiarity of his voice soothed the questions, *I must be okay now. John's here, I am safe, safe for now.*

"Do you remember the police picking you up from the hotel?" He asked.

I searched for a moment, my eyes focusing in the back of my head, a dim glimmer of the cops standing at my door and asking my name came to mind. *"Are you Holly? And my reply, No."*

"That really happened?" I asked.

"Yes, you reacted to medications, the prednisone caused the spaciness, the crying fits, the lack of sleep, and even hallucinations. We are in the hospital in San Francisco now, you're doing well and you are getting better," John said.

My body felt so weak, my feet felt like lead.

"I flew down right after we hung up," John said. I could see a tension on his face that looked new.

"You're okay now, I'm here for you," he said.

I faded in and out of reality over the next few days. Waves of confusion and spaciness, everything seemed to have an alternate meaning. The hospital machines were not just machines, they were spies for the aliens.

I knew the aliens were there. I could hear them clicking at night, with beeps and clicks they ran through the halls. It must be a secret code, a secret language of the alien race that was watching down over every move. The nurse was an alien messenger and if I let her put me in the 'circle tomb,' the aliens would read my mind. (Consequently, they had a really hard time convincing me to get an MRI).

As the days went by in the hospital, the world gradually started to stabilize into reality. The bed became the solid airbed that it was, automatically inflating and deflating for comfort. It was no longer controlled by *the pillow people* who were previously responsible for its unpredictable movements.

The nurses were no longer alien spies, they became the dayshift or the nightshift with no agenda beyond taking my blood pressure and measuring my vitals. The invisible demon that had control of the blood pressure machine vacated it, leaving behind the metal stand and cords, an inanimate array of metal, beeping, and wires. And the world around me turned back into a normal, everyday hospital.

Throughout the episode, John was there by my side, along with his mom and some of my friends. My mind continued making up stories about them as they read in the corner or ate their meals.

When my perceptions returned to normal, I found myself back in a tired reality. I felt deep exhaustion, it was hard to stay awake, and hard to put thoughts together, but after about a week, they released me from the hospital and John drove me home back to Washington and our five acres.

Over the next couple of weeks, I continued not sleeping, feeling waves of fear shake me, I was prone to episodes of panic. The hallucinations came and went as I felt whispers of alternate meanings like a blanket over reality, playing out in my mind. As the medication worked its way out of my body, reality began to stabilize. I was exhausted and spent many hours sleeping. I had pressure in my chest which seemed to cramp down on my lungs, stifling my breath.

CHAPTER 7

Dare to Believe in More

I sat in the recliner in the living room. I had to sit up in a chair because when I lay down, the pressure on my lungs hurt too bad. In the hospital I had developed a case of pleurisy, where the lining in the lungs becomes inflamed and starts to separate and any movement was excruciating, I sat still in the recliner trying not to move a muscle.

Apparently, prednisone reactions are as high as 18% that's almost 1 in 5 people who take prednisone have auditory and visual hallucinations. These and other reactions are so prevalent that there was a whole floor of the hospital dedicated to 'medication reactions.'

With the disappointment of the prednisone and the near brush with death caused by the hallucinations, I knew Western Medicine was not a complete answer for me. All they could do was prescribe me medications that I would take every day for the rest of my life and medications always created side effects.

I kept thinking of the diagnosis over and over, the doctor's words running through my mind, *"We don't know what causes Lupus. It's degenerative, it will only get worse over time, and there is no cure. But take these medications that will probably give you cancer in about 10 years, but hopefully, we'll have better medications by then."*

I thought about the symptoms, joint pain, skin rashes, and allergy to the sun. *Was I meant to be cloistered in my room, crippled up for the rest of my life?* I could feel all my hopes and dreams for the future cloud over and slip away. Despair gnawed at the edges of my mind as tears welled up in my eyes.

"It's not fair," I sobbed. The shaking of my tears triggered sharp pains that ripped through my body, like tiny glass shards stabbing through my lungs. I caught myself, *Okay, I can't cry, it hurts too much. How could I keep myself from crying?*

Holly, I heard my mind say, *"Are you going to build your future around what you can't do or are you going to believe in something more?"*

I had been imagining my future as a victim of this disease. I saw my future in terms of what I wouldn't be able to do, no more hiking, no more rivers, no more sunshine and it was devastating. I recognized I had a choice. I could resign myself to the diagnosis and adopt the Western Medicine life sentence of Lupus, or I could believe in something more.

I couldn't rely on Western Medicine to fix me. The prednisone had more side effects than I bargained for, creating hallucinations that caused me to take the pills which landed me in the hospital. Apparently, I was one of the 18% of those who have this type of reaction to prednisone. That seems like a rather high-risk rate. I couldn't put all my eggs in the Western Medicine basket. Besides Western Medicine didn't even know the cause of Lupus. If they don't know the cause, how could they find a cure?

If I wanted to change this...it was up to me to find my own answers. And I knew from my hypnosis training, before you can make any change, the first ingredient is hope. You have to see where you want to go and believe it's possible. We map out our lives in our minds before we create in reality. What you believe in you will create. If you don't like where you are in life, you can always choose to believe in something more.

I committed to changing my focus. Rather than seeing myself cloistered in my room, hiding from the sun, I imagined running through the trails by my house, hiking to the local waterfalls, and soaking up the feeling of nature, the water, and the fresh air. I imagined feeling the droplets of water on my face as the sound of the roaring water fell and flowed from one level to another in the waterfalls of Washington and watching the salmon jump upstream in the river.

I filled my mind with all the pictures I loved. As I lay in the recliner, trying not to move, I allowed my mind to take me back to the Umpqua River, seeing the turquoise clear water reflecting the green of the trees and watching six-foot salmon swimming below me as I peered into the silky waters. The towering trees above stood as sentinels of the scenery, holding the space for all the life teeming everywhere, the tangible feeling of being surrounded by the magic of nature masquerading as biological life forms.

And then I was backpacking again in the deserts of Utah, following trails no one had seen for hundreds of years. As you hike up a ridge to see canyon stone walls covered with the stories of ancient people a thousand years before, who had carved their stories in stone. Pictures and carvings on the canyon walls just waiting for someone to hear their stories, whisperings from the rock where people of another time left their mark on the world.

As I turned my mental pictures around, the future began to brighten. I felt relief as I held the vision of the sunshine of Mexico. I felt my skin soak up the warmth of the air and the gentle ocean breeze whisper across my face. I felt my feet squirming in the sands, feeling the softness of the beach and the rhythmic waves of water wrapping around my toes as the sand shifted underfoot.

A part of my mind spoke up, "You can't do that. The doctors said you have Lupus – you don't just get over it, there's no cure, you'll never be better."

I didn't know how I could overcome it and I wasn't on the beach in Mexico....yet. But I could enjoy it in my mind even now, just in this moment.

I answered my inner skeptic, *"Never is a long time and doctors don't know everything."* As a longtime student of holistic healing methods, I had heard people's stories of healings, spontaneous recoveries, and even miraculous results. And then there's the placebo effect, which shows the mind has the power to physically affect the body. It's not just a trick, real healing is happening as evidenced in the amazing results of placebo surgeries. The power of the mind is causing the body to heal, something very real is happening; we just can't explain it...yet.

"And what if I could heal completely, wouldn't that be amazing?" I asked my mind.

"Yes, it would," That part of my mind had to agree and it chimed in, *"But don't set yourself up for disappointment."*

"Disappointment is about not getting what you want," I told my mind. *But that's somewhere in the future. What about right here, right now? Maybe I won't have the sunshine in Mexico in reality. But I can have it for this moment. I can have it right here right now even as I think about it, I can have it in my mind. I have the freedom to create my inner world."*

Besides I thought, *what if you don't get your hopes up, what if you don't hold the vision of what you want? You surely won't get it if you don't believe you can have it because you won't even try. Isn't hope better than no hope? And in hope, I can enjoy my vision of the future now. Aren't these visions of hope better than the visions of being a cripple, cloistered in my bedroom, hiding from the sun and hiding from life?*

I could feel something click as that part of my mind agreed that hope was better than no hope and it quieted as I imagined Mexico and the beautiful scenes of nature, the places and the adventures that I loved, and the things I longed to do again.

Dreaming of sunning myself on the beaches of Mexico kept me from crying. My mind relaxed. My body relaxed. The pain eased bit by bit. I could step into my inner dream world and have it all now in a small, yet very real way and I could rest in the thought of it, a quiet peace.

With something new for my mind to focus on, the days sitting in the chair passed easier. Hope had taken the edge off the pain. With the sunshine and beaches of Mexico on my mind, I could enjoy my internal reveries, getting lost in the promise of someday and the wonder of *"What if I could?"* Even if the sunshine of Mexico and the rivers of Oregon were not happening now, I could have it in my inner world and I even looked with interest to each new day.

"What places of the world do I want to explore in my mind today?" I asked myself as I faced the day sitting in the chair waiting for my body to recover.

Those days after the hospital, feeling defeated and broken, I stumbled upon a key principle: Dare to hope and believe in something more.

Whether you are facing a health condition of your own, a diagnosis, a disappointment, or a limitation in your life, you have a choice. When you look into your future, it may look bleak or you may even feel tempted to give into despair.

But do you have the courage to believe in more?

Yes, you may risk the disappointment of not getting what you want, but life and healing are a process. It may not happen all at once. In the words of my whitewater guide trainers, "Where-ever you point the nose of your boat, there it will carry you." Are you pointing your boat of life to crash on the rocks or to flow with the currents to carry you through the rapids?

What about right here, right now? Are you willing to hold a vision of yourself experiencing health, relishing health, and the goodness of life? Are you willing to believe in more even if it feels like just a wish?

Wishes are the whispers of possibilities and possibilities are where miracles are born.

Perhaps you may not be ready to believe in recovering completely. That's okay. But what if you could improve your energy just a little more? Or what if you could reduce the pain and discomfort so your body could feel just a little better? What difference would that make in your everyday experience?

What if you could find greater well-being and enjoy life just a little more, even in small ways? What future are you willing to envision and hold for yourself? What are you willing to believe in?

Now sometimes when we imagine a positive future, a part of our mind says, "That's not possible, you can't have that." We all have an inner skeptic and it's doing an important job for us. The inner skeptic just wants to know what's real. And sometimes it tries to save us from disappointment, so it thinks, 'If I don't get my hopes up, I won't be disappointed.' So instead of risking disappointment, it consigns us to defeat, but notice where defeat takes us.

Let's recognize that the inner skeptic is doing a job for you. It doesn't want to be 'duped,' it wants to know what's real. But if it dismisses what it doesn't understand, it can hold us back or even sabotage our results by discounting our progress.

So let's acknowledge that we don't have all the answers...yet. The inner skeptic can help us move forward faster if we ask it to help us recognize what works for us. What helps you feel even just a little bit better? Each person's path is unique, each body is unique. We want the inner skeptic to recognize what works, so you can do more of what works. As you do more of what works, you build momentum and progress. Small steps of progress can really add up over time.

How do you recognize something is working? The subtle signs show up first, you can recognize a strategy works by how you feel. If you feel better, then something is working. There may be many strategies that help you feel better and better, even small things can add up to tip the balance toward health and recovery.

So, it's important to recognize what works for you. What helps you feel better? As you do more of what's working, you can build on small improvements every day. And let us agree that hope is better than no hope. Hope can help us feel better in the moment. Hope can inspire healing. Hope can rally your inner resources. Hope can tune your brain to recognize new answers that show up.

Hope is a key ingredient in the recipe of belief and recovery. So let us agree that risking hope is worthwhile. And if you are disappointed somewhere down the road, you can cross that bridge then. Disappointment is asking us to re-evaluate and refocus. So in the here and now: hoping, imagining, and envisioning better health cues your unconscious mind to build the roadmap to that destination. Self-healing and recovery is a journey, better to wear the comforting shoes of hope rather than the broken shoes of defeat and self-pity. If you don't believe in a better future or bring hope to your recovery, your chances of finding the path to a better future will stay hidden and obscured.

Besides, hope is just more fun. Hope can affect the quality of your life right here and right now. It brings energy, it allows optimism, willingness, and curiosity to learn new information. As we explore new avenues, we can open to expanded wisdom.

It's not about living in a fairyland, it's about creating the space for new answers. As we address the challenges of life, if we come from an attitude of curiosity and wonder, we can alleviate the mental suffering we cause ourselves by wallowing in defeat. Curiosity and wonder inspire new questions and with new questions can come new answers, better answers.

Anything you want to achieve in life, you need to give your mind directions of where you want it to take you. Our trajectory in life is mapped out by the focus of our minds, whether we are looking to change our health, our careers, jobs, etc.

The future you imagine in your mind gives your automatic mind or unconscious mind the direction of where you want it to go. And whatever you decide about your life, that's the energy that you are projecting into our future. If I believe I am tragic, then I'm feeding that energy into my life. If I believe I am blessed, that's the energy I feed into my life.

Everything in our lives was created first in someone's mind: the paint, the walls, the houses, computers, books. We map it out in our mind first before we create it in reality. And so it is with health and healing. Our consciousness offers us the ability to imagine, problem-solve, create, and explore new possibilities. And hey, the flexibility of the mind and the power of consciousness was a wide-open field in my new profession as a Hypnotist.

Reflection: How will you use your mind to shift into the life you want? Are you willing to believe in more? What's the energy with which you are creating your future?

CHAPTER 8

Meditation as Medicine

As I had imagined visiting the adventures of my life and exploring new places in my mind, I was also reminded of the skills of meditation I had learned to quiet the mind and reduce pain. It's almost like when I was focused on the pain, I didn't remember what I already knew to help it feel better. Sitting in the recliner, waiting for my body to heal, I had time to meditate.

I started with the meditation sequence I learned. I took in a gentle breath, held it, and released and imagined letting go of the cares of life. Another easy gentle breath in, hold it, and release my fears and worries with the breath to clear my mind. Then I imagined a soft healing light, like the light of the sun flowing down through the top of my head, feeling it flow through my head as I let it clear out the chatter and clutter of my mind. I imagined and felt it flowing down through my neck, letting it flow down through my arms to my elbows to my forearms, wrists, and all the way to my fingertips. Then imagining the healing light washing down through my chest and my back, letting it pour through my spine, washing through the core of my body, letting it clear out old thoughts, and old energies as if shuttling them down through my body and down to my feet.

Then feeling the lightness continue to pour through my stomach, and my pelvis, letting it flow through my thighs and legs, down my shins and calves to the bottoms of my feet. And everywhere the healing light flows, I imagined it clearing out the difficulties and bringing in lightness, ease, softness, and comfort.

And then feeling the light soak into the muscles and tissues of the body as if highlighting my body with this radiant light. Then I imagined looking into my body and seeing the places of discomfort in my lungs, I went inside my mind and imagined the area of discomfort. I noticed and imagined the outline of it, the border of it, the shape of it, even the color of the pain or discomfort.

And then I imagined making it round as my first meditation teacher taught me. When I had made the place of discomfort round, I began shrinking it smaller and smaller. I continued to shrink it in my mind, smaller and smaller, down to the size of a golf ball, to the size of a marble, to the size of a pea, to the head of a pin, to the point of a pin, to a speck and then shoot it down through my feet and into the ground to be recycled in the healing earth. The earth takes last year's leaves and turns them into nutrients for new growth. The earth is a grand recycler, nourisher, and healer.

As I continued the meditation, the pain subsided. As I imagined packaging up the pain, making it round and shrinking it smaller and smaller, the cells and tissues that had been screaming at me at first, quieted down like a child turns sleepy after throwing a tantrum. I could sleep more peacefully with less pain as my body became quieter, reflecting the quiet of my mind.

Each time I felt the stabbing pain in my lungs, I would repeat the sequence of light and shrinking the pain spots smaller and smaller and sending it down through my feet, through the floor, into the ground, into the earth to be recycled.

And I felt better and better by degrees.

As I had trained in Hypnotherapy, I understood the value of meditation to soothe the mind and body and shift into a healing state. As the mind gets clear, the body responds. When we think of stressful thoughts, the body responds with tension and activates the fight or flight response. When we are stressed, the body releases more of the chemicals that cause pain. But as we focus on calming thoughts, it inspires calming feelings, and the body responds to these thoughts and feelings.

By using the pain relief sequence, it gave me something to focus on rather than just feeling miserable. This healing light sequence and the process of shrinking areas of pain or discomfort also cues the unconscious or automatic mind to run healing sequences on the areas of pain or discomfort.

In Hypnotherapy, we recognize the language of the automatic mind or unconscious mind as imagery, story, metaphor, symbolism, and feelings. When we use the unconscious mind's own language, it takes in the positive messages at a profound level, activating the changes you want within the unconscious mind for you. Using the imagery of collecting the pain spots, packaging it out, and sending it down out of the body, activates the body's natural healing abilities. It also has the added effect of pain relief, but it's more than pain relief, it's inspiring your body to heal. In this simple, easy tool, we are acknowledging the pain as a shape and color, then shrinking it, we are metaphorically telling the unconscious mind to address and resolve the pain or discomfort.

Pain is a signal from the body that something needs attention or care, when we cover it up with pain pills, we aren't addressing the issue, we are dismissing it, ignoring it. Rather than ignore it, we can notice it, recognize it, and then ask the unconscious mind to address and resolve it. I'm not against using pain pills, they certainly helped me many times, but we can dive deeper into understanding the mind-body and resolve the reasons causing the pain.

This simple sequence also utilizes metaphor which speaks directly to the unconscious mind. As you shrink the discomfort down to a tiny spark of energy into the earth, it tells the unconscious mind to clear it out and let it go. The earth is a great healer, it takes the garbage, the waste, and last year's leaves, and breaks it down into nutrients and the building blocks for new life and new growth.

Many of the pains and discomforts we experience can have multiple layers within the mind-body-spirit system. In the healing journey, we may need to address these many layers and the deeper root issues to resolve the underlying reasons for the imbalances so that true healing can take place. However, this meditation sequence is a powerful way to communicate with the unconscious mind and get the unconscious mind to activate your body's natural healing states.

As I continued feeding my mind the positive images and messages of recovery, I relaxed and felt myself slip into those inner realms of imagination, energy, and even magic. It was more than feeling better, I was living the adventure in my heart and my being. I was seeing the beautiful, enchanted places of the world in my mind even if I couldn't have it in the real world ... yet.

The pain in my lungs subsided over the next several days and I finally healed enough to be mobile. Slowly, I started getting back to the activities of life and I settled into a different kind of normal.

Reflection: Research has shown many benefits of meditation including pain relief, alleviating depression, feelings of isolation and loneliness. It can also reduce inflammation at the cellular level, calm the nervous system, improve immune function, and even change your brain. What's your meditation practice? Check out the Resource section for the article: *"20 Scientific Reasons to Start Meditating Today."*

CHAPTER 9

Disappointment Asks Us to Refocus

I stared at the handfuls of pills prescribed by the doctors of the hospital. I had to write them down every day to keep track of what I was taking. There were medications for morning, noon, and night and if I didn't write them down, I would forget as the days blurred into each other.

I was on 12 medications for various things. There were medications for immunosuppressants, medications for my lungs, medications to alleviate the side effects of medications, medications for pain, and the list went on. I felt defeated from my recent stint in the hospital, that my trusted herbal remedies weren't enough to solve this puzzle.

How could this be my life? What was happening? It just didn't make sense, my mind ruminated.

The diagnosis was more than the symptoms, I now somehow belonged to a group of people with a debilitating disease and poor hope of recovery and I felt the futility of it. The herbal cures I had tried hadn't worked or perhaps weren't enough. I felt my world crashing in, *I had always been healthy, loved the outdoors, spent years as a wilderness guide, and was a Herbalist and Health Coach. It was a cruel twist of fate.*

Oh, the irony! I thought.

And why now? I wasn't sick before, I wasn't born with it, but all of a sudden now this?

In researching how others with my diagnosis were faring, it felt very unhopeful. I read about how the condition affected mostly women and how they had to curtail their lives with many trips to the hospital and many ending up in wheelchairs and on disability. The prognosis was not good.

According to the doctors, the medications were the only answer to suppress my body's immune system to keep it from attacking my own tissues. There is no known cause as to why the body doesn't identify its own cells. People aren't born with it, it shows up typically in the early thirties mostly in women. In Western Medicine, they don't know what causes it and so they don't know how to cure it.

According to the Western Medical model, there is no hope of recovery, only the management of the symptoms with handfuls of invasive pills, and pills always have side effects. The body is seen as the enemy, it has gone wrong and must be manipulated, controlled, and suppressed and medications are the only prescribed route.

One of the doctors of the hospital had said to me, "This medication is the best hope we have for now, it will probably cause you cancer in ten years, but hopefully we'll have better medications by then."

We have come to expect a doctor to take care of us; we see the doctor as having all the information, the knowledge, and the power. When health issues happen, we see the body as wrong and we expect physicians to save us, but the Western Medical field only focuses on the biochemical explanations.

Don't get me wrong, Western Medicine is great for diagnostics and emergency care, it has saved my life more than once. However, its track record for chronic and preventative treatments fall short of other holistic approaches and alternative methods.

Western Medicine is only one perspective and approach, but there is much Western Medicine can't explain. It can't explain why someone is still alive 13 years later after they were given only 6 months to live. It can't explain cases of spontaneous remissions or how the mind can heal the body as evidenced in the placebo effect. And Western Medicine dismisses what it can't explain.

The Western Medical approach is based on reductionist thinking, breaking down the knowledge of the body and health into smaller and smaller parts which has compartmentalized the approach to medicine into specialists with specific knowledge. So if you have a foot problem, you see a podiatrist or a heart problem, you see a cardiologist. Reductionist thinking has caused the field of science to have an amazing understanding of biology and cellular functioning at minute levels, but this isolationist thinking hasn't paid attention to how the myriad of multiple systems of the body interact and affect each other in the bigger picture of health.

With my herbal training and background, I could draw from an expanded holistic perspective. In the world of Natural Healing, it is understood that millions of years of evolution have perfected a responsive intelligence of the body that adapts to the environment. It also recognizes that the body is constantly healing and repairing its tissues. The body is creating new cells every day.

Every cell of the body has specific timelines for renewal. Cells in the stomach replace themselves every 5 days. Every second millions of new red blood cells are being made and the many cells of the blood are essentially replaced within 120 days. The body is continually healing and repairing itself. The body itself has wisdom and intelligence in how it operates. From understanding this, the herbalist's function is to give the body the right environment and building blocks so the body can naturally rebalance, repair, and heal itself. The motto from my herbal training was, "The body will heal itself if given the right environment."

We see a distinct example of how the Western Medical approach differs from holistic care in the treatment of fevers. Typically when a person has a fever, it indicates the person is sick. The pharmaceutical approach is to take an aspirin to reduce the fever. But what is the body trying to do?

The herbalist perspective asks, "What is the body doing and how can we help it in its healing course?" So, what is the body doing by creating a fever? When the immune system of the body identifies a foreign invader or bacteria, it takes a protein code from the foreign invader which it then transfers to immune cells which produce antibodies which target the virus or bacteria. The T-killer cells of the immune system then target the cells with the protein code, attacking the foreign bacteria. In response to recognizing a foreign protein to be cleared out, the body increases body temperature, causing a fever.

In our typical approach to a fever, we might take an aspirin to lower the fever. Taking a medication to lower fever interferes with the body's natural ability to address the bacteria or virus. A word of caution: *Please do your own research before attempting to let a fever run its course as there can be complications and even life-threatening situations if the fever is too high.*

As it turns out, the body is best able to create antibodies at an elevated temperature and so creating a fever helps the body on two accounts. One, raising body temperature activates the immune system allowing it to be more responsive and quickly produce antibodies. And two, bacteria and viruses are temperature-specific and only live within certain temperature ranges, when the body raises the temperature, it makes it harder for viruses and bacteria to survive and replicate.

The natural approach is a paradigm shift, recognizing the body's natural intelligence and innate abilities for healing and the focus is to support the body in its healing course. Even though you are not feeling well, your body is working for you and naturally moving toward health. The natural practitioner's focus is to empower the body, "What does the body need to do its job of healing and rebalancing?"

It's your own puzzle box of your mind-body-spirit system. What is it doing? And what is it trying to do? It's an empowering view that places power back in your hands.

What you do, and the actions you take make a difference. What you eat makes a difference, the nutrients, and the building blocks are in your hands. Your ability to rest, rebalance your routines, and build your life around your healthy lifestyle is of course key to helping the body heal and restore itself.

I swallowed the handful of pills along with my pride, resigned to my current situation.

This was temporary, doctors don't know everything and people do heal. I'd just have to refocus my efforts and come up with a plan integrating the Complementary and Alternative Medicine CAM methods that I already knew. Maybe herbs weren't a complete answer for me but there was still much I could apply with a holistic approach.

What can I do? I could start with what I knew. As I wrote out a list of: "What can I do right now?' I started to notice an inner energy and drive building within me.

I can follow the doctor's advice and take the medications. Although I knew it wasn't a complete answer for me, it did represent a body of wisdom that could help me out in my current situation.

I can be more strict with what I eat. I could continue searching for resources of natural health alternatives. There must be more to the puzzle. I couldn't believe that my body which had no sign of illness before was now on a path of degeneration and "incurable chronic illness." It just didn't make sense.

I could stress less. I'd been busy building my hypnosis practice and there was a fair amount of stress with setting up a new business. I could slow my schedule and make sure I had regular routines of eating, regular sleep, and quiet time.

I could get further testing recommended by my Naturopathic doctor. I could gather more research and come up with an integrative approach to CAM (Complementary and Alternative Medicine) therapies and create a plan with holistic professionals.

And then there were the Hypnosis and Neuro Linguistic Programming courses that I had trained and certified in, how did they integrate and fit together? I had mostly learned to use Hypnosis to change habits, like overeating and lack of motivation. In the training, we hadn't covered much on applications of healing with the body. I knew there was a lot more to explore there, but not exactly sure how to apply it all.

I had a sneaking suspicion that all the holistic modalities could somehow work together, like some bigger puzzle that we're just not seeing how all the pieces fit. As I re-oriented myself to take charge of what I could do, it was the beginnings of a plan. I reached out to Dr. Nelson to schedule testing and detail a solid care plan together.

Reflection: Is there some situation in life where you feel stuck or even powerless? Start making a list asking: What can I do? When you open yourself to the question, the answers come. Just keep brainstorming, keep asking the question and new answers will show up. Get a list of 20+ options. We have more options available than we are aware, for example: break down crying is an option, a valid one. It can clear your mind and heart and reset your energy, but it may not be your most productive option. Once you have your list, then prioritize 1, 2, 3, etc. Now you have the beginnings of a plan. What's on your CAN do list?

CHAPTER 10

Wisdom Through Multiple Perspectives

I sat in Dr. Nelson's office after the prednisone event. Dr Nelson looked at me with concern, "Well now we know that you have a reaction to prednisone, so we can take that off the table. I've been doing a little more research and here's what I've found. I know you like the details, so I'm happy to share the details with you."

She continued, "In my research, autoimmune conditions are where the body's immune system, which is in charge of cleaning up foreign invaders, mistakes the body's own tissues, confusing self from non-self. One of the theories behind this is Leaky Gut Syndrome. This is when people are eating certain foods that cause an allergy response, so the cells of the stomach are reacting to foods with inflammation. In the allergy response, the body releases histamines, causing inflammation which increases the space between the cells of the stomach lining. As it opens up the space between the cells of the stomach lining, undigested material from the stomach leaks out through this lining and into the blood. Then the body recognizes these undigested proteins, which aren't supposed to be in the blood or lymph, and then creates antibodies to clean it up."

"Because these proteins are not well digested and in the body's tissues, the immune system sees them as foreign invaders, confusing the body's tissues with these proteins and ends up attacking the body's tissues. So in short, we can test for Leaky Gut Syndrome," she said.

"Ok, that sounds good, let's set it up," I said.

"Okay, well you should also know that unfortunately because you received a diagnosis without having health insurance, you cannot get health insurance now and you'll have to pay all medical expenses out of pocket," she said in a concerned tone.

"Oh wow. I've always been healthy, I've never needed health insurance and of course as a seasonal river guide, I was a seasonal employee, what will the testing cost?" I asked.

"Let's create a treatment plan and then we can go through and prioritize it as you can afford it," she said.

I felt caught between a rock and a hard place. I needed further testing to rule out things and get a clearer picture of a treatment plan, but I really didn't have the money.

"Okay sure," I replied.

"We can also test for heavy metal poisoning, from what I've read accumulation of toxic heavy metals shows similar symptoms to those of autoimmune disorders."

"Okay that sounds good," I said.

"And then there's also the Anti-Inflammatory Diet." She said, "In the Naturopathic field, we recognize that underpinning all illness is inflammation. Your body naturally creates inflammation everyday as part of its metabolic processes. However, in illness when there is too much inflammation in the body, it affects how the body operates and can cause all sorts of problems. Inflammation can create pressure on the cells, restricting blood flow, circulation, and other imbalances which then cause more pain, more symptoms, and aggravate the condition."

She continued, "There are certain foods that cause more inflammation than others. When you eat foods, they are digested through one of two pathways. One pathway causes higher inflammation and the other pathway causes decreased inflammation," she said.

"So, adjusting your diet to avoid or eliminate foods causing more inflammation could at least keep the condition from becoming worse. By avoiding the top inflammatory foods, you can quell the body's histamine response and manage cellular reactions. Essentially, The Anti-Inflammatory Diet is about eating a whole foods diet incorporating more whole fresh fruits and vegetables, nuts, grains, and seeds and avoiding the common allergens. The most common allergen foods are wheat, corn, soy, and dairy. There are some whole foods however that digest through the inflammation pathway, there are books that now outline which foods are either inflammatory or anti-inflammatory. As your body balances, you may be able to eat more of the inflammatory foods as you feel better."

This was certainly new information to me. I already believed in whole foods eating, and it was in line with what I already knew. It sounded perhaps a little more in-depth than my previous understanding, and I was open to trying it.

"I already don't drink milk because I have lactose intolerance, but when you say give up dairy does that mean I have to give up cheese and butter too?" I asked.

"Well yes, I recommend doing an elimination diet for a window of time to really cut out the allergen foods and then you can start adding them back to see how your body responds to each food. We can also test for food allergies," she said. "However, you can have a food sensitivity, which will still cause the histamine response, without it being a full-blown allergy. And food sensitivities may not show up on an allergy test. The elimination diet helps you hone in on what foods your body may be reacting to and which foods are causing inflammation and making symptoms worse."

She continued, "As the buildup of toxins within our bodies can be a main cause of inflammation, The natural medicine approach is to assist the body's four elimination channels. The body naturally clears out waste products through the intestines, it filters out and eliminates waste through the kidneys, sweats out toxins through the skin, and even breathes out CO_2 and waste gases through our lungs. So it's also recommended to make sure the elimination channels are not clogged, keeping them open and working properly so your body can get rid of toxins," she said.

"Okay yes, that fits with Herbalist training, I was thinking of doing a detox, and it's a good way to start the elimination diet," I replied.

"Okay so to revisit your plan. We can put allergy testing and heavy metal testing on the agenda. We can also test for Leaky Gut Syndrome, and you can also get started with the Anti-Inflammatory Diet," she said.

"Yes, the elimination diet and a detox, I can get started with that. How long do you think I need to do the elimination diet?" I asked.

"Typically it's recommended for 12 weeks, you pretty much cut everything out except for white rice and maybe a little fish, then start adding foods in one at a time. You'll also want to track your symptoms, what you eat, and how you feel. Some foods can have a delayed histamine response even more than 72 hours. So from this, we can hone in on any foods that may be aggravating inflammation or making it worse," Dr. Nelson said.

"Okay, ugh, elimination diet. But it's definitely worth a try." I said. "Let's schedule the testing for maybe a few weeks out when I can pull together some money to cover it."

"Okay, I suggest testing for Leaky Gut Syndrome and heavy metal accumulation testing first," she said.

"Sounds like a plan." I felt a wash of relief, at least there was a process. The information she shared about inflammatory foods and anti-inflammatory foods was new, but it seemed to explain why whole foods eating works for the body.

"I know you are a Hypnotherapist, are you working with women for weight loss?" She asked.

"Why yes, I do," I replied.

"Well, I ask because I have a colleague who teaches clinics to set up healthy lifestyle weight loss classes. She's looking to connect with others teaching weight loss, the two of you may be able to refer to each other. Would it be okay if I gave her your number?" She asked.

"Yes, that'd be great. I'm happy to connect with her and find out what she's doing," I said. I did love how the local business community was so helpful to each other. I attended a few networking groups, where local professionals gather to build referral networks. There was a feeling of rooting for each other's success in business.

I left the doctor's office armed with a plan and feeling a little bit lighter. Here was hope again and I had a process and new information as well. I felt empowered knowing there were actions I could take to make a difference in my body and how I felt, the plan was clear and it made sense to me.

I guess it's just going to take a little longer to figure this out, I thought. I resigned myself to patience, I can let it be a process of understanding and experimenting. *That's part of being my own guinea pig, just keep trying new things until you recognize what works.*

It felt good to have a plan but also felt good to have clear recommendations from a professional I could trust, someone that could see the bigger picture of holistic care and natural health.

When I turned my mind to the question: What can I do? I felt hope after the disappointment of prednisone and the devastation of the trip to the hospital. In asking the question, I recognized there were many options and I could enlist professionals who were a good fit for me. I had new options and clear next steps with the help of a holistic professional who could see a bigger picture of health and wellness.

Reflection: Where do you feel stuck in life? Who do you know that would have good information or advice on this subject? What would be the next steps in getting help and gathering resources? As you keep asking the question, the mind continues to bring answers. Then you can sort through and recognize your best steps.

CHAPTER 11

Elimination Diet When Body Says No

I wasn't looking forward to the elimination diet, but I was curious and I was willing to try it. I didn't drink milk, but I certainly enjoyed butter and cheese and creamer. I would have to give up some of my favorite foods, but it was 12 weeks. I could do this and if it made a difference for my body, it was worth the experiment.

I bought the book, The Anti-Inflammatory Diet, and decided to do a combination of the elimination diet structure and use the Anti-Inflammatory Diet as a way to weed out inflammatory foods faster. The idea was to eliminate all foods down to a few staples, white rice, olive oil, and some vegetables so you can track what you are eating and identify any inflammatory responses your body is doing. Then each week, add just 1 food back into your diet and wait a few days to see how you feel. By paring it down and tracking how your body responds, you can pinpoint any problematic foods or food sensitivities.

I set about preparing for the elimination diet. The base of the diet was white rice, vegetables, and a little bit of fish. I cleaned out of my kitchen the foods that were on the Inflammatory list. I identified the foods that were Anti-Inflammatory list and went shopping to stock up. It's easier to make dietary changes when you have healthy alternatives available. I got a notebook so I could write down what I ate and how my body was doing and see if I noticed a difference from adding foods back in over time.

John was nice about it, but he didn't want to do the elimination diet with me and I didn't blame him. He agreed to be on the same page of the main courses with me, but he still wanted his treats, so he agreed to not leave cookies, chocolate, and sweets out in the kitchen. He would just keep them in his office so I wouldn't be tempted.

I kept notes on what I ate each day. At first, it was pretty plain: week one was white rice and a little olive oil and a little salt were also allowed. Most vegetables were okay except the ones listed as inflammatory in the book, *The Anti-inflammatory Diet*. In week two, I kept the same baseline, and I could add a little bit of tuna.

By day 10, I noticed a remarkable difference. I had significantly less achiness in my joints, even 50% less pain and it was easier to move. I could walk easier, I could bend my elbows fully. There was still some soreness in my hip, but I could walk without limping. It really was making a difference for me.

Then week 3, I added bread back in to see if it was okay. I noticed just a little of an upset stomach, it didn't seem like a problem. *Okay, maybe I could do sandwiches, they are so convenient, it's nice to take lunch to the wellness clinic where I worked.*

About a week later, I noticed the achiness in my joints was back, even undoing a lot of the improvements I had previously noticed. *Okay, maybe bread is out. I could cut it out for another week and then retry adding it back in.* It took two weeks of cutting out bread to feel as good as I had before eating it. In trying to add bread back in, there was a little more indigestion and bloating.

Nope, the body says no. I guess bread was causing more inflammation, I noted.

The elimination diet was a painstaking process, but I was hunting down clues. I noticed that I felt okay eating bread and pasta, but if I ate it 3 days in a row, I would notice more achiness and pain. It didn't show up immediately, but it had a delayed effect so it was definitely a food sensitivity.

I noticed other things too when I didn't eat bread, like my stomach felt better after meals. I would say I've always had a sensitive stomach and it just felt better. There was less irritation and less bloating when I ate in line with the Anti-Inflammatory Diet.

I lost seven pounds within the first ten days of the elimination and Anti-Inflammatory Diet. When the weight drops so quickly, it's a good indicator the weight loss is probably due to releasing water weight caused by inflammation. The inflammation response causes tissues to swell with water, thus causing extra bloating and weight. I wasn't really trying for weight loss, I mostly just wanted to feel better. But weight loss was a bonus as I had gained an extra forty pounds since I quit backpacking and went back to university to finish my degree.

It was amazing that so many symptoms seemed to disappear just by changing a few of the foods I ate. My joints felt less achy and the skin rashes that irritated me also disappeared. It was a relief to find that something so simple could make such a difference, but I was still on the chemo drugs that were suppressing my immune system to keep it from overreacting and attacking my skin and organs.

If I could feel better in my body by just changing up some foods, it was totally worth it. It wasn't a complete solution, but it was definitely an improvement. And the real question was, How often did I want to feel bloated, indigestion, and achiness?

Reflection: Do you feel bloated after meals? Are there some days you can't wear your rings? Do you have swelling in your legs and ankles? Any of these signs can be indicators of a food sensitivity or inflammation response. Are you willing to try changing some things in your diet to see if it makes a difference for you?

CHAPTER 12

Rheumatologist & What Should I Eat?

As I continued to recover into a new normal, I was also building my practice of NLP Coaching & Hypnotherapy. Even before I found Coaching, I remember John had asked me what I wanted to do in my career as I transitioned from wilderness guiding back into college courses. I replied, "I want to help people recognize how all the aspects of their lives are working together, I want to be a holistic life planner."

I remember John said, "That's not really a thing."

But those were the only words I knew to explain it. It wasn't until a few years later I found out that it really was a thing, it was called Life Coaching. It was exactly that, recognizing the bigger picture of life and seeing how all the aspects affected each other and then directing your choices and crafting your life by what nourishes you and what nourishes your soul on multiple levels.

In building my practice, I found a treatment room to rent in a massage clinic in Vancouver Washington, which I shared with another Hypnotherapist. It was easy splitting days of the week: I had Mondays, Wednesdays, and Fridays, and she took Tuesdays and Thursdays. The room had previously been a chiropractor's office with dark wood cupboards and counters. The carpet was a functional multicolor short blue carpet.

My office mate, the other Hypnotherapist had brought in a print by Salvador Dali of a clock melting in a tree. It was spot on because one of the effects of Hypnosis is a feeling of flow or timelessness, a one-hour session could feel like 15 minutes. We had a blue recliner for clients, so they could relax comfortably and prop their feet up, which added to the feeling of taking a break from the cares of the world.

I was feeling better and getting my health and energy back, especially as I was applying the Anti-Inflammatory Diet principles. However, I also continued working with my doctors and the specialists assigned to me to manage the autoimmune condition since my stay in the hospital.

I remember one day in particular, I noticed a stark contrast in how I was feeling. I had been working with a couple of clients in the morning. I am a people person and I enjoy working with clients on their life's challenges, and with Hypnosis I could also help them 'rewire their brain' out of the old patterns and into new behaviors. It felt good to help people set up new habits and navigate their own minds with greater clarity and insight.

This one day in particular, I was feeling good, I had just finished a session with a client on motivation. My client had come in feeling downtrodden, but by the end of the session, she had brightened up with hope and optimism. We had shifted her outlook on life and the light was back on in her eyes. It warmed my heart to see her shift so quickly. The thrill of watching transformation never gets old, it's always uplifting.

As my client left with new hope and action steps for the week to keep the optimism, I felt satisfied with the day's work. I wrapped up at the office and drove to my appointment with my rheumatologist, a specialist who deals with inflammation. I was hopeful; perhaps she would know something that I didn't about nutrition and how foods affect the body and could tell me more about which foods to avoid or which ones to choose or other healthy life strategies.

I pulled into the parking lot of the large medical office with a towering granite fountain out front. I unfastened my seat belt, grabbed my laptop bag, and breezed across the parking lot to the imposing doors of the grand new office building.

The building was still under construction and the elevator wasn't working. I looked at the stairs as they loomed ahead of me, two flights up. I began climbing one foot at a time. As I climbed, I felt winded and stopped for a moment. With each step, I noticed feeling achier and a little more run-down. I made my way to the waiting area and checked in for the appointment. I had to pause to catch my breath as I gave my information to the lady to check-in. From the waiting area, I was led down a hallway. Walking down the hall seemed so long as I paused for breath, finally, I was ushered to the treatment room, where I took a seat and waited for the doctor.

My rheumatologist opened the door, dressed in the standard attire: a white lab coat, stethoscope draped around her neck, and carrying a clipboard. As she walked into the room, I could feel my energy drop. She peered down at me with what I'm sure was meant to be kindness, but I felt myself responding to the tone of her voice as if my body crippled up under her concern as if she was reminding me that I was sick, indeed very sick.

"How are you doing today?" She said with a soft tone and a heavy weight of pity.

As I thought about it, I had been feeling pretty good up until I came into her office. I had been feeling hopeful, and enjoying my workday. I hadn't really noticed the pain in my joints, but it was certainly there now.

"I was feeling better today," I said.

"Squeeze this to test your grip strength," she said. I squeezed the metal instrument, she took it read a number, and recorded it in her notes on the clipboard. We went through the routine test of holding the clamps that measured my hand strength, vitals, and blood pressure.

"What's your pain level?" She asked. I had paused to think about how to respond, I turned my attention to my hands. My hip hadn't hurt all day, but now, I could feel soreness. I bent my elbow to feel how it moved, it had been good today, but I could feel a pinch as I tried to straighten it fully.

"I don't know about a 4 or 5 of 1-10 scale," I replied.

Maybe she would know more about the new information I had learned about inflammatory and anti-inflammatory foods. "I wanted to ask you; is there any special diet I should do?" I asked.

She spoke over her clipboard without looking at me as she made her notes, "No, food doesn't affect it at all. Just eat whatever you want."

I was floored, she was a specialist in inflammation. Didn't she know that some foods are inflammatory and some are anti-inflammatory? Didn't she know that dairy especially causes inflammation? Didn't she know that sugar can cause inflammation and weaken the immune system too?

I pushed it further, "Well I've noticed I feel better when I don't eat wheat or dairy. When I eat these foods I'm just not as achy, it's like the pain decreases by almost 50%," I said. "Is there a reason behind this?"

"No, food doesn't affect it. You'll always be sick I'm afraid, there's no cure for Lupus," she said.

It was like a weight of bricks dumped on my prior hopefulness and bright mood.

"Okay, I'm going to give you some lab work to do, send it over so I can take a look at it, and we'll schedule again for 3 months," she said and left the room.

I felt the heaviness of the conversation, dumbfounded as I made my way out of the office. I could feel that twinge in my right hip as I limped out to my car, compensating for the pain of it. As I got to my car, I gently folded myself to fit into the driver's seat. And I felt the achiness of my shoulder, my hip and now even my fingers felt tight and achy, pains that weren't there before. The thought crossed my mind, *I didn't feel this bad going into the office, in fact, I remember breezing across the parking lot without a thought of any aches and pains.*

On my commute home, I thought about the events of the day as I passed through the Northwest greenery on the winding road. Sure, I had woken up feeling a little stiff, but not too uncomfortable. In going to my office earlier that day, I had good energy and felt rather uplifted. I enjoyed the quiet serene space of the healing center where I worked.

Working with my client in the morning, the common body aches just didn't seem to be there. As we went through the process of hypnosis for boosting optimism and motivation, I felt the flow and ease of spinning threads of uplifting thoughts into a hypnosis process for my client to follow, as if weaving a blanket of comfort, hope, and positivity to settle around my client Melissa. At the end of the session, I saw the light in her eyes, that spark of hope, that she could embrace the goodness of being herself.

My day up there had been really good. It was certainly a stark contrast to seeing my rheumatologist. I particularly noticed the contrast between parking the car and floating across the parking lot to the office and the difference I felt in returning to my car from the appointment. I had limped back to my car with pains in my hips and aches in my arms and hands that simply weren't there before.

I relaxed into the beautiful commute home to the magical Washington acreage. I walked into the house, and my dog Riley jumped off the couch to greet me with his tail wagging. "Hi Riley, did you have a good day?" I doggie spoke dotingly while I scratched his head and put down my computer bag.

John was cooking dinner in the kitchen and looked up over the pan he was stirring on the stove, "How was your day pumpkin?"

"Well, it was actually a pretty good day. I was feeling good in the morning, I met with a client, and we had a good session. But then I went to see the Rheumatologist. That's when I noticed my mood really took a turn. This morning, I felt good, getting ready for the day and then meeting with the client, it's like swimming in hypnosis all day, so soothing."

I continued, "I felt fine when I pulled into the parking lot. Then I noticed, parking the car and walking to the office, I was fine. But the closer I got to her office, the stiffer and achier I felt. And by the time I had finished the appointment, I felt so achy I had a limp walking back to my car, I was seriously limping." I said, "It was really quite remarkable the difference between before the visit with her and how I felt after seeing her."

"When I arrived at the office, I had no problems getting out of the car and walking across the parking lot. It's like opening the door to the doctor's office, I just slipped back into fatigue and achiness. As if all the disease were sitting in the waiting room for me to pick back up when I came in. It was truly interesting," I walked into the kitchen to hug him around his shoulders while he stirred dinner.

"What did your doctor say?" John asked.

"Well the appointment was routine, but it was more than that, it was a feeling. It was how she looked at me when I was in her office, it's like a weight of pity fell on my head. And then when I asked her, 'What should I be eating?' She said, 'It doesn't matter what you eat. She said foods don't affect Lupus at all, to just eat whatever I wanted. I even told her that I felt better when I didn't eat wheat and dairy," I said.

"Oh what did she say to that?" John asked.

"She said it didn't matter, I'd always be sick." By the end of the visit, I felt worse than I had all day, even worse than the past few weeks. It was like I just reverted back to when I saw her before," I said.

"What do you think made the difference?" John asked.

"Huh, you know as I think about it, I think the last time I was in her office, I was super sick. And when I went back to her office, it was as if my mind was picking up right where I had left off, almost going back to a state of sickness when I saw her the last time. And then when she looked at me with pity, it just felt like my mind was playing right into it," I said.

"Well, you know what you are doing helps you feel better." John said, "We've figured out that wheat and dairy make it worse, so it doesn't matter what she says about it. Don't focus on what she thinks, focus on what you've found that makes a difference for you."

"Yes you're right, I'll just keep doing what I know makes a difference. But how can someone that educated think that food doesn't matter? She's a rheumatologist and doesn't know that some foods are inflammatory and other foods are anti-inflammatory? The ignorance of the medical world astounds me," I said.

"Well she knows what she's studied, she has studied pharmaceuticals and she hasn't studied nutrition and foods," John said. "And who writes the medical books? Pharmaceutical companies."

"Oh yeah. Yep, like that old saying, 'When you have a hammer, all you see is nails,'" I replied.

"Yep, people only speak to what they know, even doctors only speak to what they know," John said. "If they haven't had exposure to information outside of the pre-approved medical system, they can't really speak to it, and even ignore it."

I was encouraged by John's words. I recommitted to staying focused on doing what I knew rather than letting some expert's skepticism derail my own hope and vision. After all, I was the one living in my body, I was recognizing the effects of foods and how my body responded regardless of what the rheumatologist didn't believe or didn't know. Recognizing what worked for me had to be enough for now, and I was feeling better. Bit by bit, I was making progress and that was all the confirmation I needed.

There must be more answers somewhere. There must be a better way or more things that can help. I thought back to the conversation and her response, *"It doesn't matter what you eat, foods don't affect it at all."*

What do you mean it doesn't matter? I thought. The foods you eat are the building blocks for new cells and tissues. Of course food makes a difference and different foods affect your body differently.

I remember my Nutrition Science classes in college, the teacher mentioned that in some medical schools doctors aren't even required to take a single class on Nutrition. They only cover the main pathologies of nutritional deficiencies, such as a deficiency of vitamin D which causes rickets, or a lack of vitamin C causes scurvy. It's not their forte because it hasn't been the basis of their studies.

And even experts only speak to what they know and what information they've been given. And the different disciplines of knowledge don't necessarily update with each other. And of course, there's new research all the time, keeping up with just one field or discipline would be overwhelming.

But in any case, I wasn't going to let experts undermine my own awareness of my body. It's my body and I am the one living in it. Doctors don't have all the answers, they can't explain why some people get better and others don't. They have also been trained to see disease a certain way, as a problem to be corrected with medications or surgery. As doctors have been trained in pharmaceuticals, the main body of knowledge that they know is of course pharmaceuticals, so they tend to dismiss or discount other resources that can make a difference.

Ultimately, it's your body, you are the one who lives in it. While doctors and professionals have a certain body of knowledge, they also don't know everything about your mind-body-spirit system and possibilities for healing. New research and health information are coming forward all the time. It's important to have trusted professionals in the process, but recognize that ultimately you are in charge of your health and body. Choose professionals that support you in wellness, not in staying in sickness.

And to be fair there is a ton of new information and research coming to light all the time and it would certainly be overwhelming to try to cover it all, especially in the world of health, nutrition and medicine. As doctors are seeing patients, they may not even have the time to catch up on the latest developments. Pay attention to what makes you feel worse and what makes you feel better.

Reflection: Do you have a health issue or condition you would like to improve? What have you noticed that makes a difference for you? There may be a disparity between what your doctor says is possible and what is actually possible for your unique mind-body-spirit system. Do your own research, but even more importantly, pay attention to your body and your results. Continue to notice what works for you and prioritize what works for *you*.

CHAPTER 13

Listening to Your Body & Intuition

One of the first experiences I had with mind-body healing came from when I was in my early twenties. Backpacking with teen programs, there was a place in the desert where we did "dirt skiing." We led our kids up to a small hill which was made out of lots of small clumps of clay. It wasn't sand, but it looked somewhat like a dune, but instead of sand it was made up of these small clumps of clay.

At the end of our day, to get a little relief from the hard work of hiking, we took a break and climbed to the top of the clay hill. There was a place where you could get a running start and launch yourself off the top of the hill into the pebble-sized clumps of clay to see how much air you could get before you fell into the clay hill.

I was having a great time, I jumped off once and nearly got 15 feet, then on the second jump I went even further, I landed out 18 feet.

"Hey kids come on with me and let's jump together, there were about 3 of us in a line, I led the count, one...two...three...and we jumped. Oh yeah even more distance, but when I landed, I could hear it, a pop in my leg and I buckled under the pain of it. I tried standing up to no avail. The top of the hill where our crew and backpacks were seemed so far away. The hill was steep, no one could pull me up either. It hurt to move my leg, but there was no other way out.

I started climbing toward the top on my hands and knees, trying to keep my leg still as I climbed punching my hands into the clay mounds to brace myself for the steepness, and slowly made my way to the top. Talking with the other staff, we quickly assessed I needed medical attention. They called our support team who made it out several hours later as we were out in the backcountry off main roads and somewhat inaccessible.

When I got to see the doctor the following morning, the X-rays showed a spiral fracture in both of the bones of my leg, the Tibia and Fibula. The doctor said I would need surgery and they planned to use pins to stick the bones back together so they would heal.

After the surgery, I had my leg in a cast and the doctor gave me instructions that I shouldn't walk on it at all for the first 4 weeks to allow my body to heal. This was hard for me as a twenty-two-year-old who was used to backpacking 5-10 miles a day and I got grumpy quick. However, at the time I found a fantasy book series that totally captivated my attention. It was Robert Jordan's *Wheel of Time* series and I was hooked so I didn't hardly notice the week as I dove into reading so I could ignore my body and let it do its healing thing.

About week four, I went back to the doctor for my first checkup visit. After taking the X rays again to compare progress, the doctor gave me the news.

"Holly, your leg just isn't healing as well as it should be for how young you are. Let's give it another few weeks and see if it's making changes, if not we may have to redo the surgery," the doctor said.

I was alarmed, what if my leg didn't do its healing thing? Would I end up crippled? Okay, I thought, it was time to get serious. I had found a wilderness meditation teacher and one of the meditations he had taught us was to imagine healing light through your body. Then with any pain or discomfort, imagine the light clearing out the pain and healing the area.

Okay, I thought. I can apply what I learned and see if it made a difference. So instead of just ignoring my body and burying my mind in the book, I started a daily meditation of washing the healing light through my body and then imagining the light clearing out the area of the break.

And then I had an ah-ha moment, instead of just clearing out the area of the break, what if I imagined knitting the bones back together? I started with the healing light sequence and then imagined shrinking myself smaller and smaller and I imagined traveling down through my body to the area of the bone breaks, I could see them in my mind. I imagined then having a needle and with threads of light I envisioned knitting the bones back together. I did this every day for a few weeks.

At the next doctor visit with new X-rays to check on progress, I got the news from the doctor. "Wow, your bones have healed far beyond what we would expect, these X-rays look great! What have you been doing?" The doctor asked.

"Well I used meditation to imagine the bones healing together," I told him.

"Well whatever you are doing, keep doing it and we'll have you out of that cast sooner than expected," he said.

But in working meditation with autoimmune, it wasn't the same as an injury. There didn't seem to be a specific place to work on or a specific part of the body to be fixed. When I tried to think of the immune system, it didn't have a specific location, it seemed ghostlike and nebulous.

So although I could do the healing light meditations, there seemed to be a disconnect in applying the same type of meditation to the condition. While I believed Hypnosis and Meditation would work, I didn't have a clear idea of how to apply it in my case. So, instead perhaps I could focus on intuition.

I'm a fan of science and research, however, science can only explain the phenomena that we are aware of, but there is more possibility available in the human experience than what science has been able to explain so far. And science tends to dismiss what it can't explain. I find research fascinating, but it doesn't define the human spirit or our potential or possibilities for healing. As you are living in your body every day, the more you can befriend it and pay attention to what it's asking for, the more you can use your awareness and intuition to navigate your health and find new possibilities in your recovery.

I started with the basics, keeping a food and mood journal and paying attention to the body in a very practical way. When our diets are healthy, we eat a lot of variety, but all this variety can make it difficult to isolate any food sensitivities that can affect the body. By journaling each day what you are eating and how your body feels, over time you can start to notice patterns of symptoms. Which days does your body feel worse versus which days does your body feel better? As you look back over your history of weeks, you'll start to notice the patterns.

This is a very practical way to start paying attention to your body. Many of us tend to ignore the body until there's a problem, I did this too. But by tracking what you eat, you can notice how your body feels and your mood, this will bring you a deeper awareness of your body and what you can do, which is a much more empowering place to be rather than leaving your health results up experts who may or may not be up to date with new research.

I pulled up my notes on intuition from past wilderness classes where I had learned to expand my awareness on many levels. We learned to notice and identify intuitive messages and pay attention to inner vision. Inner vision is the inner knowing that can help with making decisions. Intuition can also help you recognize greater answers of expanded wisdom and insight.

We can also draw on intuition in the process of working with the body. Intuition is one of the most powerful tools you can embrace in your own healing puzzle. Most people have some connection to intuition. You may have heard it called inner knowing, gut response or even instinct.

Intuition is the part of you that can help you recognize if something is a fit for you or not. It's a part of you that brings to light inspiration and your next steps as well as solutions. Sometimes we think of intuition as a special gift, belonging to only special people and psychics. But chances are you've been using intuition in your life in many ways that you may have taken for granted.

When you meet new people, how do you know to either connect with the person or to avoid them? Perhaps you have some great friendships, what brought you together to connect and create the friendship? Sometimes intuition shows up as our next best step. Did you take a job you had hesitations about and then found it less than satisfying? Or perhaps you know a job would be a great fit for you and it turned it out well. These situations can all be ways your intuition shows up.

We can use intuition in everyday even subtle ways. When ordering food from a restaurant, we often talk about what "sounds good" or we think about which foods we want to eat.

Intuition can show up through each of our 5 senses. We can have visual intuition information. Like a flash of a friend's face in your mind and then the phone rings. Intuitive messages can come through your hearing channels, like a word that flashes in your mind. It can be when a song gets stuck in your head and when you think of the lyrics, you recognize a message that applies to your life, this can be an intuitive message.

Intuition can come through the body as a feeling of tension or relief of tension. You might think of the last time you were trying to decide between two choices. When you think of one choice your body may feel a heaviness or a tightness. When you think of the other choice, you can feel relief from tension or lightness.

Intuition can come through the sense of smell. These messages may be more subtle, but intuition can come through them as well. For example thinking, "What do I want to do today?" And then you smell pine and think of a pine forest. This can be an intuitive message to take some time in nature to allow the mind and body to decompress.

Intuition can come through our sense of taste. You may notice it when you're deciding what to cook for dinner or choosing food from a menu at a restaurant. Some foods just sound more enticing or some foods, even though you like them, are just not appetizing at the moment. When you think about choosing foods you are imagining how they taste and how they sit with your body. But your mind is considering more than that, it's connecting with tastes, with flavors. And if your mind is tuned to intuitive eating, it's also considering what nutrients, vitamins, and minerals your body wants and needs.

There are other intuition channels as well for sensing life force, auras, energies, and beyond, but the 5 physical senses are a good starting place. One channel of intuition may be clearer for you than the others. Intuition is a skill that gets stronger the more you pay attention to it, the more you practice it, and the more you follow through on its messages.

In our Western busy-minded culture, we tend to overschedule ourselves with work, with todo-ings and the busyness of life with little time for self-reflection and quiet space. We haven't prioritized the quiet of the mind and self-reflection that allows intuition to come through more clearly.

By creating time in your day for quiet space and self-reflection, you can create space for connecting more with your intuition and strengthening your intuitive senses. As you pay attention to your inner messages and clarify your intuitive messages, intuition becomes more noticeable and more reliable.

Intuition can be confusing sometimes. Its subtle messages can also come through our energetic and emotional systems. So if you grew up in a home where emotions were ignored or covered up, it can create emotional clogs, like when junk clogs the drain of a sink. If we've been covering up our feelings, ignoring or avoiding our emotions, this will interfere with the quality and clarity of the intuitive messages we receive.

Emotional intuitive messages can be very subtle and in order to notice the messages that come through, it's helpful to notice your emotional baseline. If you are sensitive to other people's emotions, this is your intuitive channel at work. This can also be confusing because some of what you feel emotionally may not be yours. You may be picking up other people's energies and emotions, but this information can come through your own emotional system. It can be useful to create some energetic boundaries or ways of clearing your mind and energetic system to recognize your own baseline, and clean it regularly.

Intuition also uses the same channels the unconscious mind uses to communicate information with us. The language of the unconscious mind and the language of intuition are essentially the same: story, imagery, metaphor, symbolism, and feelings, these are our primary language. The language you speak is a secondary code using sounds (words) to describe your inner experience. This primary language is what Hypnotists use in speaking with the unconscious mind to help it take in the positive messages more deeply and change behaviors.

When we are in busy mind with our todo lists and tasks, we are typically in a beta brainwave pattern. When we are in beta brainwave pattern, characterized by 13-30 cycles per second or Hertz, Hz. In beta brainwave pattern, the brain has a lot of neurons firing randomly, we may experience scattered thinking, difficulty paying attention, and have a hard time staying focused. This is our conscious, active, daily state of mind.

However, when we calm the mind and create a peaceful and relaxed state, our brainwave patterns slow down and synchronize activity across the brain hemispheres, creating an alpha wave pattern characterized by 8-12 Hz. We show more alpha brainwaves when we are resting, relaxing and meditating. It also becomes easier to remember information and memories, easier to think clearly and focus, and we are more tapped into creativity and inspiration. In alpha brainwave states, our body starts accessing natural healing states and it's easier to listen and notice the more subtle intuitive messages.

As we continue to relax our mental state into Theta brainwave pattern, 4-8 Hz, is evident with light sleep and deeper meditation states. As we increase the body's natural healing abilities. Delta brain wave pattern is .5 – 4 Hz, characterized by deep dreamless sleep.

All these brainwave states are natural, the brain circulates through these patterns when we sleep at night. In our daytime waking hours, we have learned to spend most of our busy time in the Beta brainwave states.

As you relax and clear your mind, it becomes easier to notice and clarify your intuition. Meditation is one way to clear your mind and create space for intuition to show up. There is however a conundrum that meditation seeks to clear all thoughts, which can be refreshing. But when we want intuition information to come through, we don't necessarily want a completely blank mind. With Hypnosis we can tune the mind to notice and connect with intuitive messages, clarify, and hone our intuitive abilities to be more clear and accurate.

As noted earlier, your intuition messages can come through the body, we use this channel most often when we are choosing foods to eat. Stories of pregnant women craving weird things like pickles and ice cream illustrate this intuitive sense. Some of our cravings for certain foods can be the body wanting or needing specific nutrients. Some of our cravings however, come from our emotional system, but these too can be intuitive messages if you interpret and process them correctly. These cravings also get garbled if your emotional system is backlogged.

As we recognize the body has a natural intelligence, we can start drawing on the many resources of this intelligence and wisdom. Through many millennia and generations of humans living in bodies and adapting to our environments, the body holds a vast archive of wisdom.

The body knows how to heal itself; it knows how to knit cells and tissues back together. Your body has automated programs and sequences for healing. When you get a cut on your finger, it's not the band aid that knits your skin cells and tissues back together, the band aid just keeps the cut clean so your body can work its magic.

Your body has a grand intelligence, it knows how to heal itself.

Consequently, the state of mind where Intuitive messages can come through is also the body's natural healing state: The alpha brain wave state. In the alpha state, the mind is calm, clear and more open to creative solutions and inspiration.

Tapping into the intuition of your body can be as easy as asking the question, "What does my body want to do today?" And notice what comes to mind: thoughts, pictures, images, words, feelings.

Connecting with your intuition and clarifying its inner messages can help you find your path through illness more quickly. What works for one body may not work for you, or it may not work at the current time. Sometimes there is a sequence or order to resolving the issues of the mind-body-spirit system. You can recognize whether a doctor or a treatment is a good fit for you or not.

Ultimately, you are in charge of your body and you get to choose what is right for you. Being informed with more options simply allows new possibilities to show up. When we know treatment options, it's easier for intuition to highlight the next steps.

Intuition is a skill like any other and it can also be practiced, strengthened and clarified to become a more trusted resource. If there is one skill I could share or instill the importance of, it would be intuition. With intuition, you can recognize your path and your answers for your own body and your life.

See Resources section for Bubble of Light Meditation to start creating inner quiet and notice your intuitive answers. This can also help you clear your energetic and emotional system as well.

Reflection: Keeping a food and mood journal is a great activity that I encourage students in my healthy lifestyle classes and programs I teach. Pay attention to what you are eating and write it down, also pay attention to what you are feeling physically as well as emotionally and track it.

Meditation can clear your mind and start tuning your awareness into your intuition. Where in your life and routine can you create 15 minutes for quiet space and reflection? Dedicating some quiet time for your mind will allow your intuitive messages to come through more clearly.

You may already have intuition operating in your life, how does it come through? Which intuitive channels are easiest for you? Keeping a meditation and intuition journal can help you recognize and notice the subtle messages of intuition.

CHAPTER 14

Connecting with Your Intuition

Intuition is the one skill that can really help you the most in navigating your path to healing the body. One of the methods I found super helpful for connecting with intuition is through journaling. By taking the time to journal, you become more aware of your own thoughts and feelings that are running in the background of your mind. As you recognize the negative patterns and beliefs, you can change them or even update them to better habits and patterns through working with the unconscious mind and using its language.

There are a few different methods of journaling that can be helpful. One strategy recommended in the book, *The Artist's Way* by Julia Cameron, this strategy is to handwrite 3 pages every morning, she calls this "Morning Pages." When you do this exercise, write whatever comes to mind by hand and just let it free-flow. Just write without thinking, without directing it or censoring it, just write whatever comes to mind. Brain dump, write out whatever is in your brain. Don't correct it or worry about punctuation. Let the thoughts flow and get them down on paper. Let yourself be in the flow of consciousness, flowing from one thought to another.

In the book, The Artist's Way, she recommends this strategy as a way to clear your creative channels and get those creative juices flowing. It can be a helpful practice for writers, musicians, artists or anyone who wants to activate their creative mind. Incidentally, when we are in creative space, our intuitive mind becomes activated and more clear, this is where we are open to inspiration.

Cameron also mentions another benefit of 'Morning Pages' in that you start to get tired of listening to your own complaints and negativity. After a while, you'll start to ignore the negative talk and just move forward anyway.

If your mind continues with the same thoughts over and over, it's showing you where your mind is stuck. If you've noticed your mind replaying a past event over and over, it's showing you either a brain habit such as self-blame or negative thinking, or it may want to bring your attention to resolve something. These thoughts then affect your emotional system, you may feel down, lacking confidence, or depressed. Your emotional system shows you the quality of your thoughts.

In this way of doing free writes, you can see what brain habits your mind is up to. You'll start to notice your own mind's patterns. You may also notice recurring ideas that aren't logical but feel true and you'll start to notice how your emotions follow your thoughts.

This 'brain dump' process can also help with emotional clogs, like hair that gets caught going down a drain. If you are avoiding your emotions and not letting them flow through, or if you are taking on other people's emotions and not clearing them, they can accumulate and garble your clarity. You can also see how the recurring thoughts are creating your own recurring feelings and emotional habits like anxiety, depression, and poor self-esteem.

I've found these exercises useful to actually slow down my thoughts and see them on paper. As I would let my mind free flow and write it down, I started to recognize the negative thoughts that kept recurring. Recognizing the negative habits is the first step in clearing them and letting them go.

I gave this exercise to one of my clients and the following week, I asked her how the journaling went. She reported that she didn't like the exercise because she started to realize how negative her mind was and then she had judgments about this negativity which took her mind into self-blame. Well to the NLP Practitioner or Hypnotherapist, once we know the pattern of these negative self-talk scripts, we can change them. But most people don't recognize their inner negative patterns because they are familiar or we are used to them like background noise.

In my process, I added a few more steps to clear out the mental clutter and unclog the emotional system. Once you've done your brain dump pages, then go back through your 3 pages and start highlighting the negative patterns that you see.

You can also recognize some of that negative self-talk as other people's opinions or just bad ideas and just cross them out. Keep in mind these are just old ideas that got stuck, most people have them running in the background of the mind to some degree unless you change them.

Many of the negative thoughts that keep showing up are beliefs or thinking errors, especially if they are recurring. Mental blocks are the negative beliefs stuck on repeat and running automatically in the unconscious mind.

You can also question any ideas that aren't true and cross them out. When your mind says things like, "Why do I always say the wrong thing?" You may notice you feel embarrassed or feel bad. You can ask yourself, is this really true that I ALWAYS say the wrong thing?

Of course it's not always true. You're noticing that sometimes and some situations you might say things you don't intend or that are inappropriate to the situation, but it's not ALWAYS. The mind tends to generalize. Generalizations such as 'always, never, and forever' are clues that these thoughts and beliefs aren't really true, the mind has just generalized or catastrophized the idea to save bandwidth. These generalizations are of course not helpful, but as you recognize them now, you can dismiss them as untruths.

Using the exercise of free writing, then go back through and underline or highlight the negative thoughts and belief patterns that you notice. These brain habits are recurring beliefs that are affecting your mind, your clarity, and your emotions.

Also going through this exercise, you might want to notice the emotional theme of each section. From this, your mind will start to recognize your brain's thoughts and habits and you'll notice your emotional ups and downs through the day reflect the thoughts you indulge in. Are you indulging in what is positive and uplifting? Or are you indulging in the problems of life, where you feel stuck and what is wrong with the world or worse yet, what is 'wrong' with you?

These recurring negative beliefs are also responsible for the inner layers of stress we experience, which the body responds to. These recurring beliefs are responsible for the energy (physical and emotional) that we generate in our bodies and the energy of these negative thoughts can then interfere with the body's natural flow and life force. If this continues over time, this energetic interference then blocks the body's flow of qi, the life force energy, disrupting systems and resulting in illness or dis-ease conditions.

Reflection: Go through the exercise of free writing. Go back through and notice: What negative thoughts or beliefs do you notice your mind replaying? What mental blocks and thinking errors do you recognize? How are your emotions tracking your thoughts? What would you like your mind to be saying instead?

CHAPTER 15

Journaling: Ask the Questions

Another journaling method is to pick a question of something you want answered, then write it down on a clean sheet of paper. Then let your mind go to quiet space or meditation and sit with the silence.

Get in a clear state of mind. I like to use the healing light sequence, imagine the healing light pouring down through the top of your head, through your body to the bottoms of your feet. Let the light clear out the old thoughts and feelings, let your mind connect with the higher wisdom and insight. I like to imagine drifting up through the column of light, higher and higher to the place of higher wisdom and insight. Then from that place of clarity, lightness, higher wisdom and insight, ask your question.

Notice whatever comes to mind: thoughts, pictures, images, words and feelings. All of these can be useful messages from your intuitive mind, your expanded mind. Give yourself a few minutes to sit with whatever comes.

Then write down whatever comes to you. Let your thoughts flow. When you pause or have gone through a sequence, you can use the healing light to clear your mind again and ask the same question again. Again, notice whatever comes to mind and write down whatever comes even if you think it's a silly answer.

As you ask the questions, your mind will find the answer. Keep asking the question and your mind will continue to find more layers of answers, there can be many layers and many answers.

For example, If I ask myself this question, "What can I do to feel better?"

Answer: Take a pain pill.

"What can I do to feel better?"

Answer: Take your medications.

"What can I do to feel better?"

Answer: Clear your mind.

"What can I do to feel better?"

Answer: Let go of stress.

"What can I do to feel better?"

Answer: Relax.

"What can I do to feel better?"

Answer: Connect with Peace.

You can see from this example there can be many answers that are valid and would work for you. You can also see how we might not be recognizing all our answers and there can be answers within answers. When you open the space and the intention of higher wisdom and insight, it will be there for you.

If you are new to intuition or have felt like you've tried intuition in the past and it didn't work out, you may have some mental blocks with your intuition. However, as you intend and clear the channel of your intuition, you can strengthen it, like building a muscle. The more you practice it, the stronger it gets.

The quality of the question you ask relates to the quality of the answers you get. Sometimes we ask a question that is too vague or doesn't warrant the quality of answers we are looking for. Open-ended questions are best to start, then you can use yes or no questions to clarify. Here's some examples of how to adjust your questions to get more open and expanded answers. The quality of your answers has everything to do with the quality of the questions you ask.

Here's an example: Can I get better? This question elicits a yes or no response. The word "can" relates to possibility, in the space of possibility anything is possible with the right resources and understandings, but you may not be ready for all those steps at once. Make sure the question you ask is clear, if you don't like the answer, clarify the question or pick a new question.

A better question might be: What can I do to feel better?

Here's another example of a question that's somewhat vague: Which job should I take?

Here, even the word *should* shows the question is asking someone else's opinion or judgment. Who's opinion are you asking? Should I take the job? Well, it depends on what results you want. There can be many factors involved such as your skills, abilities co-workers, the strength of the company, and the environment that could make it a good fit for you or a not so good fit.

A better question might be: Is this job choice a good fit for me? Am I a good fit for this job?

Here's another example of a question that is too vague: Will this relationship work out?

This question again is directing the mind to a yes or no response, so adjusting it to a more open question could bring you better insights. Well, what do you mean by "work out" and what do you want? Does "work out" mean having some fun times together and friendship, or does that mean intimacy and or marriage and partnership? You can see the question itself has a buried expectation. Also with relationships, there are many choices along the way. Choices in how we communicate, choices in what we prioritize and choices about what we are willing to work through with the other person when our emotional triggers come up.

It may be a better question to ask: What is the nature of the connection with this person? This is a more open question, allowing for greater responses rather than just a yes or no answer. It can be helpful to use yes or no questions to clarify information that comes up. And mostly our relationships are about the journey, not a destination.

Sometimes people think their intuition doesn't work because they pick a romantic partner, and it didn't "work out." We can feel betrayed when a friend no longer wants to connect with us, when a lover decides to leave or when life takes an unexpected turn.

Think of intuition like a breadcrumb trail. It's often showing you your next steps, not necessarily the whole destination. Life is a process of learning, growing, clarifying, and adjusting. What "worked out" for a window of time may no longer work for the both of you over time. When we choose partners that "don't work out" typically it's because there was something in that relationship that you needed to learn, navigate, or clarify so you could move forward in your relationship growth. Maybe that relationship was exactly the experience you needed at the time.

If you've felt burned by your intuition in the past, you may have turned it off, shut it down, or have some mental blocks to clear out. You can use the 'free write' exercise from the prior chapter about your intuition to help you find any blocks so you can clear them. Spend the time just free writing about intuition and see what comes up.

Intuition works best when your mind is clear and calm, you can use "Bubble of Light" Meditation to clear your mind and take you into a light meditative state.

See the Resources section for a Self Hypnosis Exercise to speak with your unconscious mind and update your intuition. Here's some phrases you might use with the Self Hypnosis Exercise to reprogram your unconscious mind about intuition:

- As I notice intuition, it can work more clearly for me.
- In the past, my intuition hasn't been as clear as I would like, but I'm willing to notice and recognize when intuition shows up.
- In the past, I felt my intuition wasn't working, but I am willing to notice small impressions of positive actions I can take in moving forward.
- I can trust intuition is working for me when I pay attention and follow through on impressions.

CHAPTER 16

Synchronicities Show Up: Gluten-Free Living

I got a call from Lisa, the woman my Naturopathic Doctor had mentioned, she was helping clinics set up weight loss classes and we planned to meet for coffee to talk more about how to refer clients to each other.

I walked into the coffee shop, ordered my coffee and I saw a woman with blond hair sitting at a table with a laptop who fit the description: blond hair, yellow shirt, and reading glasses. I walked up to her. "Are you Lisa?" I asked.

She smiled pleasantly, "Why yes. Thank you so much for meeting with me. I'm looking forward to hearing more about what you do and how we might be able to refer clients to each other," she said.

I sat down with my cup of coffee. "So, my Dr. Nelson says you are helping clinics set up weight loss classes?" I asked.

"Yes, I've been working with a program for about five years now, it's a weight loss program backed by science and research. I help health professionals set up, teach the classes, and run the groups. Dr. Nelson said you might be a good fit for working with the program or at least we might be able to refer clients to each other. We can talk about that more, but first I'm so curious, how does Hypnosis work?" she asked.

"Well, most people say they want a certain goal, 'I want to lose weight or go to the gym,' but then they don't follow through on what they say they want. People are often wanting to achieve changes in life, but then they procrastinate, put things off 'til later or just fall off the wagon. Partially this is because motivation doesn't last. But also for most people there's a disconnect between what we say we want and the actions we take," I said. "In understanding hypnosis, a good model is to think of an iceberg. You've heard that phrase, 'it's just the tip of the iceberg?'"

"Yes, of course," she smiled.

"Well, this refers to the portion of the iceberg we see above the water is a much smaller part, it's only about 10%, this smaller part represents our conscious mind. At the conscious level, we are logical and rational, but the larger portion of the mind operates below the surface, the 90% of the iceberg that we don't see. So, when we say, 'I want to lose weight' or 'I want to eat healthy,' we pick that goal from our conscious mind, but the unconscious mind isn't logical and rational, it's running old habits on repeat. You may have the conscious goal to eat healthy, but if your unconscious mind is running a 'craving sweets program,' which part do you think will win?" I asked.

She laughed, "So true, I've said the same thing, 'I'm going to eat healthy,' but then I've fallen back into old habits and I teach classes on it."

"Yes, exactly. Most people have noticed the disconnect between the conscious and unconscious minds. I like to call the unconscious mind the automatic mind because it's in charge of whatever is running automatically: habits, cravings, even procrastination and sabotage are encoded there. We can have a conscious goal, but if the unconscious mind is not onboard, you will likely continue to struggle or feel like you are fighting yourself."

"So, hypnosis is one way that we update the unconscious mind with our goals, getting the larger part of your mind onboard with what you want so that your automatic mind will run new programs for you," I explained.

"You said hypnosis works with cravings? That's really fascinating because as I've been teaching these healthy eating and weight loss classes, cravings are really the one thing that takes people off the program," she said.

"Oh yes, this might be a great way we can refer clients to each other," I said.

"And sabotage too. I see the students fall off the wagon even when they are getting great results with the weight loss program I teach," she said.

We continued to talk and share about our businesses. As I heard about Lisa's weight loss program, I learned it was founded by a woman, Dr. Shari Lieberman who had a Ph.D. in Exercise Science and another Ph.D. in Nutrition. The program had long-term weight loss results, it wasn't based on calorie counting, but based on understanding how foods affect your body and specifically how foods impact your blood sugar levels as evidenced by testing and the Glycemic Index of foods.

She brought with her Dr. Shari's book, *Dare to Lose* to show the research about how foods affect the body and how to achieve lasting weight loss by keeping your body in fat burning zone. The program focused on avoiding foods that spiked your blood sugar quickly, which causes a release of insulin. Insulin is the hormone, the carrier that takes glucose (the sugar the body uses to run all its systems) into the cells and tissues to be used. However, if the body has too much available sugar at once, then it stores the sugar as fat, saving it for later. By focusing on whole foods eating instead, limiting processed foods and foods that raise your blood sugar, the body could rebalance and people could achieve long-lasting results and stop yoyo dieting.

I was fascinated. She let me borrow the book to review it so I could check out the research for myself. Some of the concepts were new about the Glycemic Index and how processed foods affect blood sugar, but it seemed to be scientifically showing why whole foods eating is good for you, which was in line with my Herbalist training. We made a time to reconnect so I could return her book and take a deeper look at the program and possibly teach the classes.

As I reviewed the program, it was the first weight loss program I had seen that really considered the quality of foods rather than just cutting calories. It was a system that I could endorse, that I felt really good about. I loved that the program embraced whole foods eating and the quality of foods, rather than just counting calories. It was a plug and play system, based off of Dr. Shari Lieberman's book and the program included support materials for running the 6- or 12-week class formats.

It was in this program, I learned more about the effects of gluten sensitivity for some people. I knew I felt better when I didn't eat wheat, but this really explained why. The program talked about the difference between a food sensitivity versus food allergy response to wheat, which is Celiac disease. Celiac disease is when the gluten protein in wheat agitates the digestive tract and intestines causing cramping, abdominal distress, and diarrhea. I had heard about Celiac disease, but it's only about 1% of the population that have the actual Celiac diagnosis.

The symptoms of gluten sensitivity may be subtle so you might not even recognize them especially if you are eating wheat regularly. Symptoms can include headaches, brain fogginess, stomach upset, bloating, indigestion, achiness in joints, swelling of tissues including swelling of ankles or fingers. Symptoms can show up even 72 hours to one week after you've eaten gluten. Because of this delay, it can be hard to detect food sensitivity which can be an underlying cause of bloating, inflammation weight gain, and other health issues as well.

I was surprised to find that as many as 1 in 5 people are estimated to have gluten sensitivity, that's 20% of the population. In Dr. Lieberman's later book, *The Gluten Connection,* she shares the research showing people who have a chronic illness or autoimmune disease tend to have higher rates of this gluten sensitivity.

From doing the Elimination Diet and Anti-Inflammatory Diet, I had certainly noticed that it made a difference for me to stay away from wheat, this program just expanded the knowledge further. Gluten is a protein found in wheat, rye, oats and barley. The program recommended cutting out all of these sources of gluten, even the ones where wheat was only a minor additive such as in soups, stews, salad dressings and soy sauce as even a little bit can cause an inflammation reaction. So I decided to do a 2 gluten-free week trial as well.

At the end of the 2-week trial, I could wear all my rings, I lost about 7 lbs. in the first two weeks. That doesn't really happen with fat, healthy fat loss is only 1-2 pounds per week, but what it does show is the release of water weight. The inflammation response causes the tissues to swell and hold onto extra water, so seeing a big release of weight within two weeks shows a reduction of inflammation and releasing water weight.

I'd love to say that from there on, I was gluten-free 100% and I had no more symptoms of Lupus. But it wasn't that way. I didn't have as much achiness. I felt better, but I wasn't back to my vital self. However, the symptoms were less, a lot less and I felt I wasn't nearly as exhausted as before.

And the cravings got in the way for me too. I wasn't always good with my diet, even though I knew better. Gluten is everywhere, you must be determined to avoid it. And baked goods were my weakness. It took me a while to practice the discipline to say no when someone brought double chocolate chip cookies to work or when cake was served at a family party, it seemed rude to pass up the birthday cake. Even though I knew gluten-free eating made a big difference in how I felt, I still found myself sliding backward.

I was excited to see results for myself and curious to see how it would work for others. With my background in Herbalist training, and my passion for health, and after seeing the difference it made for me, I was convinced with the program and with the help of Lisa, I started teaching healthy lifestyle classes. It was nice having a structure, I didn't have to reinvent the wheel.

Reflection: When you start asking the questions, your mind starts noticing people, opportunities, and resources that are your next steps. Notice the synchronicities of life, they are also your intuition coming through for you as your mind is inspired to be drawn to what's good for your path.

What synchronicities do you notice? Write your stories of your own synchronicities in your Intuition journal. The more we pay attention to the synchronicities, the more we can follow that breadcrumb trail of intuition.

CHAPTER 17

Healthy Lifestyle Classes

Lisa partnered with me in leading the first series of healthy lifestyle weight loss classes. I could use the larger yoga room at the wellness clinic for my classes. I got the word out with my business networking groups and the women from the massage center. The material was pretty straightforward. The class structure offered the Low Glycemic Eating program, and we started with a 6-week series.

My first class was small, but it was manageable with 6 students. We met weekly covering the content of the program, and discussing the principles of the Low Glycemic Index. Along the way, I added in some tips for managing your brain with NLP and Hypnosis.

It was week three of the class and I introduced the gluten-free 2-week trial. I explained the gluten-free trial meant cutting out wheat for 14 days and eliminating the foods where gluten was often hidden as an additive, like soups, salad dressing, and even soy sauce. I explained the symptoms, the sensitivity to gluten, and that the symptoms could show up 72 hours to a week later because it can have a delayed effect, it can be a hidden factor in why they aren't losing weight. It can also cause symptoms such as upset digestion, inflammation, and even other health issues.

I could see the deer in the headlights look in my students' eyes. One of my students Cindy piped up, "What are we going to eat then if we aren't eating wheat and we're already eating low sugar? That means no pasta, no sandwiches, no sugar, so what's left?"

I could feel their uncertainty in the room. "The key to making healthier eating easy is in having good substitutes for what you're eating now. Let's do the next class at the gluten-free store. We can meet there and shop for foods to substitute for wheat. For now, pick a day on your calendar to start your 2-week gluten-free trial," I said. "We might have to get a little creative, but there are other options," I added.

I could feel the tension in the room relaxed a little bit, but they still weren't convinced.

"Well, you know I'm not saying you'll never have a cookie or sandwich again. I'm saying commit to the two weeks and see if it makes a difference for you. Then you can eat a little bit of wheat to see how it affects your body. After the 2-week trial, we can talk about adjusting it in your life if it makes a difference for you."

I saw them nod their heads in agreement.

"Okay so next week, we'll meet at the gluten-free store to shop and stock up. Take a look at your calendar for the weeks after that and pick a time you can do the gluten-free trial," I said. "Try to coordinate with your calendar around family celebrations. For example, if you have a family member's birthday coming up, wait 'til after the birthday party to pick your wheat-free weeks. Or if you have travel plans, it's best to target a date after your travels."

The next class, we met at the gluten-free store to stock up on the alternatives so we could be prepared for the 2 wheat-free weeks. Most of the students planned to start the gluten-free trial the next day. Anytime you are making healthy lifestyle changes, it's best to set yourself up for success before you start by having healthier options available.

We found some gluten-free pastas, crackers and bagels. At the time, even with a store dedicated to gluten-free alternatives, the pickings were slim.

We talked about what foods to switch out in their regular habits for gluten-free trial to be successful, mostly they just needed to switch out sandwiches and pasta. Once you know good alternatives for what you are normally eating it becomes easier. So instead of sandwich with 2 slices of bread, we talked about wrapping it in lettuce. Or taking a salad to work instead of a sandwich. At the time salads started to appear in fast food places as well. So we talked about choosing healthier alternatives and being really strict for two weeks and focusing on foods that you like that fit the Low Glycemic Eating guidelines.

I explained, "A challenge with doing gluten-free alternatives is these substitutes are typically high glycemic rating on the Glycemic Index. For example, gluten-free bread is usually made from white rice and tapioca and is highly processed, so the body converts it to sugar quickly, which then spikes your blood sugar. But for the process of the 2-week trial, just notice if cutting out wheat makes a difference for you and then you can adjust and find alternatives to create a good balance in managing your blood sugar levels afterwards. Once the trial is done, then you'll know if you feel better eating gluten-free."

We got ourselves stocked up with healthier choices and plans for good substitutions for the 2-week trial and set to reconvene class the next week at the massage clinic.

At the next class after doing the gluten-free trial, everyone filed in and took their seats.

I asked, "What are you all noticing from eating gluten-free over the past week?"

"I noticed the less pain in my knees, my rheumatoid arthritis pain is way down after one week," said Evelyn.

"Well over this last week, I did notice that my stomach wasn't feeling bloated after meals, and I lost 5 pounds in just one week!" Suzanne piped in. "The only thing I really changed was not eating wheat."

"That's really great to notice, the 5 pounds is likely that extra inflammation and water weight." I chimed in, "It had the same effect for me."

"I've been sleeping better, and I don't seem to have the brain fog in the afternoon," said Sarah.

Most of the class had noticed some effects and even significant results after just one week, feeling less bloated, more at ease with digestion after meals, and less swelling in fingers and ankles. We went on to talk about the day's plan of adding in mild exercise and strength training to support a healthy lifestyle and boost metabolism for weight loss.

"Okay keep it up one more week so the body can clear out the residual effects of gluten, see you next week," I said to wrap up class.

The following week the ladies walked in and took their seats. I welcomed them in and started class by checking in, "Okay, what did you all notice after doing the two-week trial?" I asked.

Evelyn said, "My rheumatoid arthritis pain has totally cleared up. I can play on the floor with my grandkids and I can stand up again without help, this is huge for me! If this continues, I may not even need the knee surgery."

Suzanne chimed in, "I didn't know I could feel good after eating a meal, I always just felt bloated and uncomfortable. Going wheat-free I feel good after I eat, rather than bloated and sluggish."

Sarah said, "I just notice I feel better, more energy and it's like I think clearer too."

Judy said, "I didn't really notice a difference, but I did lose 2 pounds this week, so I'm happy about that."

"Well, not everyone has a gluten sensitivity, but now you can see how it affects you and the effects can be subtle, so it really helps to clear it out for two weeks. But you can now see if it made a difference for you by improving digestion, clearing brain fog, reducing inflammation and promoting weight loss."

"And now you don't have to do it forever, but how often do you want to feel bloated, indigestion and brain fog?" I asked. "Sometimes I ask myself, is piece of cake worth feeling that way? And sometimes I decide it is, but mostly it's not."

Suzanne queried, "Well what do we do about the cravings? I know what is healthy, it's just the cravings that make it hard."

"We're talking about motivation for fitness today, but next class I'll adjust it to include a Hypnosis session on cravings, how would that be?" I asked.

They agreed and from there, I started to write and plan my own classes, marrying the science-based nutritional content with the NLP and Hypnosis skills and it was the beginning of the A Lighter You: Hypnosis for Weight Loss System.

As I was teaching the healthy lifestyle classes, my students were learning about how foods affect the body, but I also recognized they were struggling with habits and cravings. Some of the brain habits they were fighting against were the very things I had seen in myself and my Hypnosis clients as we made changes to healthier eating. Even though they knew what foods were healthy, they still struggled with old habits, cravings, stress eating and emotional eating for comfort or happiness.

I also found that the healthy eating curriculum wasn't as streamlined as I wanted, and it didn't even talk about the importance of getting in your greens, support for digestion and superfoods, so I also created my own healthy eating guide. It incorporated principles from Dr. Shari Lieberman's program, but also included the key principles from Nutritional Vitalogist Certification and my Herbalist background.

In this guide, I wanted to make it super easy for my students to replace processed foods and find great alternatives so they didn't have to feel hungry and deprived. I wanted them to experience the joy and fantasticness of healthy foods and feel the health, energy and vitality in their bodies. This guidebook became, A Lighter You! Health Coach's Guide to Nutrition which I later changed the title to A Lighter You Healthy Eating Made Easy.

Teaching the classes made me aware of how much misinformation there was in advertising and what we think are healthy foods. Even so-called "health foods" can be loaded with sugars beyond what is good for the body, for example, yogurt. Many commercial yogurts have 30 grams of sugar. To put this in perspective, a Twix candy bar has 26 grams of sugar, so eating yogurt can have the same effect on your body as eating a candy bar, and yet it's touted as a healthy food. Unbelievable!

I was excited to share the nutrition information and see such great results for the women in my class as they too were changing to a healthier lifestyle. They had been disappointed with weight loss programs in the past, but as we went through the weeks, it really demystified weight loss, and they experienced results. And as a teacher on my own journey of a healthier lifestyle, it was nice having camaraderie in making the changes.

By incorporating a gluten-free, low-sugar diet, and adding lots of healthy fruits and vegetables, I was feeling better and my energy was returning. I could go for walks and mild exercise. It wasn't a total solution to the condition, but it was a good start, and it gave me hope that there were elements I could control, and that I could affect this condition and my body. There were things I could do to feel better. I could give my body more of what it needed to rebalance, recover, and heal. I loved offering the classes and seeing the difference it made for the women. I also loved watching the ah-ha moments along the way and contributing to the content with my tools and skills of hypnosis to offer a more complete program.

Although changing my diet wasn't a complete solution, it was something that helped me feel better quickly and it gave me control over the condition. I had less pain, and more energy and I could function better. And of course, there were cravings, sweets, pastries, and cookies were my weakness.

Why do we crave foods that we know aren't good for us? Especially when we know that certain foods make us feel bad or affect our health and vitality.

Cravings aren't logical and rational, they come from the deeper mind, the automatic mind and that is why they are so hard to fight against. It's the unconscious mind that creates the impulses for unhealthy foods, even when we know consciously that it's hurting the body and makes us feel bad. It's the cravings that can take us off track even when we are noticing results.

Recognizing the challenges of cravings and motivation, I then created A Lighter You Mind Body Hypnosis Weight Loss CD series to address the mindset for creating healthy lifestyle change with Hypnosis. One of the CDs in the set, Curb Your Cravings, focused on resolving cravings by educating and rewiring the unconscious mind to choose foods that are good for the body, rather than choosing for taste or choosing for "comfort" and other emotional reasons.

As you feed your body better, your body complains less and you both feel better. So, focus on what you know and keep doing what you know. Notice what helps you feel better, you can know that something is working for you by how you feel. If you feel better, it's working. As you focus on what works, you can do more of what's working and create an upward spiral.

By focusing on what works, you can feel better by degrees and build back into your health, energy, and vitality. What's good for your body is good for you and what's good for your mind is good for your body as we'll see in the next sections.

The anti-inflammatory and gluten-free diets were helping, I had reduced joint pain, and I could function better. I still had some achy days when I couldn't walk straight, or when I had to hold my arm at a funny angle to not aggravate the pain. I still could not push myself when exercising, even twenty minutes was too much of an overload and I would have to take a nap for 2 hours. However, I was keeping a food journal to recognize the patterns that made it worse and what made it better. I was still taking immunosuppressant drugs and chemo drugs prescribed by my doctors, but I kept the hope it was temporary, and I was finding better solutions.

Reflection: Would it be worth it to make small changes in what you eat if it could reduce your body pains by 20% or even by 15%? Yes, it's worth it. Is it worth it to swap out foods for healthier options if you could improve your energy by 30%? Why yes, yes, it's worth it as you feel better even by degrees. And even small improvements can help your overall quality of life. You don't need to starve or deprive yourself, but if you can make simple changes and get your health and energy back, is it worth it? I can tell you resoundingly, Yes it's worth it!

What diet changes are you willing to explore to feel better? What's your plan for recognizing food sensitivities? The key to changing what you eat is to have healthier substitutions, you can check out the healthy lifestyle program, how to curb cravings, and make easy changes with the healthy eating guide at: www.ALighterYouSystem.com/free

CHAPTER 18

Self-Reflection to Notice Patterns

My morning routine included waking up, pouring myself a cup of coffee and having some quiet time to reflect or meditate. Then I would head to the office to see the clients for the day. I enjoyed the quiet office setting. The other practitioners in the wellness center were massage therapists, so it was peaceful and even serene. In the afternoons and evenings, I went to the Vancouver City Chamber events to meet with the local business owners of the community to make connections and network.

One morning, I woke up and sat with my coffee overlooking the meadow encircled by the 60-foot-deep green pines. I watched the mama deer walk across the green grass with her twin fawns. I loved using the morning quiet hours to reflect and set up my mind for the day.

I wrote in my journal about my mood, my emotions, and how my body was responding. As I looked over my food journal, I started to notice that the day after I went to networking events, I felt more achiness and stiffness in my joints. I hadn't noticed that before, but I thumbed through my journal to the past few weeks and there it showed up again. I was doing well with the Anti-Inflammatory Diet program, but I noticed a definite pattern.

I sat with it in meditation, asking my mind, *"What is causing more pain on the days after networking?"* I closed my eyes and let my mind go blank.

A scene came to mind. I was 10 years old, standing in front of 28 teenagers in a church meeting, the silence was deafening. I was stumped, searching my mind for the words to a poem I had selected to share, but the words wouldn't come. I had taken the time to memorize it, but the words wouldn't come.

"The sun lights the sky with a gentle warmth...." I stammered as my mind went blank. I felt my face go flush, I didn't know what to do, so I started the poem over, maybe I could pick it up again. But I got to the same place and the same stuck.

"The sun lights the sky with a gentle warmth..." and then nothing.

I stood there, in the silence for what seemed like hours, *if only my mind could remember the words. Come on mind, remember the words, remember the words....* but the words had flown away like the bluebird in the poem. *The bluebird...the bluebird...nothing.*

Still nothing, I could feel the rush of heat into my face, it must be beet red. *Come on mind...the bluebird, what about the bluebird...*

I stood there, uncertain what to do in the longest most awkward silence of my life. The crowd of girls stared back at me with blank expressions, none of their faces could give me the next line of the poem.

I didn't know exactly how long I was in front of the class, it seemed like forever, the blank stares shifted and turned restless as they started to elbow each other and snicker.

My shoulders fell as I resigned my efforts, my mind wouldn't give up the words. Embarrassed, I said nothing and slumped back to my seat in the back row. The meeting continued as if it didn't happen, I felt my face still radiating the heat of embarrassment as I tried to be invisible.

I was a little bewildered by this memory, it was so long ago. I had many successful speaking events since then, like the year that I won a competition in state with the American Legion contest or when I won second place in a statewide debate competition.

"Why is this memory of embarrassment coming up?" I asked my mind.

I thought of the networking meetings. When it came time to introduce my name and business, sure, I felt a little nervous, but nothing to raise an eyebrow at. Apparently though, introducing myself and networking was somehow triggering this shadow of embarrassment from the past memory. Although I felt okay in the networking events, it was causing a stress reaction. And this subtle stress could be the cause of why my body felt worse the day after those events.

"Stress can cause inflammation," the words of the naturopathic doctor echoed in my mind.

Somehow being in the spotlight, even just for 30 seconds was triggering some kind of internal stress reaction. The stress, although almost imperceptible to my conscious awareness, was then triggering extra inflammation, causing the symptoms and even the pain and achiness.

So I asked my mind, "What is the stress here with speaking?"

Answer: *Speaking is embarrassing, scary,* I felt my mind say.

This underlying fear must be the cause of underlying stress, which must be aggravating the immune system causing a mild flare-up. It didn't make sense though; I was in Toastmasters. I loved doing the improv speaking, speaking for two minutes on a random topic. I enjoyed knitting together the words and meanings, creatively connecting the dots of two seemingly unrelated topics for the audience. Of course, my Toastmasters group was only 10 people. The symptoms were telling me that something was getting triggered.

As I thought about it, the business chamber event was typically close to 100 people. Interesting, I had been noticing a skin rash over the last little while, perhaps it was the size of the group that was triggering the underlying stress and creating more inflammation and more symptoms.

Me: "What is this about?" I asked my mind.

I could feel a twinge of fear.

Whisper in my mind: *It's not okay to stand out. Fear, Fear of being seen. Fear of being embarrassed.*

Interesting, although at the conscious level I was okay, the unconscious mind could be running the fear pattern at the automatic level, causing the reaction of stress and inflammation in the body. I understood how the unconscious mind works, it's very fast at processing and when we are in a situation that's similar to a past event, the brain picks up the memory file of the past. So even though we tell ourselves, "I am confident, I am in control," the unconscious mind is still referencing and responding to the emotional past history.

I wasn't about to stop networking meetings and building my practice, I knew my business was my life purpose. I'd just have to find other ways to alleviate stress and the associated fears of being seen. Perhaps I could take myself through an NLP exercise to take the edge off the fear of speaking and embarrassment.

Reflection: Is there some symptom or condition of the body you want more insight into? Give yourself some quiet time of meditation, sit with the silence, and ask, "What is this about?" Notice whatever comes to mind, thoughts, pictures, images, words, and feelings can all be useful information. Journal about what comes up for you.

CHAPTER 19

Recoding Stress Triggers & Fears

I met Kevin at a networking luncheon where business owners gathered to connect, talk, and learn about each other's businesses to build community and refer clients to each other. When Kevin heard I can help the mind get over fears using Neuro Linguistic Programming and other tools, he was intrigued and we set up a time to talk further.

Kevin mentioned he was new to the insurance field and although he was accomplished, he felt nervous about reaching out to new businesses. When he heard that NLP could recode and rewire the brain, he decided to give a session a try.

I welcomed Kevin into my office and motioned for him to take a seat.

Kevin had short dark curly hair and was dressed in a suit jacket and tie. He was tall, with an olive complexion and charismatic with a winning smile, white teeth and bright eyes. He had an air of self-assuredness and so it was a little surprising when he disclosed some fear of sales.

"What is the sales process like for you?" I asked to get some background.

"Well as new agents, we look up businesses to approach, they must meet certain criteria. I find a good candidate, walk in the front door and try to strike up a conversation with the front desk person so that I can get on the schedule to see the boss. Then I have a chance to pitch the boss and show him the benefits of what the insurance program can do for their employees. Then we set up a time to present the program to the employees and then hopefully they sign up."

"So where in that process does the fear come up for you?" I asked.

"Right in the beginning. I pull up to a new business, park the car. In the car, I feel really comfortable and confident. I know I have a lot going for me. I use positive affirmations, 'I can do this, it's easy to get new accounts.' And then when I feel pretty good, I walk up to the front door."

"And then what?" I asked.

"As I grab the door handle, it's like my blood runs backward," he said. "I feel it all through my body. It's irrational, I know I shouldn't feel that way, but there it is."

"And then what happens?" I asked.

"Well then, I feel small as I stand in the front of the office, I see the secretary, the gatekeeper. It's like she's just waiting to reject me and kick me out," he said.

"So how does your body feel and what else do you notice?" I asked.

"My hands feel clammy, I can feel myself shake on the inside. On the outside I appear calm and collected, I just smile and try to make conversation, but I feel that nervous, shaky feeling," he said.

"With a process from NLP Neuro Linguistic Programming, we can look for the memory files where your brain has coded this fear response, the place it first started and then recode it. Would you like your mind to recode this for you so you can feel at ease and comfortable while prospecting?" I asked.

"Yes of course," he said.

"So stand up with me, we are going to imagine a line here on the floor that represents your life. The past goes this way and the future heads out the door," I said as I motioned an imaginary line on the floor. "Now we will mark this place as the present moment and stand here with me in the present moment," I said. "Where do you feel that fear response in your body?" I asked.

"I feel it in my chest and in my gut," he said.

"Okay, place your hand on your chest to tell your mind to stick with that feeling and now walk backward with me as your mind identifies the first place this old feeling of fear first started for you, and tell me what comes to mind." We stepped backward several steps, and he paused.

"It feels like it's here. A memory is coming up, I think I'm 5 years old, it was my first day of kindergarten school. My mom had just dropped me off at the school for the first time and she left. It's the first time I've been without my family," he said.

"And what's going on there?" I asked.

"It's like chaos. I'm in a room of strangers, some kids are crying in the corner, and a few running around, I just want to go find my mom, but she's gone. There's a couple of teachers in the room trying to keep order."

As Kevin accessed the memory, I could see the fear reflected in the tension of his face and his posture as he described the situation. "Okay step to the side here, shake it off for a minute," I said. Kevin stepped to the side and shook his head and arms and the tension eased.

"This is part of how the brain works. We have an experience, and the brain packages up the memory: the sights, sounds, sensations plus the emotions we feel at the time and the brain files it all together into the same memory file. Then when we are in a situation that is similar, the brain says, 'this looks like the time when…' and it pulls up the old memory file and we feel the same feelings from the first event, so we can feel upset all over again, even though it's not happening now. A lot of what we feel isn't really about the moment, it's about our whole history," I explained.

"At the conscious level, we are logical and rational, but the unconscious mind is referencing a whole lot more than just the present moment." I continued, "Think of the unconscious mind holding the grand archives of the mind, all your memories are coded in those deeper files, when we are in a situation that's similar, the brain says, 'Oh let me get that file.' The brain thinks it is helping. Yes, we are anthropomorphizing the brain just a little bit here."

"This automatic fear response was more useful in our evolutionary history, if we heard a rustle of leaves and got chased by an elephant, the mind creates the association: the rustle of leaves means danger. Then when we hear the same sound, the mind automatically brings up the fear response, preparing the body to fight off an attack or run away. If we had to think about it, rather than respond instantly, we would likely be short-lived," I explained.

"So, when you are walking into a new office, the brain says, 'This looks like the time when I was left all alone, without my family and it brings up the 5-year-old memory. Now this is happening almost instantly. What you're aware of is the conscious level, grasping the door handle and then feeling the fear response," I said. "Think of the mind as a highly compact supercomputer able to process large amounts of information very quickly and it's running this connection automatically."

"Wow, that makes sense," Kevin said.

"Now, as the older wiser self, looking back, what would you tell the 5-year-old Kevin about this first day of kindergarten?" I asked.

"That it's okay, I'm just meeting more people and life is just expanding," he said. "Life was first about me and my family, but as you grow up, you get to meet more people."

"That's right, life is expanding who you know, expanding your social connections and sometimes it may be uncomfortable, but it's part of life and growth. What's a time when you were in a group of strangers, but you made some good connections or friends?"

"When I went to a family reunion. I didn't know everyone there, but they were all smiling and having a good time, and everyone was open and accepting. It was all family, just a larger picture of family, they made me feel accepted and that I belonged."

"And what message can you share with the 5-year-old about the family reunion?" I asked.

"The future is bright. Strangers are just friends you haven't met yet," he said. I watched his body relax and his posture straighten and open up as he beamed a smile.

"And if there were an image or symbol that would represent that for the 5-year-old, what would that be?" I asked.

"A pair of sunglasses," Kevin said.

"Great give the sunglasses to your 5-year-old self, and let's take a snapshot of that family reunion and blow it up into a big picture and imagine all those family and friends are with you in the background, how does that feel?" I asked.

"Feels really good," he said, he was still beaming.

I motioned him to take a step back onto the imaginary line, "Now becoming the 5-year-old self with all these messages, surrounded by family, the sunglasses, knowing life is okay and connections are expanding, how do you feel now?" I asked.

"It feels great, I can relax," he said.

"And what becomes important to the 5-year-old self now?" I asked.

"Well, I can see there are other kids who feel uncomfortable, so rather than feel isolated, I can just go make some friends," he said.

"Great and imagine doing that now," I said.

"Yeah, it feels really good. I did make a really good friend in that class, Jeff," he said.

"Wonderful, so now we are going to grow up through time, but only as quickly as your unconscious mind is able to make the updates at all the levels and ages of you as we move forward through time, integrating these positive messages: the future is bright, strangers are friends you haven't met yet, growing through the years of you," I guided Kevin to walk forward on the imaginary line, "walking all the way back to the present moment as your unconscious mind integrates those changes and comes back to now."

"So now that we've helped that 5-year-old mind address the fear and create a new association with sunglasses, and 'strangers are friends waiting to happen.' Now think of walking into the next office to prospect, but now you have all of this, the sunglasses, your family, the family reunion, and even your friend Jeff. As you walk into the office to chat with the secretary, how does it look and feel to you now?" I asked.

"With the sunglasses on and the sense of family, I can just relax and be myself," he said.

"What if the secretary says no?" I asked.

"It's not a big deal, maybe the next one is a better fit. But when they see how good the program is, of course they'll set up the meetings," he said. I could see his confidence radiate through his posture.

We finished up the session and made plans to schedule the next session.

When Kevin came back in for the follow-up session he said, "This is amazing! I was able to use all the images we set up, I just walked into new offices, only felt the old fear once or twice like a small twinge, but I was totally able to bring myself back to focusing on the family reunion, my relatives and the sunglasses. I went to 10 new offices and landed 5 appointments to talk with bosses."

In Kevin's case, we gave his mind new things to focus on represented by the sunglasses. By giving his mind new images and meanings, we recoded what his brain was focusing on at the unconscious level so his automatic mind could think differently about that event. So now that his mind had the imagery and symbolism, he could stay feeling confident and radiate his charismatic, award-winning smile while prospecting.

With the old fear out of the way, Kevin was excited about making new contacts. He went on to meet all his sales quotas and even won two contests that same season for the most registrations, taking his wife on much-needed vacations to Hawaii and Mexico.

In this situation, there were some simple level changes to address by recoding the memory file responsible for the automatic fear response that Kevin was experiencing. Once his mind had new meanings and associations for meeting strangers, his mind was able to experience it differently and let his natural confidence shine through. From that place of feeling confident and positive, he was motivated to find new businesses and achieve his sales goals. Here's what Kevin had to say:

> *"Working with Holly made clear some of the phobias I had about prospecting new clients, finding energy where I couldn't before for key presentations. Structuring my work day and week to maximize my potential. Not only did I meet all my sales markers, I won the incentives and a cruise, but I also maximized my time and created work-life balance that allowed for more quality time with my wife and kids."-Kevin, 39.*

Kevin could have wasted a lot of time and struggle just trying to "make himself do it." If you have to battle your mind for what you are trying to achieve in life, it will burn you out. How much better to address what the mind is focusing on and give it a new focus to assist you in thinking differently, feeling differently so that moving forward is easier and more natural?

Inspired by Kevin's story, I asked myself, "What does my 10-year-old need in order to relax and not feel embarrassed when speaking in front of a group?"

I changed the memory of reciting the poem and getting stuck to imagining bringing cheat cards with me that I could refer to. I added in the feeling of all my later awards and accolades to my 10-year-old self and I felt like a rockstar. This was just a little glitch on the road of life, and I had learned along the way.

Reflection: Where do you feel subtle stress or fear? What patterns do you notice in your food, mood, and symptoms journal? What is your mind focusing on and what do you want it to do differently? What images, pictures, and symbolisms remind your mind to stay focused on that state of being that you want? Can you imagine doing the change now?

CHAPTER 20

The Body Responds to What You Think

I met with my breakfast networking group, we were about 12 business professionals. We ordered breakfast and the organizer of the group opened the meeting.

"Welcome everyone, Nancy will be doing our thought of the day and then Holly will be doing the 10-minute presentation, educating us about something in connection with her business."

"Ohh shoot! I didn't know I was speaking," I said. My food arrived in front of me, I must have forgotten to write it down. Well okay, I guess I'll just share what I have been learning."

"Do you want to skip this week and do next week?" Ken, the organizer asked.

"No I can do it, I'll just share what I've been learning about the stress and relaxation response," I said. I guess I would get to see how well my handy work on de-stressing myself would go in this surprise speaking moment.

It came to my turn to speak, I stood up and instantly accessed the healing light, it's so great I could use it in my mind as I thought about it. I started, "The body responds to what you think! Now hold on Holly, some of you might be saying. Isn't that pseudo-science to say that 'your body responds to what you think?' Well, let me explain. We know that the body physically responds to stress through the autonomic nervous system."

"There are two parts to the autonomic nervous system, the sympathetic and the parasympathetic. Think of them as a spectrum, operating opposite of each other: when one is engaged, the other is relaxed."

"The sympathetic nervous system engages when we are stressed, and the body activates the 'fight or flight' mode. It prepares the body to physically fight off an attacker or run away. The body releases stress hormones, adrenaline, and cortisol among others into the blood. Hormones are communicators, telling the body to run certain functions. These stress hormones cause the body to increase heart rate and respirations and directs blood away from the organs and to the muscles of the body for quick action," I explained.

"So what causes us stress?" I paused to allow my colleagues to respond.

"Family."

"Deadlines."

"Bad insurance policies!" Bruce piped in.

"Not having a retirement plan!" Karen added.

We all chuckled. I continued, "These are common stressors: family, coworkers, deadlines at work, jobs, money. I never heard mention of a hungry tiger or a rampaging elephant, but our bodies respond to modern-day stresses through the same pathway as if we are being chased by a tiger or an elephant. The body activates the same pathway of the 'fight or flight' response that our ancestors used to survive."

"The stressors we experience in today's world are not immediate danger, they are imagined threat or perceived threat. But in our everyday life, fighting the boss or running away from traffic are not typically going to work for us. And so we sit in this chemical stew of stress hormones, and we try to calm ourselves down or we distract ourselves with a snack, have you heard of stress eating?"

"The parasympathetic is the other end of the autonomic nervous system, this is the 'rest and digest' response. When we are stress eating, we are actually trying to activate the relaxation response as a way to calm ourselves and get out of stress," I said.

"The things that cause us stress now are not inherently dangerous: family, coworkers, deadlines, etc. But it's more *how we think* about these things that are causing the stress," I paused for effect.

"We can recognize that the mind has thoughts and then creates a chain of thoughts and meanings in the background, it can sound like this, *'What if I don't get my work done on time? ...then the boss won't be happy with me... then I'll be on the cutback list... and then what if lose my job? If I lost my job... I won't be able to pay my bills. What would happen then?"*

"And the mind continues expanding the story of what if-ing until we imagine scenarios of losing the job, the house, or significant other. These mental pictures communicate this imagined reality of loss to the unconscious automatic mind and the body responds to these thoughts and mental pictures. When we think of the negative events, the body releases the stress chemicals, and our body physically responds."

"So we can see through the stress response that the body physically responds to the thoughts we think. There is the influence of stress from outside of us, like traffic or deadlines. However, most of our stress comes from within our own minds; what the mind imagines actually creates the stress we experience. The mind can be running these stress or fear patterns automatically at the unconscious levels, so we don't even notice these thoughts because they are happening so fast, what we do notice is the feelings they leave behind."

"If the thoughts we think can cause the body to go into the stress response, then could we also use our thoughts to engage the opposite of stress, which is the relaxation response?"

"When we are relaxed, the mind and body focus on healing and repair. The body physically responds to relaxation by decreasing blood pressure, slowing the heart rate, recycling the stress hormones, and healing and repairing cells. It's in the relaxation response that the immune system creates new antibodies and updates its abilities to respond to foreign invaders. Knowing this, can we also enroll the mind to quell the stress, create inner calm and harmony, and from that affect the cells of the body to behave better in doing their jobs?" I asked.

"Why yes, yes it can. This is what Meditation and even Hypnosis are all about. Meditation and Hypnosis use similar states of the mind. There's quite a bit of research showing the link between meditation and how the body responds. When we start going into meditative states, the mind clears and the body responds by the relaxation response, even our brain wave patterns change."

"In our everyday busy mind, the brain operates in a Beta brain wave pattern characterized by 12.5 to 30 cycles per second or Hertz. As we calm the mind and body, the brainwave pattern slows and synchronizes activity across the brain, showing an Alpha brain wave pattern, known to be 8-12 cycles per second. As meditation or hypnosis states deepen, the brain wave activity continues to slow and synchronize to Theta brain wave pattern, 4-7 cycles per second."

"As the brainwave patterns slow and synchronize, moving from Beta brainwave states to Alpha brainwave states, the mind starts to think differently. Beta brainwaves are characterized by scattered thinking and difficulty with paying attention. As we move into Alpha brainwave states, the mind becomes clearer, opening up creativity and inspiration. Alpha brainwave states are associated with clear thinking and finding creative solutions. The body also responds with the 'Relaxation Response' by lowering heart rate and lowering blood pressure."

"The blood moves from skeletal muscles to the organs and the brain, facilitating digestion, absorption and the body begins to prioritize healing and repair activities in Alpha brain wave states. The body updates the immune system and works on creating antibodies. Theta brain wave states take the mind and body deeper into the relaxation, healing, and repair states. These are all natural states of the mind and body. We go through all these brainwave patterns while we sleep at night. This is all outlined in Dr. Herbert Benson's book *The Relaxation Response*."

"An article from Psychology Today, "20 Reasons to Start Meditating Today," cites the research showing how meditation affects the brain using Magnetic Resonance Imaging. Some of this research shows meditation alleviates depression and loneliness, it can also increase compassion and well-being. Meditation has been shown to manage and reduce pain. Meditation naturally takes us into the Relaxation Response, engaging the parasympathetic nervous system and causing the body to go into healing and repair mode. This is where the body's energies are focused into digestion, absorption of nutrients, repairing cellular damage, creating new cells, and updating the immune system."

"The research also shows that meditation over time can actually change your brain. So you can clearly see now that the body responds physically to what we think about. Most of the source of stress we experience comes from within our own minds. When we clear up our stressful thoughts, we can clear up anxieties, worries, and even phobias," I said.

"We can do relaxation activities, making time for yoga, journaling, and meditation. But these activities only address the symptoms of stress, not the source. If we really want to clean up levels of stress in the mind and body, we can address the source of stress instead. With NLP & Hypnosis, we can do this by quickly setting up new habits of relaxation and inner calm. We can keep our inner calm even during stressful situations. We can set up the inner states of calm which the mind can tap into and use in difficult situations and stressful times."

Would it be okay if I walked you through an example of this using the "Healing Light Bubble Sequence," I said. I saw heads nod around the table. I then took about five minutes to walk them through the process.

"And coming back to your everyday awareness, notice how you are feeling now rather than before we started?" I asked.

"Yeah, my mind feels clear," Bruce said.

"I feel really calm and light," Shari chimed.

I saw their heads nod around the table.

I checked in with my nervous system, it felt calm and clear. I had an inner calm that I could feel in the background of my mind with the resources I had set up previously for my mind. This surprise speaking event showed me the changes I made for my own mind had worked for speaking. There was no embarrassment, my face wasn't flushing red and I could feel the inner calm and clarity shining through.

Reflection: What's your morning self-care routine? How can you use meditation to quell stress and clear your mind to start your day and build up your inner states of harmony and well-being? In the places where you feel triggers and stress, what resources do you want your mind to take on for you so your mind and body can respond differently?

CHAPTER 21

Food Sensitivities as Stress Patterns

One of my clients, Tammy, recently graduated high school and was moving into college. Her parents wanted her to have positive study skills while attending college and to balance succeeding in her studies while having fun in college.

Tammy and I met by phone through our work together. We started with addressing habits and patterns around studying and learning as she was applying herself to college courses.

About our 5th visit, we started like any other, "What would you like your brain to do for you?" I asked.

She said, "I just have a hard time avoiding all the foods I have allergies to at the college. My parents bought me the meal plan, but I find it hard to find foods I can eat."

"And also I need to work on brain fog in the afternoons, somedays I have a hard time staying awake. I even do the head nod in my classes, one day I fell asleep at my desk. My brain just won't pay attention. I've skipped some classes to go to my dorm and take a nap, but I can't keep doing that," Tammy said.

I knew that food sensitivities could make a difference with brain fog particularly. "Well, Tammy, what foods you are allergic to?" I asked. Thinking we could create a strategy to avoid one or two foods and find healthier options.

"Well, I'm allergic to peanut butter, milk, bananas, strawberries, bread, melons, pineapple, and peaches, the canned ones, but I can eat fresh ones," she said.

Hmm, I thought, this list was certainly longer than I expected. Maybe there was a bigger pattern involved. I decided to look for the deeper pattern of what the brain was coding.

"Okay," I said, "just sit back and relax allow yourself to get comfortable. You can do this with eyes closed or eyes open," I said.

"And now imagine that familiar bubble of light washing down through your head, clearing out the mental clutter, let it wash through your body all the way to the bottoms of your feet, and now imagine that bubble glowing out around you, radiating that light around you one foot, two foot," I said.

"And now in your bubble, let your mind take you back to see the time and place where your mind first started the pattern of allergies to these foods," I said. "What do you see?" I asked.

"Hmm, I see I'm five years old, my mom dropped me off at daycare," she said.

"What is going on?" I asked.

"Well, there's only one adult, and there's a kid is crying in the corner," she said. "My mom just left and left me with these strangers," she said.

"What is your mind saying about this situation?" I asked.

"I feel alone. It's saying I'm alone," she said. "I don't know if Mom is coming back," she said. I could hear some distress in her voice.

"What else is going on here?" I asked.

"Well, I just feel nervous, I start to cry," she said. "But the teacher tells me not to cry and gives me a strawberry," she said.

"Then what?" I asked.

"Well, I don't want the strawberry, I want my Mom, but I eat it anyway," Tammy said.

"Okay, what else do you notice here?" I asked.

"Well, it's lunchtime and they are feeding us peanut butter and jelly sandwiches," she said.

Hmm...my intuition piqued, this sounded like the allergy list she gave me earlier. "What else are they feeding you for lunch," I asked.

"Oh yeah, there's melons too and pineapple," she said.

"What is the five-year-old self feeling?" I asked.

"Scared, trying to calm down. I don't know if Mom is coming back, why did she leave me?" she said, her voice starting to quaver.

"Okay as your older wiser self, you know Mom came back and you can see she always loves you," I said. "Go ahead and tell your five-year-old self what she needs to know about Mom leaving you at daycare," I said.

"Yes, of course she came back, I do feel loved by my family," she said.

"Have your five-year-old self look forward through time to see you as you are now, knowing you survived, that your family always loves you, you are safe and cared for," I said. "How does it feel now?" I asked.

"Better, yes this tightness in my stomach just relaxed," she said.

"Wonderful to notice that, and now the five-year-old just really wants Mom. If the five-year-old could be with your Mom, what would she feel? I asked.

"Loved," she said.

"Yes and when your Mom isn't there physically does she stop loving you?" I asked.

"No, she loves me," she said.

"So we can recognize the love continues whether people are present or not, right?" I asked.

"Right," she said.

"Okay, so as the five-year-old self, imagine a ray of light shining from your heart to Mom's heart that represents the love you feel for her and feel the love coming back again. Can you imagine that?" I asked.

"Yes, I can feel she loves me," she said.

"Now with this connection to Mom, let's also add rays of light for each member of your family, knowing you are loved wherever you go, you are always loved even when your people are not physically present," I said.

"Yes, I feel that," she said.

"Now that the 5-year-old self feels always loved, what would you like her to know about staying at daycare while Mom goes to work?" I asked.

"She needs to know she's not alone, she can relax, know she's loved, and she can even have fun and make friends," she said.

"Wonderful, were there some fun activities at daycare? What were they?" I asked.

"I liked to draw and color and some days they'd let us do finger painting and singing," she said.

"Okay great, so now seeing all those lunch foods on the table that your mind had associated to this discomfort with daycare and the feeling of being alone. But now that you know you aren't alone and you can feel your family's love for you, that you are always connected with their love even when they're not physically present. And now we're going to replace all the fear with the awareness that you are safe and there are fun activities to do like finger painting, making friends, and singing. And you probably would have been bored at work with your Mom wouldn't you?"

"Yes, the adult world is boring for five-year-olds," she laughed.

"And now bring all these activities in front of those foods and now ask your unconscious mind to clear out all the fears associated with those foods until they are bright and colorful, even let them radiate brightness, how do they look to you now?" I asked.

"It looks good, the foods are really bright, they look actually kind of fun," she said.

"Okay and now we are going to ask your unconscious mind, now that it has removed the associated fears from these foods, it can send them out to recycle in the way you already know. Can your mind and body now recognize the goodness of these foods to nourish your body?" I asked.

"It feels like yes," she said.

"Wonderful, thanking your unconscious mind for working with you and working for you," I said. "And now that your unconscious mind can recognize the goodness in these foods and that they can work with your body and can mean fun, how does your body feel about them now?" I asked.

"My body feels good," Tammy said. "I want to try them again."

"Okay wonderful, is there any place within Tammy that is not okay with these foods or does it feel clear?" I asked.

"It feels clear, except for something," Tammy said.

"Tune into it, ask your unconscious mind to project a picture of it onto a movie screen in your mind's eye," I said.

"I see bread…..I feel like my body is saying no to bread," she said.

"Wonderful, again thanking your unconscious mind for working for you and with you," I said.

"And now just see the cleared foods and the brightness of them, just tuck them into the background of your mind, feeling the goodness of them, the clarity of them, how does that feel?" I asked.

"It feels really good," she said.

"Okay, now just coming back to your everyday awareness, back into your body feeling renewed, refreshed, all the way back now, as your unconscious mind integrates to all the places, ages of you," I said.

"Okay, that was interesting Tammy that those foods were ones associated with daycare. It sounds like your child's mind associated those foods with the high alert and the fears of being alone," I said.

"So now do I just try eating the foods?" Tammy asked.

"Well, it depends on how safe you feel with eating the foods, did you have an anaphylactic reaction or just irritation? If you had only mild symptoms you could try just one at a time, then wait about 72 hours to make sure there are no symptoms from it. Even though you had mild symptoms, it's best to be safe and have an epi-pen available, do you have one handy?" I asked.

"Yes, she said. "I keep it for bee stings."

"Great. Allergies are interesting, they can show up for no apparent reason and they can disappear for no reason. The mind is coding a food or a thing like a dog or cat, it's coding it as a threat when there is no threat, the threat is how the body responds to the food or the dog or the cat," I said. "So we just recode how the mind thinks of them and allergies can disappear," I said.

"That's so interesting," Tammy said. "I'm going to definitely give it a try this week."

"Only test one food at a time. You could also contact your doctor to arrange a medical allergy test to make sure it's clear," I said.

"Well, the only symptoms I really get from eating the foods is a swollen tongue," she said. "It doesn't affect my airway," she said.

"Okay sure, you can also use the body intuition check to just make sure," I said. I took her through a couple of minutes of showing her how to ask her body and unconscious mind if the foods would be okay, she got "Yes." We also went through some strategies for avoiding bread on campus and getting healthier options. She also committed to speaking with the admin of the cafeteria to see if they could offer gluten-free options and lettuce leaves for wraps. We wrapped up the session, Tammy agreed to action steps for the next week to support her progress with healthy food options and her studies.

I thought about the autoimmune condition in light of allergy responses, there were definitely similarities. When I had flare-ups I would get a rash, that's a skin irritation. Sometimes it would be itchy which is similar to hives, but not so extreme. I also thought back to the cases I came across where a woman stopped eating potatoes, and her Lupus cleared up. And the other case where a woman stopped drinking artificial sweeteners and her Lupus cleared up. Perhaps allergen foods were a bigger factor in the autoimmune condition than I had thought. Certainly, food sensitivities or allergies could cause extra stress on the system creating a stress overload, aggravating the condition.

The Anti-Inflammatory Diet was helping and when I ate clean and whole foods I certainly felt better, but also it didn't seem to be a complete answer. I had seen the theme of underlying fears associated with allergy cases like allergies of dogs and cats that I had cleared with NLP tools. It was interesting to understand allergies to foods in a similar way. It made sense, the mind codes a food as a threat when it's not really a threat but the body reacts to it. And perhaps there's some tipping point of unconscious stress and fear patterns that then affect how the immune system operates.

Reflection: Pay attention to your food and mood journal and notice if there are times of more digestive upset. If so, what's your history with these foods and is there a past event causing associations of underlying fears or stress? As we resolve the past, the mind then recodes the associations and we can tip the unconscious patterns toward more inner calm and harmony. As the mind achieves inner calm and harmony, the body will follow.

CHAPTER 22

Positive Intentions of Cravings

I knew that nutrition and eating healthy were important to how the body functions, even foundational to health. I knew eating an Anti-inflammatory diet was helpful, I knew it made my joints feel better and I had better energy.

But although I knew the difference it made for me in how I felt, why was I still tempted by cravings? Why did I still give in cookies and sweets? Why couldn't I just stick with the program?

As a professional, I was helping clients overcome cravings, so I looked inward for my own patterns. In meditation, I cleared my mind and went to that relaxing state where the deeper mind can communicate, where inspiration can be heard and I settled into the inner quiet.

"I ask my mind to bring forward the parts of my mind in charge of the cravings," I said. "What are the cravings about?" I asked.

Inner voice: *I don't want to be well.* That was weird, of course, I want to be well, but my training told me to have patience and listen deeply to understand.

Me: "Why not?" I asked.

Inner voice: *Hurt. Slow down.*

Me: "So my mind is craving wheat so that I eat poorly and feel bad, in feeling bad I slow down?"

Inner voice: *Yes, sad,* whispered some part of my mind.

Me: "I'm not sad. My life is really good," I talked back, arguing with myself. "I love my work. I have a supportive partner. We have a comfortable home, five beautiful acres overlooking a meadow where the deer wander across the lawn every morning. We have a wonderful deck that looks out across the acreage where we sit and watch the night sky."

Me: "I have everything I want, John, my big German shepherd Moki, my cat Chupacabra, I love my home life, I love my environment. I love my life." I said.

Inner voice: *Sad.*

Me: "Okay, what is 'the sad' about?"

Inner voice: *I'm not okay.*

Me: "Of course I'm okay. My life is good. I may not be out on the rivers anymore, but there's so much to love, so much to appreciate in my life. I'm not sad."

Inner voice: *Sad.*

Me: "Okay, what is this sad all about?"

Inner voice: *Hurt. I want to hurt.*

Me: "What do you mean you want to hurt? Why would you want to hurt?"

Inner voice: *It's sad, hurting shows my hurt.*

Me: "Okay, what is the hurt? Where is the hurt?"
Inner voice: *Seven years old.*

I breathed into it. I asked my mind to take me back to the hurt of seven years old, where was the hurt? I could see the bubble but it was dark, I couldn't see it. Asking my mind to peel it back, what do I see now? Nothing. I couldn't see anything.

I knew what it was. When I was seven years old, I was traumatized by neighborhood boys who did unspeakable things. It first surfaced years ago when I was diagnosed with IBS, Irritable Bowel Syndrome.

Years ago, I had lived in France for a little over a year and when I returned to Utah, I felt somewhat lost and displaced. My parents had divorced while I was away and they had moved to different cities. My friends had all moved away to different towns and I was left with rebuilding my life. So I started with what I knew and I went back to work for wilderness programs. I had a couple years of experience as a wilderness guide and counselor backpacking with troubled teens before I left, I still had contacts in the companies and it was easy to get a job there.

My mother was building a cabin in the hills of Utah which bordered national forest. It didn't have water or electricity or flushing toilets, but it had a roof. The camping world was familiar, living out of a backpack and nature was sort of my thing. The cabin sounded perfect, a little plot of earth with open arms and blue skies in the warm embrace of the Utah mountains.

I was camping at the cabin in the hills outside of town. I had a small Geo Metro that I drove into town about 9 miles away to get supplies. I loved the land, the juniper, and the smell of the sagebrush. I split my time between camping at the cabin for my weeks off and then working for a week on the wilderness trail. The wilderness programs operated year-round, and I worked mostly in winter. Yes, it was somewhat brutal weather in the Utah winter snow, but we had good gear and good support staff.

The summers I left open to teach wilderness survival classes and follow the primitive skills gatherings. And I loved the summer months on the land, the warm sun, the blue skies, and the quiet of the mountains. The property bordered a national forest so there was little foot traffic, just an occasional horse and rider would wander through as they had missed the main horse trail up the road.

Working with wilderness programs was familiar, I settled into the groove of working a week on the trail with the teens and a week off at the cabin. But after working a few weeks on the trail, I started to notice my stomach was just cramping all the time, it felt irritated. It was irritated after meals, it was irritated at night, and it seemed to be getting worse. I wasn't sure what to do.

I finally made an appointment with a local doctor, and he diagnosed it as IBS, Irritable Bowel Syndrome, and prescribed medications. The medications helped a little bit, but not enough. It was more than uncomfortable to be out camping with stomach cramping and diarrhea, especially when you had to dig a hole each time you went to the bathroom.

I spoke with my sister who lived nearby, and she recommended I see a psychologist, one she had also worked with. I did a few sessions with the psychologist who also happened to have hypnosis training as well. He took me through a light hypnosis state, similar to meditation, and asked, "What is this stomach cramping and irritation about?"

My body shook with fear, and I burst out crying, deep heart-rending sobs. And that was the first time this abuse story from my childhood came to light. It was overwhelming and intense, I didn't know it was there. We had looked for the reason behind IBS and this memory just popped up.

The emotions were overwhelming: it was horrifying with so much confusion, terror, and hopelessness. Working together we unraveled the story that seemed to be a bottomless pit. From working through the trauma of this extreme abuse, the IBS got better until it just disappeared. I had no more need for medications, and I was able to continue working on the trail with the wilderness programs again.

Life continued that way for a few years until I followed a wilderness program to Bend, Oregon where I met John. After about a year working there, I went back to school to finish my degree in psychology at Portland State University and John bought a house in Washington about an hour away.

As I had asked in meditation," What are the cravings about?" I learned the deeper positive intention of the cravings for the allergen foods was to make me feel bad so I slowed down. My mind was continuing to crave unhealthy foods, sabotaging myself so I would feel hurt in my body. The hurt in my body reflected the inner emotional layers of trauma that were not yet resolved. Pain, whether physical or emotional, is a signal that something needs care or attention in the mind or body. As we pay attention and resolve the emotional hurts of the mind, the body can follow into rebalancing and healing.

In NLP we say to look for the positive intention of the parts of the mind causing sabotage, what are they trying to do? It seemed a part of my mind was trying to get me to pay attention, to slow down so I would do the inner work of resolving more layers of the hurts still internalized within. It felt daunting to try to clear it on my own. This would make sense, however, that the Lupus symptoms were being perpetuated by unconscious fear patterns, causing stress and inflammation and this old story was a viper's nest of trauma, fear, and confusion.

The traumas from the past were resurfacing, it felt too overwhelming to go looking on my own. I sat in meditation asking, "Who would be helpful in helping me resolve this history?" I sat in silence. A flash of a recent friend came to mind. He had come to one of the stress relief workshops at the yoga center.

I called to make a time to network with Rich. He also had a similar background and training in NLP & Hypnosis, perhaps we could compare notes on traumas.

When we met at a coffee shop, I heard his explanation of Thought Pattern Management. He shared his own story of what he had overcome and all the tools and strategies he used, some worked better than others. One strategy he found highly useful was Thought Pattern Management, a modality based on principles of NLP & Hypnosis, but with a slightly different focus: to teach the mind strategies and automate its processes using the body's natural intelligence.

He said, "Sometimes the mind holds onto past negative events because it recognizes there are positive learnings from those events. But if it hasn't fully processed or resolved the old history, the negative ideas or energy of it will continue to replay in the mind and be expressed through the body.

Once the mind learns to 'recycle' the negative past events into positive lessons and learnings, it can make peace with the past and let it go. It can do this at the unconscious level, we don't even need to know consciously what it's recycling, it can just do it for us."

I was intrigued and we set up a time where Rich would take me through the process so I could see how it worked for myself. Through the process of Thought Pattern Management or TPM I felt I was able to release core fears that my mind had been holding and even uplevel to a new level of well-being.

With advanced processes of TPM, it can even run 'recycling' automatically, changing our energy levels and lifting the baseline of our well-being. As so many of my clients have found huge benefits from TPM processes, I've made it foundational to the work that I do. With the first single session we can teach the mind to learn its way out of the emotional loops we get stuck in like anxiety and depression by teaching the mind to let things go and recycle.

Reflection: When we experience traumatic events, it requires more than just knowing the old story, we need to help the brain and unconscious mind resolve and recode the events. Just talking about the event doesn't necessarily help it clear. If your meditation practice uncovers a traumatic story, please seek the help of a qualified professional.

With the advances in NLP and TPM modalities, there are easier ways to resolve and clear traumas at the unconscious levels, without the need to re-live the old stories, which can be re-traumatizing and cause emotional and physical reactions of the mind and body. We can resolve even traumas and layers of stress at the unconscious levels, addressing and resolving traumas more easily without the need of re-telling the details of the negative story. We can teach the unconscious mind strategies for recycling the old stories so the mind to sort it, resolve it, and recode it, which then allows for new habits of well-being in how the mind-body-spirit system responds.

If you've had experiences with past negative history resurfacing, we sometimes think the previous work we did, "didn't work." While we may have found relief at different times or with different modalities, there can be multiple layers of the mind affected even from a single event. Especially traumas can affect multiple layers of the mind. The unconscious mind operates like a jar with many marbles.

So while you may find relief with a modality or clearing up one or two past traumatic events, you may not have addressed and resolved all the layers of it. If trauma resurfaces, it's your mind showing you what is left to be resolved. Take heart, it can be a process, and recognize your progress along the way. The mind cleans up in layers.

As so many of my clients have found huge benefits from TPM processes, I've made it foundational to the work that I do. With the first single session we can teach the mind to clear up past history at the unconscious level in a way that is gentle and allows the person to be safe, comfortable and secure. With this strategy the mind learns and then automates its ability to get out of emotion loops, ease the inner stress and establish and maintain higher levels of well-being.

There are several processes within NLP I have also found super useful in addressing and resolving traumas in a content-free strategy. In recent research, some of the NLP processes went through clinical trials to test the effectiveness of these processes in working with veterans diagnosed with Post Traumatic Stress Disorder, PTSD. The NLP tools passed with flying colors, see the Resources section for the website link to see research results and brain scans.

Reflection: Illness often asks us to slow down, be more clear with ourselves, and resolve unconscious layers of stress. We can recognize symptoms of the body as messages from the unconscious mind. Your mind and body are working for you, what is it trying to tell you? Create time for inner reflection, meditation, and intuition. Recognize the symptoms of the body are the unconscious mind bringing you messages about your state of being and asking for awareness or resolution for your next level of healing.

CHAPTER 23

Irritable Bowel Syndrome: Mind-Body Stress

Ryan walked into my office, a dapper 30-year-old with dark hair, dark eyes, and a clean-shaven face. His suit jacket and slacks announced he was a young professional. We shook hands in greeting, I invited him to take a seat in my office.

I reviewed his paperwork and asked, "So what brings you in today?"

He said, "I've had Irritable Bowel Syndrome for years. It seems to come on when I travel. I just moved here from New York and my new doctor thinks it's stress related. I've been through all the tests and there's nothing physically wrong with me. The medications help somewhat, but not all the time. Ultimately, I'd like to not take medications and my doctor suggested I try Hypnosis to reduce the stress and he recommended you."

"Well, I'm so glad you came in Ryan. Yes, most of our stress comes from within the mind. When the mind runs automatic stress patterns, it certainly can affect how we feel and how the body responds. So tell me, what are the symptoms you experience?" I asked.

"Well IBS comes and goes, but I get stomach cramps, my intestines start to hurt and cramp up and then I just have to go to the bathroom, I get diarrhea. And it's crazy, even if I've already gone to the bathroom, my body thinks it has to go again."

"So when do you notice these symptoms coming on? What makes it worse?" I asked.

"Well, I notice it when I get stressed. When I travel it gets really bad too, so I stopped taking trips at work in my sales job. I also notice it if I have to speak in meetings," he said.

"Any other things you've noticed that make it worse?" I asked.

"No that's pretty much it, speaking, stress, and traveling. If I could get some help with this, it would make a huge difference for me. In fact, there's a promotion I'd like to apply for, but it means more travel. I don't know if I can take the promotion with my body acting like this," he said.

"It sounds like you've noticed traveling is a trigger, so tell me about travel, what are your earliest memories of traveling?" I asked.

"Not very good. As a kid, my parents got divorced and my mom was always moving around. She had a hard time keeping a stable job and I remember as early as 6 or 7 years old, packing and unpacking a small brown suitcase. We stayed with relatives a few months at a time, I often slept on the couch and we just kept moving each couple of months," Ryan said.

"That definitely explains the stress related to travel. It sounds like your mind is associating that history of life being unstable and chaos with travel rather than seeing travel as fun and adventure," I said.

"Yeah, I guess that makes sense," Ryan replied. "I really would like to enjoy travel, my fiancé loves to travel and I would love to enjoy it like she does. But anytime we go somewhere, I have to make sure there's bathrooms available and I just feel so nervous about it, I can't relax," he said. "I tell myself travel is supposed to be fun, but it doesn't seem to make a difference to my body."

"At the conscious level, you can say 'travel means fun and adventure,' but the unconscious mind is running the old program of 'travel means instability and chaos' and your body is reacting to the stress of that," I said.

"And now tell me, what does it mean to you if you have to speak in a meeting?" I asked.

"Do you mean how do I feel about it? Well, I get really stressed."

"So thinking back to the last time you had to speak in a meeting, what was your mind saying right before you had to speak?" I asked.

"Well, we were sitting around a conference room table, I had to get up and go to the bathroom again. I was worrying about my turn. I guess I was thinking, 'I don't want to look stupid.'" Ryan said.

"What have you tried so far?" I asked.

"I've tried getting myself pumped up before the meeting before I speak. I've said, 'I'm not going to mess this up.' But when it's my turn to speak, I have to rush to the restroom," he said. "It's so embarrassing. Even though I make sure to go to the restroom before the meeting, it doesn't matter."

"Yes, I can see a pattern. I look for the pattern of brain habits running in the background that are causing these stress triggers. Then we can start changing the brain habits and help your mind switch to referencing the positive things you want your brain to be doing for you instead. The mind informs the body and the automatic mind or unconscious mind informs the body automatically," I said.

I continued, "Sounds like you have a pattern of worry about 'looking stupid' when speaking and then running a fear loop around it. Worry is usually about projecting our fears into the future, 'what if this happens, what if that happens,'" I said. "The worry causes anxiety and then the body responds to the anxiety and stress with the symptoms."

We then went through a few different sessions to train the brain out of stress habits and patterns, teaching the mind how to learn its way out of the old patterns of stress, worry, and anxiety. The unconscious mind integrates change more quickly through its own language, so if we want the unconscious mind to take on a new behavior or a new focus, we can make it more memorable by wrapping it in a story or metaphor.

In asking the unconscious mind to replace the internalized stress with instead inner calm, I asked Ryan to bring up a positive memory of a time and place he felt calm. He described a wonderful memory of a beautiful mountain lake, watching ducks float on the water.

I then created a Hypnosis session for Ryan's mind to take on an inner habit of calm, using the memory and the image of the ducks. We asked the stomach to take on the feeling of relaxation, like floating above the water, so that he could carry the calm internally. The duck's feet can still be working underneath, swimming, paddling, and guiding the duck even while working very fast under the water, suggesting that Ryan's stomach could remain calm and effortless as if floating on water, even as Ryan was busily moving through his day.

The images of the duck and the lake gave his mind a quick cue to get back to the inner calm we created in the hypnosis session. I also recorded the session so Ryan could continue to listen and refresh his mind-body system.

After a few weeks, Ryan came back to check in.

"What have you noticed in the past weeks?" I asked.

"This stuff is amazing! I just don't have the stomach cramping during meetings, I feel more confident with speaking. I'm feeling so much better, I'm going to try traveling as it can really help my sales career. I have a trip scheduled with my fiancé, so we'll see how it works and if all goes well I'm going to go for that promotion!"

"That's great, have you also been using the hypnosis recordings we did for you?" I asked.

"Oh yes, I used them religiously for the first week, but then it was just like my body had it. So when I started feeling nervous in a meeting, I just pictured the duck floating on the water and my stomach would calm right down," he said.

"Great! I love to hear that you are using the skills we set up for you. Any other problem spots?" I asked.

"No. I'm really excited about this upcoming trip and I keep thinking how I have choices as an adult, that I get to choose travel as fun and adventure, I really think I got this," Ryan replied. This echoed how we had reframed travel from being a youngster, bouncing from place to place with his mom. As an adult, he got to choose travel for fun and adventure and still keep stability in his life. We had used the image of his brown suitcase, packing it with images of fun, travels and adventures.

"Wonderful. Well I'm here if you need a touchup, but as everything sounds like it's on track, just keep using the imagery and you can use the hypnosis recordings as a refresher as well," I said.

Sometimes issues are a little more complicated than a few sessions, it depends on how many 'brain tangles' are involved. When we look at the brain as running a series of habits, it becomes a whole lot easier to untangle stress, worry, and anxiety patterns that are aggravating the mind-body system. It's all about helping the mind switch its focus from thoughts and habits causing stress to focus on better thoughts and habits that support how we want to show up in life. And especially addressing these patterns at the levels of the unconscious mind.

What the mind focuses on affects the body. Some of our stress habits and patterns are more obvious in the specific situations causing the stress that Ryan was experiencing. But some stress habits and patterns that are running automatically can be so subtle they aren't recognized. What we do recognize are the feelings or effects the stress patterns create and especially if the stress affects the body.

The doctors had no medical explanation for the IBS, but in understanding brain habits, we recognized that the body had created a habit of internalized stress and anxiety patterns. After only 5 sessions, Ryan reports he's symptom-free! Here's what Ryan had to say in his own words:

> *"I found new tools that I could tap into, a greater ability to handle life situations more comfortably and with less stress or worry. My body has been*

doing great from the work we did and the positive imaging and attitude you've helped me create and enforce has been helping so much!" — Ryan, age 32

In Ryan's case, by helping the mind-body replace stress with inner calm and by addressing the meanings of the mind, causing stress which were running in the background, he could then create habits of inner calm to replace the internalized stress. He could access his confidence, his talents, and think clearer, and the body responded by feeling calm and comfortable.

It felt so satisfying to hear the excitement in Ryan's voice and watch his eyes light up as he explained his results and his aspirations for the future. Ryan did go on to get the promotion and take the traveling job, increasing his income and being able to truly feel good in his body and enjoy his work, even when speaking and traveling. It was so satisfying to see him overcome this hurdle and move beyond the limitations of his mind to embrace a bigger picture for his life and bring his dreams into reality, I was thankful for being able to play this small part in his journey.

Reflection: What stress triggers are you noticing and what is your mind saying about them? See the Resources section for research on IBS, Irritable Bowel Syndrome, and Hypnosis.

CHAPTER 24

Acupuncture As Energetic Modality

I walked into the small clinic, and Cristina was there, greeting me with a warm smile. She had long dark brown wavy hair and blue eyes that sparkled in the natural light from the windows. She was dressed in soft blue scrubs.

"Come on in," she said. She invited me in and motioned for me to sit at a wooden table next to an open window. "Would you like some mint tea while we go over the intake paperwork together?"

"That would be lovely," I said.

She made the tea and placed it in front of me. She took a seat at the table with me while I started to sip the hot liquid. As she went through the questions from my paperwork, I felt relieved that she was open to trading services acupuncture for hypnosis, it really helped to have a skill I could offer and could offset some of the medical care costs.

I spent a few minutes telling her the backstory of my condition and defining what results I was hoping for. I filled out the paperwork and handed it back to her. She took the clipboard, looking over my responses.

"Okay I think we have all the notes here," she said at looking up from the clipboard. "We have a treatment plan now."

"I've experienced Acupuncture before, but honestly I don't know that much about how it works," I said.

"Well, in the Chinese Medicine model, we recognize the symptoms are only a small part of what is going on in the body. There can actually be many factors affecting our health. The causal factors of illness include everything in our life: our balance of life energy, the food we eat, our relationships, our social support and connections, and so on," she said.

"In the Chinese approach, we use needles on specific energy points of the body, these are called meridians, to activate the body's life force energy or chi. It's about balancing the energetic systems of the body and resetting the energy communication of the body's systems," she said. "This energetic balance allows the flow of qi, releases blocks, and restores the body's natural harmony between systems."

"Most people are worried about the needles, but it doesn't hurt if you do it right," she said. "The needles are so small you can't even feel them. So let's get started." I followed her down the hallway and into a cozy room with a massage table, covered with a terry cloth sheet.

"You can keep your clothes on for this, just take off your shoes and get comfortable on the table," she said.

I jumped on the table and settled in. She turned on soft music with running water, the environment was just so peaceful, I could feel myself starting to relax. She dimmed the lights to a soft golden glow from a lamp in the corner.

"Do I keep my eyes open or closed?" I asked.

"Whatever you want, some people like to just close their eyes and rest," she said.

She maneuvered around the small room, inserting the needles quickly with skill, placing about a dozen of them. "Okay, now we just let the needles set for about 30 minutes, you can just relax and rest. I'll come back to check on you and take them out for you later. So for now, just relax," she said and left the room.

The sound of the water in the background took me to a place near a favorite stream listening to the trickle of the water. With my eyes closed, my mind started going to that familiar place of hypnotic relaxation that I had experienced many times in meditation and in my work.

I relaxed into it, feeling the flow of breath, imagining healing light flowing through me. As I was imagining the light, I felt and noticed the finer energies flowing between the needles. It was like my mind could picture it, a blue electrical light moving between the needles, and I could actually feel it and I felt the needles buzz in my arms and through my scalp with tingles in a comforting way.

I was fascinated, I had experienced acupuncture before when I had a shoulder that had locked up when I was guiding on the rivers in Bend, Oregon. In just a few sessions with acupuncture, I was able to move my arm and get my range of motion back when other things hadn't worked.

But this, I could see and feel the energy system and the flow of it through my body, it felt soft and soothing. I decided to be a curious observer, what is this? what is it showing me?

I drifted in and out of a haze of blue-green energies and the relaxing rhythmic music with the sound of the stream flowing. It felt like the music was moving through my body and from each needle, like a soft web of blue-green threads pulsating between the needles.

I lost track of time as I ebbed and flowed in the energies and the music.

"How are you doing?" Cristina's soft voice was next to me. I opened my eyes and looked around.

"Good, I think," I said as I was coming back to the sound of the music, the running stream, and the softly lit room.

"I'm just going to remove these needles, and we can schedule for our next visit," Cristina said as she moved around the table. "Sometimes people notice effects from acupuncture immediately and sometimes over the next few days, just pay attention to how you feel."

I left the acupuncture office, feeling the inner quiet and still feeling the energy buzz. It was a soft feeling, a quiet flowing feeling. It felt good to relax and take a break from the world for a time, but I was curious to see how it would work. *What if it was all interconnected somehow? The energetic system, the life force, the mind, the body how did it all fit together?* I wondered.

The next day sitting with my journal, watching the meadow, I reflected on how I felt. I did notice the rash that had been on my leg was now clearing up and I felt I had more available energy, there was a subtle underlying level of well-being.

Reflection: Do you have a resistant symptom or illness? Research is showing amazing results with Complementary and Alternative Medicine, CAM modalities. Expand your approach to self-care and healing by trying a new modality. Clear your mind and meditate for 15 minutes or more, simply ask the question, "What's the next CAM modality that would be a fit for me?" In the healing journey, we may need to draw on multiple approaches. Use your intuition to recognize what's your best next step?

CHAPTER 25

Healing the Heart

Paul was an older gentleman in his 70s with white hair and a little extra around the middle. He was a client with one of the massage therapists in the wellness clinic, he found out I worked with hypnosis and he was interested in changing cravings and losing weight. We started working together on creating healthy lifestyle habits and changing cravings.

On our fifth visit, I greeted Paul in the waiting room and walked him back to my office motioning for him to have a seat in the reclining chair.

"So Paul, thank you for coming in today. What do you most want your brain to do for you today?" I asked.

"Well, I've been noticing great results, I no longer have cravings and the session we did last week around not eating bread really worked. It's like I just don't see the appeal of it anymore. I know I could eat it if I wanted, I just don't want it. So that's all working really well," he said.

"It's amazing isn't it, what the mind can do for you?" I said excitedly.

"Yes and I was wondering, is there anything we can do for my heart?" He asked.

"Well tell me what's going on with your heart?" I asked with curiosity.

He said, "I had a heart attack last year. I just met with my cardiologist, and he said according to the scans, there is tissue death on the back of my heart from the heart attack, making my heart work harder and I could likely have another heart attack. Do you think the body could heal it?"

"We can certainly ask the mind what it can do and see if we can maximize your body's healing around it. It's your expanded mind that knows the possibilities and healing potential of your body," I said. "So let's get started."

We started into the session. I directed Paul into the first part of the relaxation sequence of hypnosis, a light trance state. He was still aware, just deeply relaxed.

I could see the deep relaxation as the lines of his face went soft and smooth. "And now Paul, feeling deeply relaxed and at ease, I want you to imagine that you can turn your eyes inward as if you can look through your body, even looking to see the area of the heart that was affected by the heart attack, can you see it?" I asked.

"Yes," Paul answered.

"Okay wonderful, now imagine as if you can shrink your awareness smaller and smaller and travel through your body to that place of your heart. If it had a color where the tissue damage is located, what color would it be?"

"It's dark, it's black," Paul said.

"Okay, now imagine going to that place of your heart, noticing the edges of it, the shape of it, and ask, 'What is this about?'" I directed.

Paul said, "I feel sadness." I saw the lines of his mouth go slack with emotion.

"Ask the sadness for just a moment, focusing on it, and ask, 'What is this sadness all about?'" I asked.

"Sorrow. I feel sorrow for all the intolerance of the world." A tear welled up at the corner of his eye and rolled down his cheek.

"Tell me more about this sorrow," I prompted.

"I've had so many friends who are gay, and they have experienced prejudice, and intolerance and have even been disowned by their families. I feel the pain of sadness that humanity is so lacking in love. It feels sad that humanity is so judgmental that they would turn against their own families, their own children," he said.

I didn't know the answer, it felt sad to me too. I knew this required a higher answer and it was beyond me. It wouldn't be enough to say, 'Don't be sad.' When part of the mind gets stuck or takes on mental blocks, the stuckness is only one perspective. To surpass it and move beyond the stuckness, we need higher wisdom, so that's where we went next.

"See and feel that familiar ray of light shining down through the top of your head, like a column of light, bringing in higher wisdom and insight. Now feel yourself rising up through the column of light, rising up above the earth, higher and higher, travel up through that column of light, and let it carry you all the way up to higher wisdom and insight. From that higher perspective of wisdom and insight, see your personality self down on the earth plane below struggling with the intolerance of humanity. As your higher self with wisdom and insight, now what do you say to your personality self on the earth plane below?"

The corners of Paul's mouth started to lift up into a glowing smile. There seemed to be a new light and radiance in his skin, "I see now that humankind is evolving and that it becomes more tolerant and loving, but this is bigger than my lifetime. It may take decades or generations, but humanity is moving toward greater love and acceptance and caring for everyone, not just those who agree with us," he said.

"Wonderful, is there anything else?" I asked.

"Yes, even those who turn away from love now, it's not their whole story. It's just a small part of their process," he said. "I can offer them love and compassion even though they are caught up in judgment and cannot see beyond their judgments to recognize greater love."

"What is an image or symbol that represents this wisdom for you?" I asked.

"A gold ring for hope," Paul said.

"Okay, wonderful, package up that lesson and insight into that gold ring, and now travel back down the column of light into your body and give that gold ring to your heart, let that gold ring fill the space in your heart where the black used to be and let it radiate out it's message: "Humanity is evolving to more love, it's just bigger than my lifetime. And now letting this message radiate throughout all parts of your mind-body-spirit system. There is hope for humanity, humanity is evolving into higher wisdom and greater love. And now check in with your heart, how does it feel to you now?"

"It feels better, lighter, more hopeful," Paul said with a gentle smile.

"Asking your unconscious mind, now that this area of your heart has cleared out the old beliefs, is it now possible to heal the damage of your heart?" I asked.

"It says yes," Paul said.

"Asking your mind is it willing and able to heal this damage in your heart now that you are embodying this higher perspective?" I asked.

"Yes, it couldn't before because of the block, but yes now it can," his face brightened.

"And asking your unconscious mind, your expanded mind, how long will it take to fully heal and repair this area of your heart? Years, months, weeks?" I asked.

"Months," Paul said.

"How many months, notice the first number that comes to mind," I said. The automatic mind is much quicker at processing so the first response comes from the unconscious mind, whereas our logical brain likes to think and reason and takes more time to process.

"Three. Three months," he said.

"Wonderful, thank your unconscious mind for communicating with you and taking on all these positive changes into all the places, levels, and ages of you, and now come back to your everyday awareness," I said.

On the next visit, we recorded a Hypnosis CD for Paul to listen to, in which he visualized his heart repairing the damage and him experiencing optimal health. Paul agreed to listen to the CD every day for the next 30 days. It was a few months before he would meet with his cardiologist, so we set up a time to meet after his next doctor's visit.

About 4 months later, Paul walked in, his eyes twinkling. "I have amazing results to share with you," Paul said. "I went to my Cardiologist and had new scans done to see how my heart is doing.

Paul was beaming, "The Cardiologist said he couldn't believe it, he said, 'your body isn't supposed to be able to heal heart tissue, especially tissue death, but it healed it.' He could hardly believe the new scans. My cardiologist says, I now have a totally healthy heart!"

"Wow, this is fantastic, so exciting! isn't it amazing what the mind-body-spirit system can do, who knows what it's really capable of?" I replied.

This isn't supposed to happen in Western Medicine. I remember in my pre-med classes we were told that heart tissue doesn't heal, once it's damaged, it's damaged. However, when we remove the inner blocks and apply some principles of direction for the unconscious mind, perhaps it opens up new possibilities for healing that we just haven't tapped into or previously understood.

Your unconscious mind or expanded mind knows what's possible for your body and your path of healing, so we can just ask it, "What's possible here?"

This is a powerful example of how our thoughts and emotions affect our health and healing. Utilizing the mind, we can address the stuck energy in the body and transform it into higher wisdom. As we clear the mental blocks and replace them with higher wisdom and insight, the body can rebalance and even heal itself. It's the body that innately knows how to heal and has the automatic programs to do it. Sometimes it just needs the blocks removed and the activation to heal itself.

After our sessions, Paul went back to teaching yoga at 70 years old and said he had more energy and felt better than he had 30 years ago. In my last contact with him, he was continuing to teach yoga in Vancouver, Washington. Here are his own words about the sessions we did.

"I originally began working with Holly to increase my health. I had a heart attack the year before and from the

tests, it showed tissue damage on the back of my heart. I had less energy and wasn't able to be as active as I was before. Holly and I worked on a program, focusing my mind on healing as well as changing my eating habits. As we made changes and I worked with the hypnosis audios for healing, I found I had more energy and was able to be more active. My doctor has also decreased my medications. Now, 6 months later, I got the report from my Cardiologist, and he said, 'The tissue damage is gone, your heart is now considered normal.' They were amazed at my heart's recovery. I have so much more energy and this is the best I've felt in years." – Paul, Vancouver Washington, yoga instructor.

The negative thoughts and beliefs that cloud our clarity and our happiness create energetic interference in the body and over time can lead to symptoms and take its toll on our health. When we recognize these mental blocks as the energetic and emotional interference causing stress and disruption in the body's systems, we can then address and resolve this interference and direct the mind and body to work together in the process of rebalancing and self-healing.

Reflection: What if our bodies have a greater capacity for healing than what we've previously been aware of? What if the mind-body-spirit system has greater abilities of rebalancing and healing once we clear out the inner blocks of the mind? Create quiet space and ask your mind-body-spirit system, "What is the next level of healing possible for me? What do I need to let go of to achieve this?" Notice what comes to mind, you may also want to journal about the responses that come up.

CHAPTER 26

Fibromyalgia as Stress & Pain Habits

Jessica had been referred to me by a local doctor who helps clients reduce multiple medications and find more natural solutions to their health issues. She had long brown hair and a youthful face, probably in her early thirties. She had a slight frame and wore yoga leggings and sandals.

"What brings you in today?" I asked.

"Well my doctor says that maybe part of my fibromyalgia attacks could be stress-related and he referred me to you, he said that you could possibly help me change the stress patterns," she said.

"We can certainly identify what brain habits are making your stress worse and how to help your brain switch to new habits and patterns that support you," I said. I looked over the intake paperwork, I could see multiple symptoms marked: anxiety, lack of sleep, worry, yes all these would be affecting her stress levels.

"What are your stress levels like on an average day?" I asked.

"Well, I don't know pretty high I guess. I've been working through a big project at work and it's been really stressful," she said. "So it's been harder lately."

"Some of the stress we experience comes from the outside world, like deadlines and expectations. But most of the stress we experience comes from within our own minds, what the mind is running automatically in the background and the meanings it makes up about what's happening around us," I said.

I continued, "There are stress habits, things the brain keeps thinking or repeating that make it worse. So, I'm going to ask you if these common mental blocks resonate for you. Keep in mind, they are just ideas that got stuck and everyone has some of these running around in the back of their mind. Just notice if they feel true for you and rate it, scale 1-10 with how true it feels, 10 being high, 1 not at all true. Just pay attention to the feeling of it," I said.

As I had worked over the years, I heard common themes associated with stress and anxiety patterns, so I took her through identifying the most common ones to see which of them were active for her. "Think of this phrase, 'I have to get everything done, does that feel true?' I asked.

"Yes, that feels true, about an 8 or 9. Every day I have all this work to do and I can't seem to get it done," she said.

"What about, 'I need to be perfect?'" I asked.

"Oh, that one for sure. I mean I know no one is perfect, but it still feels like this bar I have to measure up to, so it's a 10," she said.

"Notice that phrase you just said, I don't measure up?" I asked. "Rate it on a scale of 1-10 with how true that feels for you."

"Yes, that one too, feels like a 9 or 10." She said. Her face was starting to show the tension of the thought, a reflection of the tangle of her mind.

"What does it mean about you that you aren't getting things done every day?" I asked.

"Oh, it feels like I'm just spinning my wheels and not making progress. It feels like... I can't do it...I can't succeed...like I'm failing I guess," she said. The emotion reflected on her face as her eyes started to tear up.

"Keep in mind these thoughts aren't really true, they just *feel* true. Everyone has some form of these recurring negative thoughts and feelings, but as we find them we can also help the mind change them," I said.

"Okay," she said as she wiped the tears with a tissue and regained composure.

"And now tell me how much do you worry; worry sounds like 'what if this, what if that?'" I asked.

"Well I don't know, I guess I worry about this big project at work, I think what if I don't do this right, what if there are legal issues...I guess I worry a lot about the work," she said.

"So now we have a good list here of what to help the brain change and what's causing extra stress. These thought habits along with the worry patterns feed anxiety and stress. So now tell me about what happens before a fibromyalgia attack. What do you notice before it comes on?" I asked.

"Well, it just seems like I start to get a headache and then the headache turns into a migraine, and then with the migraine, I have to go to bed and my body just feels pain all over. I can't get out of bed for three days and I just feel miserable. I can't do anything because of the pain," she winced.

"Oh that does sound frustrating and painful, I'm sorry you've been experiencing that," I said. "What sorts of thoughts and feelings come up before the migraine, what triggers have you noticed? Even think of the last time you had an attack, what was happening before it started?" I asked.

"I think I just get really stressed, I start feeling overwhelmed," she said. "I have all this work to sort through, I have a continuously growing to-do list," she said.

"And what else does your mind say before a fibromyalgia flare-up?" I asked.

"I guess when I'm overwhelmed, my mind says, I'm not doing it right, I can't handle this," she said.

"Yes, I can see it's not just about the work, but your mind is causing more stress with those thoughts. Stress can certainly build up and cause physical pain or illness in the body. It's likely that your mind-body system picked up the habit of creating migraines when you get stressed, it probably started somewhere in your history. The migraines can serve to take you away from what's causing the stress. Sometimes the body creates health issues as a way of avoiding the things causing us stress. When did migraines and fibromyalgia first start for you?" I asked.

"They started when I was about 13," she said.

"What were the causes of stress in your life then as a thirteen-year-old?" I asked.

"Oh, my parents wanted me to go to church and I remember not wanting to go. I remember arguing with them, but they were so insistent that I had to go to church. Every Sunday was a battle, I hated going. And then I got tired of arguing about it, I think I just kind of gave up. That's about when the migraines started," she said as her eyes went soft with reflection and the glint of a puzzle piece falling into place.

"That could certainly be enough for the mind to set up a habit to 'save you' from going to church but also possibly a habit to avoid conflict," I said.

"Yeah maybe. Jessica replied. "But it doesn't make sense. The work doesn't go away when I get an attack, I just have more to do that piles up. When I take three days off in bed, it's not helping me, it's hurting me," she said. "Why would my mind do that?"

"The unconscious mind doesn't necessarily make logical sense. Sometimes it just continues running old programs and it doesn't get the updates as we grow older. It doesn't recognize as we grow older that we have more choice in our lives or that the old patterns it has been running are outdated," I said. "It just continues to run habits and patterns even when they aren't working and even if those patterns are causing symptoms or pain," I said.

"Let's see how we can help your mind change these habits and stress patterns," I said.

"Think of these stressors like a tangle of yarns, each thread represents a negative thought causing the stress. There can be many threads and they are all wired in together. As we've been talking and recognizing the patterns, we are identifying the multiple threads and the brain habits they represent. Then we can start changing these patterns over to better ones that work for you and your body," I said.

"It can be a process to help the mind untangle the old habits and patterns and learn better strategies, but the mind also learns very quickly and we can help it set up new habits even within a few sessions," I said. "So while it is a process, change can also happen quickly."

We went through the process of teaching the mind the strategy of learning its way out of worry and once it learns the strategy, the unconscious mind can then automate it. So instead of trying to catch yourself, 'Oh I shouldn't worry' and trying to change your mind, it just runs the new pattern instead.

These automation strategies are from the modality Thought Pattern Management or TPM which focuses on teaching the mind so it can make its own updates even automatically, hypnosis trance isn't required for them to work.

At the end of the first session, I gave the homework, "Okay Jessica, I want you to journal for about 10-15 minutes each morning, just let it free flow. This will help us recognize more of the negative thoughts and beliefs to change. And really pay attention to what brings on the migraines. So if you have another flare up, I want you to notice what are you thinking? What are you saying to yourself before the migraines start? Even take some notes on what you notice so you can bring them in with you to the next meeting along with your journal," I said.

"Yes, I'll try," she said.

It was a couple of weeks before we were back in session. I checked in by asking, "Okay what have you been noticing about your thoughts, feelings, and migraines?"

"Journaling exercise was really hard, I noticed how negative my mind was. I didn't think I was that bad, I got frustrated with it so I only did it a few times," she said.

"Well let's recognize it's not that 'you're bad' or that your mind is bad, it just has old ideas that got stuck," I said. "We'll use your journal to identify the negative beliefs so we can change them."

Jessica continued, "Well on the positive side, after our last session I just felt not as irritated as before, like I could just let things go easier. I was able to work on my work files in small sections, just 30 minutes at a time as you recommended. I'm being more productive and not as overwhelmed. I'm just feeling less stressed overall," she said.

"So stress levels these past couple weeks, scale of 1-10, how would you rate it?" I asked.

"About a 5 or 6," she said. "I still feel stressed but it's not like before, it doesn't feel so overwhelming."

"Great, that's a good start. So today let's take a look at your journal to identify the negative ideas and beliefs that keep recirculating in your mind," I said. "I want you to flip through the pages and circle any of the negative phrases that pop out at you, especially the ones that recur. What do you see?"

She flipped through her notebook, "Oh... hmm...I'm not good enough, I can't do it....can't get everything done.....I can't handle it."

"Okay, so again, these are just old ideas that got stuck. So let's start with, 'I can't handle it."

"And now, go ahead and say that phrase out loud, 'I can't handle it.' Where do you feel tension in your body with that phrase?" I asked.

"I feel it in my chest and shoulders," she said.

"Imagine you could pull all of that energy out of your chest and shoulders, sucking it out and holding it out in front of you in your hands, if it had a shape and a color, what would it be?" I asked.

"It looks like a red, bumpy blob," she said.

"And now this red, bumpy blob that represents the parts of the mind holding this old idea, 'I can't handle it,' what does it actually want?" I asked.

"It wants freedom," she said.

"And imagine that freedom, what does that get for you?" I asked.

"No pressure, I could relax," she said.

"And the ability to relax, what does that get for you?" I asked.

"I can relax and be myself," she said.

"And relaxed and being yourself, what does that get?" I asked.

"I can be myself and honor myself," she said.

"And what does that allow you to have, do, or be that's even higher and more important?" I asked.

"I can honor and love me as I am," she said.

"Wonderful, and now recognizing that these parts of the mind that have been holding the old idea, 'I can't handle it,' what they really want is no pressure, to relax, so you can be yourself, honor yourself but ultimately, they want love of self," I said.

"But notice these parts of the mind holding the idea, 'I can't handle this,' they aren't creating love of self are they?" I asked.

"No, they're not," she said.

"What are they actually creating by this idea, 'I can't handle it?'" I asked.

"It creates pressure and migraines and feeling overwhelmed," she said.

"So we know you can access a feeling even as you think about it, so feel a healing light pour through the top of your head, through your head into your heart and letting that light flow through your heart pouring out to all this red, bumpy blob stuff, just giving all of those parts of you all the higher wisdom and insight, giving them all the love they need and notice as it transforms into its highest potential, what is it turning into now?" I asked.

"It's turning into a diamond," she said.

"Wonderful, now as its transformed self as the diamond, what gifts can this help you with?" I asked.

"It can help with knowing my strength," she said.

"Wonderful now that it has achieved its highest potential, is it willing to help you achieve your highest potential?" I asked.

"Yes," she said.

"Great, go ahead and place the diamond now that it's transformed back into the body where the old stuff came from, and let's give it a new message to do for you instead of the old idea, 'I can't handle it,' what would be a better message now?" I asked.

"I can figure it out, I'm strong," she said.

"Wonderful and tucking that diamond into your chest, let it radiate into your shoulders and let it radiate throughout your mind body spirit system with its new message, 'I can figure it out, I'm strong," I said. "How does that feel to you now?" I asked.

"Oh that feels better, I even feel tingles in my arms and hands," she said.

"Oh great, these belief changes also change your energetic system," I said.

"Yes, I can feel it, I feel different, lighter," she said.

We then went through a series of changing the negative beliefs and the patterns that showed up in her journal. Clearing the belief systems causing stress habits in her mind updated her unconscious mind with new automatic thoughts and feelings and also shifted her energy system as well as her outlook.

As we worked through the negative beliefs and inner stress habits, Jessica started feeling better. After rewiring the thought patterns running automatically that had been causing stress, her spirits lifted and her posture straightened, by the time she left the office, she looked lighter and more alive. We made a plan to address the belief systems and teach the mind to remain calm in stressful situations. We wrapped up the session and made plans to meet the following week.

She arrived for her next session, I welcomed her at the door and we sat down in the room. I noticed a lighter presence about her as if she was more open, even brighter.

"What have you been noticing since our last session?" I asked.

"I just don't get as stressed. When my mind starts to say the old messages, it then turns to the images and the positive focuses we set up," she said. She continued, "So I've been doing better, but then I noticed something weird. I went to visit my parents, they live a couple of hours away. Me and my husband drove down to stay for the weekend, but then I started having another migraine so I came home early, this was the first attack I've had since we started working together."

"What did you notice about your thoughts and feelings before the migraine showed up?" I asked.

"I guess we were arguing about religion. It was frustrating, they were so focused that their way is the only way. I got frustrated and didn't want to argue so I just left for a walk. The next day, I woke up with the start of migraine, so we left that day rather than stay the weekend as we planned."

"What were you thinking and feeling during the argument?" I asked.

"Well, I felt my parents' disapproval of me for not following their religion. I felt like I couldn't speak up like I couldn't say anything in my defense. I felt frustrated, I just clammed up and then I think I just shut down."

"And when you had the migraine symptoms is that when you decided to leave?" I asked.

"Yes, we cut the visit short because of the migraines and we drove back a day early," she said.

"Sometimes we think the body is against us or that the unconscious mind is sabotaging us, but when we look a little deeper, we can see that it's actually trying to help us, it just doesn't know what to do instead. So often the health symptoms we experience are either trying to signal for us to pay attention or to show us the habits and patterns that aren't working. In your case, it sounds like the unconscious mind is using migraines to get you away from stress in the moment and conflict or arguments can certainly be a stressor, especially conflict with the people we love," I said.

"Oh yeah, I can see it now," she said. "But if it causes me stress when I see them, do I just limit when I see them? We are supposed to go stay for the holidays, but it might be just too much."

"That's one way of dealing with it, just avoiding stressful situations. But what if your mind could set up new habits around your parents and how you communicate with them, what would you like to be thinking and feeling when you talk with them instead?" I asked.

"Well, I guess I'd like to say what I want to say, I don't want to agree with them just to appease them, because then I don't feel true to myself. I guess I want to keep strong in myself and still be able to speak up," she said. "But I don't want to fight either."

"We fight when we feel frustrated or threatened, but what if you didn't feel a need to defend yourself or fight?" I asked.

"Well yes, if I can be myself and say what I want to say without fighting that would be better," she let out a sigh at the wish of it.

"Let's go through a process of setting up a positive communication habit so you can stay grounded in yourself, say what you want to say, but also show up the way you want. So you can be in line with your ideal self or higher self, especially in difficult conversations," I said.

We went through the session setting up positive communication habits along with grounding and centering while also connecting with her ideal self or higher self. As we practiced the new communication habit, I could see her posture straighten and her mind found the words to stay strong to her own inner truth while still being respectful and kind.

She was able to spend the holidays with her family, focus on the best in them, and have a wonderful holiday even though they still don't agree on religion. There were a few times she had to take a break for herself to reset her mind and recenter, but she reported feeling stronger in her ability to show up in a way more aligned with her ideal self.

Sometimes we avoid the things causing us stress when we are better served in working through the stressors, which then uplifts our mind-body-spirit system to new levels of insight and well-being. She felt not only better in communicating with her parents but found greater ease in other conversations as well.

It was a process of unraveling the stress habits, recognizing the patterns, and changing the mental blocks. However, in working together, she learned to identify and change the thought patterns that were causing stress. By alleviating stress patterns at the source, the brain habits causing stress, we changed the automatic responses, which reduced the stress load on her body. This then created new messages for the mind and body, which then resulted in new physical responses of the body. We also reinforced keeping inner states of calm while the outside world was busy.

Working with Jessica did require her commitment to working through the multiple layers and tangles of brain habits. However as we identified and resolved the unconscious mental blocks, she was able to create new habits and strategies which then informed the body into greater well-being and ease. Here's what Jessica had to say about working together in her own words:

> *"My first appointment with Holly Stokes, I was hopeful, but cautiously optimistic. I felt like she understood my deep sense of pain and personal suffering: that which you only receive from someone with profound personal experience. I began journaling as Holly had recommended. As time went on, I began noticing changes in my journal entries. My feelings were beginning to come out of myself easier, and my thoughts and feelings were something I*

could put into words. Before meeting Holly I didn't realize I had aversions to discussing my deep feelings and that I lost my voice in certain relationships and specifically in family settings with my in-laws, parents and siblings.

I feel like I am now the person I want to be. I feel like I know and understand myself in a way that I never have before. Holly has truly saved me. She has been with me throughout this entire process. I feel like I have found myself again. Which I didn't know was even possible after suffering from Fibromyalgia for 17 years. My emotional intelligence has grown exponentially throughout this process with The Brain Trainer. I strongly recommend Holly Stokes, The Brain Trainer because the feelings of deep suffering and pain are no longer a part of my everyday life. I offer my warmest most heartfelt and sincere thank you to you Holly and your dedication to your work. You have paved a way for me to live my life in peace and happiness." –Jessica

Aside: I wouldn't say that 'I saved Jessica' it was her own body-mind-spirit system that did the actual healing, we just helped the brain set up new habits, patterns, and programs, it was ultimately her own system that did the rebalancing and healing.

The mind and body are connected. The thoughts we think have physical effects on the body as the body physically responds to stress. If you have a habit or pattern either of the mind or the body, what are the thoughts you recognize before the pattern shows up, before the body responds? See if you can identify the string of thoughts that are underlying the symptoms.

Illness can be the expression of multiple threads of negative thoughts and beliefs running automatically that are all wired together. By understanding these multiple threads and elements, we can work through the layers of the mind to create updates for the mind and also updates for the nervous system and the body.

Reflection: Illness can have multiple brain habits and patterns involved. What stress triggers do you notice? What brain habits and thoughts are causing the stress or making it worse? What is your body's response to the stress? Is your unconscious mind trying to 'save you' from something by avoiding stress?

Update Mental Blocks through ART to Love Process

This ART to Love process is a favorite tool I use both with myself and with clients. It's simple and easy to remember once you've experienced it a couple of times. The creator of this process, Rich Aydelott is a trusted friend and colleague and gave me permission to share this with you. If you share it with others, and please do, please also give him attribution and credit for this powerful tool.

A.R.T. to Love From the work of Rich Aydelott, Thought Pattern Management Trainer, Master NLP Practitioner, Hypnotist, www.AmazingLifeWellness.com

The A stands for Awareness. The first step of any change is to bring awareness and acknowledge the aspect to change. The R stands for Resources. Think of resources as whatever the mind needs to make this change: confidence, well-being, higher wisdom, insight, etc. T stands for Transformation. Transformation is the shift, when we shift from problem to solution state, we not only find the answers but we heal the misperceptions and untruths that have created the mental blocks which then cause the energy blocks, which then affect how the body responds.

I find this process so brilliant because rather than fighting against ourselves, this process can help you understand and transform the inner mental blocks and programs of your unconscious mind quickly and easily.

This powerful process draws on the power of love to heal our minds with clarity and inspiration which then also affects how we feel and influences how our bodies function. This process can quickly dissolve the obstacles, change negative patterns, and engage your mind and body system for higher levels of well-being.

The A.R.T to Love created by Rich Aydelott

Step 1: Identify something you'd like to change: an obstacle, a mental block or limiting belief, a fear or a recurring negative thought.

Step 2: Imagine pulling it out of your body, pulling out all the energy of it, and holding it out in front of you. If this stuff had a shape or a color, what would it be? (Some people see a visual, a color, or an image, but other people may experience a texture or a feeling of it or even just a sense of something).

Step 3: This stuff represents a part of your mind that's holding onto this old idea. Now ask it, "What does it want? What is it trying to get?" Once you ask this question, notice the very first thing that comes to mind, even if it doesn't make sense. The first thing that comes up is your unconscious mind answering.

Step 4: If it could have what it wants, what will that get for it? Keep asking this question until you get to the higher purpose or feeling. Every part of us is trying to get something positive even if that part of the mind has an inappropriate or outdated strategy.

Step 5: Imagine, sense, or feel a healing light pour through the top of your head, let it flow into your heart, and let it pour through your heart out to the image in front of you, giving it all it needs, all the love, wisdom and insight, to transform into its highest potential. What is it turning into now?

Notice the image, colors, sense or feeling of it. Continue flowing the light through your head through your heart and out to the old stuff until it transforms. What is it transforming into now?

Step 5: Now that it has fully transformed, what is the gift this part of your mind can bring back to you? What can this part of your mind be doing for you instead of the old idea?

Step 6: Now that it's achieved its highest potential, is it willing to help you achieve your highest potential?

Step 7: Integration. I also like to ask the transformed part, "If there were a better message for this part of the mind to be holding for you, what would it be." Now that it has fully transformed, invite the new image, color, or feeling back into your body with all its gifts, talents, and resources as its transformed self, along with the positive message it can be running for your mind instead. Let that radiate throughout your mind-body-spirit system as your mind makes the updates into all the levels, ages of you.

I've found this process so simple, so concise, and yet highly effective. For some of our stickier mental blocks, such as mental blocks about the self or the "I'm nots" you may have to run through it a few times as the mind tends to update in layers and there can be more than one part of the mind holding onto the old ideas.

Journaling exercise: Clear Mental Blocks with the A.R.T. to Love

Because we live in our minds and bodies, we may not notice our mental blocks as they often just feel true. So sometimes we have to dig through to find those old ideas that aren't working for us. Some of the mental blocks and programs of the mind that run automatically, we've just taken them in and adopted them as truth. This journaling exercise can help you identify mental blocks your mind has picked up so that you can transform them.

Pick an area where you feel stuck and freely write whatever you think about this stuck place. Let the words flow out onto the page. Don't correct spelling or grammar, just let it flow. Give it at least 10 minutes of free writing.

Then go look back over what you wrote and notice any negative recurring thoughts. I like to highlight or underline them. These negative thoughts are the old mental blocks that got stuck. Identify the ones you'd like to shift and then walk through the A.R.T. to Love process steps.

As you clear up the negative thoughts and thinking errors that your unconscious mind took on, you will clear the mental blocks and update your energetic and emotional system. You can feel the effects of this process quickly. It's a great way to update those places where your mind got stuck.

As you clear out the old thinking and replace it with more inspired thoughts and higher level ideas and beliefs, you'll find greater ease in your mind, greater well-being in your body, plus feel less reactive to the things that cause stress in your life, making it easier to carry your inner calm with you.

Reflection: Pick a belief, thought, feeling or idea to transform. Then walk it through the A.R.T to Love process. I like to record in my journal the notes of the new phrase and any images or symbolism of the insights that come up.

CHAPTER 27

Transforming:
I Don't Want to Be Here

I walked into my friend's massage room, the dim lighting and the serene music welcomed me into the treatment room. "What would you like to work on today?" Andrea asked.

"Under the shoulder blades, it just feels so tight even painful," I said.

"Okay we'll see what we can do to release that muscle tension," she said as she motioned me to the massage table and shut the door.

I undressed and inserted myself into the sheets of the massage table. Andrea knocked on the door and I gave the yes to usher her back in the room.

The massage table and clean sheets were comforting. The areas under my shoulder blades felt so painful, like a deep hole. As Andrea was working out the knots, I kept getting the thought over and over, *"I can't."*

It felt as if a spear had gone through my body underneath the shoulder blade and now there was an energetic hole there.

Andrea said, "I keep getting the image come to mind of a volcano, with molten lava underneath, but the top of the mountain is getting no heat, no circulation. Then I had the thought of a spear, a flash came to mind of being in a gladiator's ring. Does this mean anything to you?"

"Huh we must have synchronized thoughts, I also thought of a spear going under my shoulder blade, I don't know why my shoulder is so tight, I haven't done anything different," I said.

The image of the volcano made me think of power. With Lupus, it's as if I was weakened, I didn't have the strength or endurance, my muscles tired quickly and with small efforts, I would often feel exhausted.

"I think it's some 'I can't' going on, like helplessness or hopelessness," I said. "So, gladiator ring fits that feeling, like I have no options, hopeless," I said.

"Okay yes, we'll ask the angels to help out with this one, "she said. "I'll be quiet now so you can just allow yourself to go into that inner relaxation and healing state."

I believed in angels, I had certainly felt guided during certain windows of my life, it felt reassuring. I could feel a lightness going through my body, I tuned into my body focused on the places holding tension, and directed the lightness through.

I continued to notice and follow the energies as they flowed around my shoulder blades and through my body, I felt lighter and lighter as Andrea worked out the knots and my muscles relaxed.

After the massage, I went home and sat out on the deck looking across the green meadow and the tall pines standing as sentinels. The fresh air filled my breath and the many deep colors of green and sunlight seemed to bring comfort to my heart. I settled in for a meditation and turned on some favorite music.

The beautiful sounds of the music helped me to stay focused. As I listened to the sounds, I focused on my breath. I became aware of places that were holding tension. In my mind's eye, I imagined focusing in on those places and breathing into them.

As I did, emotions surfaced. Sometimes I couldn't put words to the emotion, I just let it release as it came through. Breathing into the center of the emotion, letting the emotion flow through, breathing it all out. I let the tears come as if a geyser broke loose and I let myself cry it out, still breathing into the center of it, until it ran clear, and there in the very center of it, was a quiet stillness.

Feeling the emotion pour through, it was a sadness. In other meditations, sadness had come up as well, it was as if the symptoms of Lupus, the swelling of tissues, and the achiness represented, "my body is sad, my body is crying." I listened deeper to the sadness, *what do you want?* I queried in my mind.

Inner voice: *"I don't want to be here,"* a whisper of a thought, it was a familiar theme.

Me: "Don't want to be where in Washougal?" I questioned.

Inner voice: *"No"*

Me: *"In this relationship?"*

The part: *"No, I want to go home."*

Me: *"Go home where, to Utah?"*

The part: *"No dummy, I want to go home to God."*

With years of working through the extreme abuse from the boys when I was a child, wanting to die seemed reasonable for some parts of my mind.

Me: "Why?"

The part of my mind must be young, 'dummy' wasn't a word I would normally use. The unconscious mind operates more like a jar of marbles, the marbles can represent memories or aspects of ourselves that have picked up old ideas, mental blocks, beliefs, or attitudes that got stuck.

The part: *"So much hurt, cruelty and pain in the world. People are killing each other in wars, people are destroying life, with no respect for life and living. Sadness for the world. I miss God and the peace of heaven and the beauty of the other side."*

Me: "Would the part that doesn't want to be here be willing to shift its focus from the pain and hurt of the world to see the beauty of life, to see what is beautiful, what is kind and gentle in life? I am here for a reason. I might as well stay focused on the beautiful." I imagined giving those parts of me God's Garden, a place of beauty where everything is alive and we are all laughing and happy. Extending God's Garden from my heart down to my feet. I noticed my feet weren't connected to it, they were separate, okay just reconnect the feet.

Me: "Can you carry God's Garden with you? And as you look out at the world, you see it's full of people, bright beings who are also carrying God's Garden. As you see all these people, you are not alone, we are not alone. Bring the garden with you and we can be a part of a vast group of bright beings creating God's Garden on earth, living with kindness, compassion, and understanding."

Inner voice: "Ok that is better, but what about all the pain in the world? Why does God let the horrors happen?"

Me: The words of a friend echoed in my mind, "God is love. The horrors happening in the world are the absence of love and the absence of God. When people are disconnected from God, they act from pain and ignorance. We are meant to bring God's love into the world, to let it shine away the darkness. The darkness cannot be where the light shines. As we shine love into the world, we heal the ignorance, we heal and transform ignorance into wisdom and light."

I imagined giving a pair of glasses to the parts of me that see the pain in the world. "As you look through, see the higher purposes of souls. The pains we experience are avenues for learning and growth. The cruelty and pain is the absence of love, the absence of God."

I don't believe we have to go through pain for our lessons, but many of us choose that avenue and it's okay. It's okay to go through the bumps of life. It's all learning and it's all growth.

Me: "Let the fears come forward into the beauty of the garden of higher love. Let them see the beauty of life, the miracle of living, and the miracle of love. When we bring love and light to ignorance, we transform ignorance, we heal it."

As I scanned through my body, I noticed that seemed to be where my legs didn't connect, like the light I could bring through my body wasn't going to my legs. I let the words echo into my tailbone and sent the connection through my legs.

Me: "It is okay to be here, it's safe to be me. it is good for me to be here, there is light and love here, there is beauty here, I can shine light here, I can help here."

I then began moving in my body, stretching and moving how my body wanted to move, adding in yoga poses and with each movement saying the words aloud. I felt energies shift through my body as I moved and whispered on the deck surrounded by trees and sunlight. I gave a snapshot of the beauty of the meadow to those inner parts of my mind, the beauty of being right here, in this place, this moment. I felt the magic of being fully present in the moment, fully connected.

I then thought of my body's reaction to sunlight and spoke aloud to my body, "I harmonize with sunlight. I harmonize with life. The light of the sun sustains life and nourishes me."

I continued to move fluidly, intuitively in the flow of it, appreciating moving, stretching, and feeling, appreciating my body. I let myself flow with intuitive stretching, moving as my body wanted to move as my Kripalu yoga teacher had encouraged. After a timeless flow of moving, I returned to my deck chair. I then thought to add my partner, John to the inner garden, the sanctuary of peace and ease. Why hadn't I thought to do that before?

Inner voice: "Because it will hurt when he's gone."

I answered: "The love and connection continue even though the people who share spaces in our lives may not be physically present, the love continues. The higher perspective is that love continues, even when people are not in your life. Let the love continue."

I then checked in with myself, *"I ask my unconscious mind to review the original causes of Lupus are they all now resolved?"*

"Mostly," the inner whispered.

Me: "Are all the original fears connected with Lupus now resolved?"

Inner voice: *"Yes."*

Me: *"Is there any reason to keep the symptoms of Lupus in my life?"*

Inner: *"Yes as a reminder to slow down and be intentional, as a reminder to pay attention to the body and be intentional with your mind, where you focus is important."*

Me: "If I set aside time during the day for meditative practice, would the symptoms of Lupus be willing to reduce and even disappear?"

Inner: *"Maybe."*

Me: "If my unconscious mind could give me a song as a cue or reminder to slow down and check in within rather than alerting me with symptoms of aches and pains, would that be okay?"

Inner: *Yes, Okay.*

Me: "What song would my unconscious mind like to use to mentally remind me to slow down and be intentional?" I asked my mind.

The words from Simon and Garfunkel played in my mind, *"Slow down you move too fast, you got to make the moment last just kicking down the cobblestone, looking for fun and feeling groovy."*

I giggled and replied, "That's perfect."

This imagery and symbolism worked for me. As you explore the language of the unconscious mind, you'll find imagery, symbolism, and metaphor that you can tailor to your own inner meanings and inner world. This is an example of the change-work, rather than getting angry at ourselves or our emotions, let's bring the light of compassion and understanding to those aspects of us that keep holding onto old thoughts, old emotions, and old wounds. As we bring understanding and compassion to these parts of ourselves, our minds, and our bodies, we can ask, "What is needed? What is wanted? What perspectives have we imagined to be true that could be upgraded?"

We can ask the inner parts of the mind running old thoughts and emotions to switch its focus, updating to higher wisdom and insight. This is the essence of evolving ourselves and the inner work that is required in the inner journey of healing.

We can update the unconscious mind or automatic mind more quickly using its own language: story, imagery, metaphor, symbolism, and feelings. If you have a health issue or symptoms, what's the metaphor for it? For example, if your feet hurt. What is it that feet do? Movement, walking, traveling, going places, going forward. So, the message of it might be feeling stuck, not moving forward, and resistant to taking the next steps.

Whether it's a part of you that is holding pain or a system of the body that is not operating as well as it needs to, any symptom or illness is simply a call for attention (awareness and care). We can recognize pain as a signal that something in the mind-body-spirit system needs extra care, awareness, and support. Once you recognize and clarify the message, you can transform the mental blocks and resolve the issue that your mind is bringing to your awareness.

Reflection: Pick a symptom, If the symptom was a metaphor for you, what would the message be? How can you bring extra care and support to the part of your body expressing the symptom? If there were a belief or thinking error behind the symptom, what would it be saying?

And the years passed in a gentle haze of Hypnosis with clients and with myself as I continued doing the inner work of clearing stress patterns and building inner resources of calm. I continued to update the inner places of my mind using the skills of meditation, journaling, Hypnosis, and Neuro-Linguistic Programming, and Thought Pattern Management to clear my own mind-body-spirit system.

CHAPTER 28

Every Life Has Rapids

I woke up one bright morning in February, feeling refreshed. Walking into the kitchen, I saw the beautiful bouquet of roses that arrived yesterday, John had sent them for Valentine's Day. I felt so blessed as I got my morning cup of coffee and sat down at my desk that overlooked our 5 acres. I got ready for my morning meditation, relaxed, and sat back in my chair. I loved looking out over the green, plush grass and watching the evergreen trees circling protectively. My chickens were already up and scratching in the yard for worms. I could see the mama deer at the edge of the meadow grazing on the plush Washington grass in the morning sunlight. A day like so many others, I sighed with satisfaction, enjoying the moment, soaking it in.

I relaxed into my chair and asked myself, "What is today about for me?"

"*Letting go,*" whispered across my mind.

Letting go, *that's weird, whatever does that mean?*

I sat down to journal and another thought impression came to mind, '*Check his emails.*'

Okay that was weird, in the ten years I'd been with John, I'd never checked his emails. He didn't even like me answering his cell phone, it seemed weird to check his emails, it was his business, his privacy.

Well I wouldn't know if I didn't take a look and it's probably nothing, I thought to myself. *I'll just take a quick look and put my mind at ease.*

I opened up his emails, he always leaves the computer open. I started scrolling through, there was a receipt for my flowers, *"ahh sweet"* I thought, but then also a receipt for chocolate-covered strawberries. *Wait, I didn't get chocolate-covered strawberries? He probably sent them to his mom.*

I opened an email from Vanessa to John. She said, "Have you talked to your girlfriend yet? Sometimes I just drive around at night, crying, I miss you. I can't believe you didn't tell me you were in a relationship."

Then I opened more emails, from John to Vanessa and more and it became clear.

Whoa, my head reeled, I felt the ground fall out from beneath me. Confusion swirled around me like a whirlwind, a barrage of thoughts bombarding me.

John has a lover, a girlfriend? How long has this been going on? And how did I not know, how did I not intuitively know something was wrong?

I don't know what was more hurtful, that he had an affair or that he was talking to her about me, *what was he saying? He hadn't said anything was wrong between us, sure he had seemed more withdrawn lately, but he was a quiet guy anyway, not prone to share his feelings unless you wrangled them out of him. He hadn't said anything to me, he was my best friend or so I had thought.*

My whole reality with John was a sham. How could he do this to me, to us? I could imagine him talking to her about me, it felt like a knife in my heart, and each thought just stabbed in deeper. I flew into the kitchen and threw out the bouquet of fresh roses all over the deck to rot and die there, a fitting image for him to see when he returned home.

I staggered back to my office room and collapsed in a puddle of tears. And then the panic set in, panic and anger. *How could I face him? He was away on business travel, but what would happen when he came home? I don't know if I can handle it.* I felt so devastated, so angry, so betrayed. I threw a bunch of clothes into my small car. *My friend Rachel would know, she was a relationship coach, and she'd know what to do.*

I called Rachel on the way over to let her know that I was on my way to see her. I arrived at her house, she led me to the kitchen where we talked. Rachel had me calm down and start thinking more rationally. John wasn't a violent person, in fact, we rarely argued. Rachel reassured me I would be able to face John when he came home, but I just needed to be clear about what I wanted to say and how to manage that conversation. She reminded me that it wasn't the end of the world, although it felt like it and to go about my regular business and routine.

Thinking more rationally, I drove back to my house to wait, it would be the next day before he was back in town. I tried to put it out of my mind, but the whirlwind of thoughts continued to bombard me. *How long had he been seeing her? Why did he pretend that everything was okay with us?* I busied myself with work.

John called a couple of hours later, "Hi pumpkin, I'm just getting to the airport in Phoenix, I have one more leg of the trip and then I'll be home tomorrow. Did you get the flowers I sent?"

"Yes I got the flowers, along with the email to your new girlfriend," I said.

"What are you talking about?" John asked.

"I read your emails to Vanessa and the chocolate-covered strawberries. When were you planning on telling me that you had a girlfriend?"

"Nothing happened," he said.

"No something happened alright, I'm not stupid, I read your emails!" I screamed through the phone.

"I'll be home tomorrow and we can talk about it," he said.

"I don't know what there is to talk about, it seems pretty clear to me," I said vehemently and promptly hung up.

He tried calling back a couple of times, but I wasn't ready to talk...I couldn't answer the phone. When I thought of him, I kept switching between panic and betrayal. *What would I do now? Are we really over?*

I didn't know which was worse, the fact that he was having an affair or the fact that he'd been keeping it from me for six months pretending that we were okay, while apparently talking about me behind my back. *I had no idea, I had thought we were still best friends,* all the while he was dating this other woman.

I felt like such a fool. *How could he do this to me? How could he do this to us? We had a life together or so I thought. I was happy, wasn't he happy? Apparently not.*

How could we just be over, just like that? Why had I let myself rely on him? Why had I let myself depend on him and where would I go now?

What would happen to me now? All this was his: the land, the house, and even the dog. Was I just going to get thrown out on the street? And I felt angry, angry at myself, how could I have not known? I must have chosen the wrong guy, why didn't my intuition tell me he'd cheat on me? My emotions kept spinning between disbelief, anger, shame, and despair.

When John came home it was mostly awkward. I didn't know how to be around him anymore. Everything I thought we were, we were not apparently. I felt so triggered just being around him or knowing he was in the next room.

CHAPTER 29

Surprise, Full Body Hives!

A few days passed in a swarm of thoughts and anxieties. With the news of John's affair, everything seemed up in the air. Life felt chaotic, *what could I rely on now?* Worries gnawed at me mixed with the judgments from the religion I grew up with and swarmed threateningly like a nest of bees that had been disturbed.

Of course, I knew logically these old ideas were someone's opinions that had been handed through the generations until I had inherited them through my family. *"A woman is not complete without a man. It's a shame to be single and alone. If you're not married you will be a spinster."* I had been single until I met John when I was 28. I felt the judgments of imagined bystanders. Although no one I knew would see me this way, the thoughts hurt just the same.

I continued to make time for my morning meditations and journaling, but I couldn't calm my mind down, I couldn't focus or find the inner quiet space. About the fourth morning after John came home, itchy spots started to appear on my arms and legs. The spots grew to white bumps the size of pencil erasers, and the spots grew and erupted into full-body hives.

It made sense that it was probably the stress causing the outbreak. I contacted one of my local healer friends, Sherrie, a Native American Reiki Practitioner and Hypnotist. I explained the outbreak and she invited me to come to her office for a session that evening to work on the hives that covered my body.

"Hi Sherrie, I seem to have broken out with a case of hives all over my body," I said as I showed her the bumps on my arms.

"Let me look at you," she said. She took my arm and pulled up the sleeve, there they were, big white spots polka dotted over my arm, I lifted my pant leg to show that I was covered.

"Oh yes, it's a good thing you called me, I can see how miserable this would be," she said. "Did anything happen recently or did the hives just show up?" She asked.

"I just found out this past week that John has been having an affair," my voice quavered through the words and I felt a lump in my throat. "I thought we were happy, I had no idea."

"Oh wow that's big news, I'm sorry to hear that. How long have you two been together?" She asked.

"Almost ten years now," I said. "I just thought we were special, I thought he was the one for me," I said in a broken voice as the tears ran down my cheeks.

"And then the hives showed up this week?" She asked. "You know this isn't a coincidence."

"Yes I know, it's probably the stress of it with everything," I said.

"Yes, well let's clear this energy out and reset your system. So take off your shoes and hop up on the massage table here, I'll dim the lights and we'll get started," her voice had a soothing tone.

The lights went comfortably dim, and I reclined on the table and relaxed. It felt good to be in a different space that wasn't home, wasn't near him. I closed my eyes.

"That's right, just close your eyes, relax, and take a break from the world. Clear your mind, take in a deep breath, and exhale letting go. Right here you are safe and you can just relax," she said. "And another deep breath, breathe in and hold it … and exhale just relaxing all the way down. Relaxing into your inner world and the quiet."

It felt good to breathe, it felt like opening my lungs up when I didn't even know they were compressed. I relaxed into the breath and relaxed into her words. With my eyes closed I could sense her hands moving over my head. There was a softness like a purple wave that seemed to slowly, softly wash through me.

I could feel tensions start to ease and by degrees, tensions relaxed and dissipated.

She said, "I'll just share what I pick up as I work on you.....fears...... there are fears like what happens to me now, where will I go?.... There's something like feeling outcast, cast away. We just want to bring love to these places of you that are worried. You're okay, here and now you are safe.....you are safe in your body, you are safe in your life." She continued to work in silence, I continued to follow the energy as I felt it flow through me and around me, like swaddling me with a soft blanket.

"Your energy has been scattered....scattered with fears......scattered with worry.....just bring it back to now, bring your energy back to you....Bring your energy back to you.....back to safety...you are safe... you are okay even in chaos, you are safe.....safe." She continued to echo the calming words and I felt imperceptible constrictions in my body relax into the sound of her voice.

She continued in silence as my awareness drifted in and out in a play of soothing soft purple waves. After some time, Sherrie woke me gently by holding my feet.

"You awake Holly?" she whispered. "You can come back to the room now."

"Yes, thank you," I said as I started to stretch and move.

"What did you experience during the process?" Sherrie asked.

"I certainly felt peaceful, I noticed a purple energy and also it seemed like there were more people in the room than just you and I," I said.

"Yes, that's my team, not everyone can pick up on that," she said. "They are my spiritual guides, angels and helpers that come in to help me work."

"I definitely feel more calm, I feel less chaos in my mind. My mind feels more clear, just an underlying feeling I'm okay," I said. "I feel more centered, more balanced."

"Wonderful, your energy looks a lot better," she said. "You had a lot of fears to clear out, it was like your mind was spinning with fears, so we cleared that energy."

"I certainly feel better," I said. I pulled up my shirt sleeve to look at my arm, I ran my hand along my arm, no bumps. "Wait, there's no hives, there's no bumps on my arms!" I felt around the base of my neck and chest, all I felt was smooth skin. "There are no more hives, wow this is amazing! I didn't think it would happen that fast, but they're gone."

"Your body responded really well to clearing out the anxieties, so it worked pretty quickly for you," she said. "It was your unconscious mind expressing the fear and not feeling safe."

"Well that certainly makes a lot of sense, I really don't feel settled. I've lived with John now for 6 years and he's been my rock for ten. Just all this affair stuff really took me by surprise, like the carpet pulled out from underneath me," I said.

"I'm sorry you are going through this," she said. "Well your energy is clear now, but you know it's really important to take care of yourself through this time. Take quiet time, journal and when you recognize fears coming up, make sure you clear them. It's like your system just got overwhelmed with not only John but past fears were triggered too," she said.

"What past fears?" I asked.

"Well 'not safe was' there, but also 'outcast' came up. You felt rejected, and outcast even as if your survival was on the line….it was like a fear you couldn't survive alone. I think it was a past life event where you were an outcast from a group," she said. "I think it all just overwhelmed your body."

"Wow, okay, that's interesting. I've had the feeling of 'outcast' before. I never really felt I belonged when I grew up, so I just kind of kept to myself with a few close friends."

"Self-care is important, take time to journal or meditate. As emotions come up, make sure to clear them and let them go," she said. "Especially if fears come up, keep telling yourself you are safe and you got this, whatever happens, you got this," she said. "And I'm always here if you need a touchup."

We wrapped up the session and I drove back home, my 45-minute commute from town gave me time to self-reflect. I let myself drive home carrying with me the relaxation and calm I felt, no use in trying to figure out everything right now. I turned my attention to what was working in my life, what I could appreciate. I enjoyed seeing clients and working with NLP & Hypnosis, I loved the work and felt deep satisfaction in lifting others to recognize their worth and value and see the higher possibilities of their lives.

My friend Rachel offered that I could stay with her until John and I could sort out what we were going to do. At least we'd both have our own space to find our footing and maybe my body wouldn't get so triggered and have such stress reactions. I didn't want the stress and anxiety to cause a flare-up of the autoimmune condition.

I spoke with John about taking a break, I could move in with Rachel until we decided one way or the other. He agreed and he also agreed to couples counseling with me, maybe this was what we needed, and maybe we could sort through it all.

My friend Rachel had a spare room, it was comfortable, but it was sparse. All I had with me were the essentials: a bed, a closet full of clothes, and my laptop. But at least I wouldn't be triggered seeing John, or feel so awkward at night when we shared the same bed. *Oh yeah, he'd actually been sleeping on the couch for the last 3 months, why didn't I notice that red flag?*

At least I could relax into my own space in the spare room at Rachel's and get my head clear. I was thankful for the quiet of my little room in Rachel's house. She was a little older than me, she also ran her own business, mostly online. She had a nine-year-old boy who was in school during the day, so the house was quiet.

In the weeks that followed, Rachel's place was a treasure trove of books on love, communication, and relationships. I dove into reading all I could. I settled into a new routine, splitting my time between reading in my room, consuming psychology books on relationships, and seeing clients in my office in Vancouver. I began to feel more settled within myself, even while so much was up in the air.

I found it odd that I suddenly had a lot more time available, there were no dishes to do, no big meals to cook, and no extra laundry. I wasn't watching Television or cop shows, which John had going nonstop. He said he liked the background sound of people talking, it set his mind at ease. My commute was now 20 minutes rather than 45. I liked having more quiet space and less television time. And I loved the quiet which I filled with reading and working on hypnosis materials.

Without all the extra demands of living in a house with a boyfriend and television, there was just more time and more space. I came and went as I pleased and it was really peaceful for a few months. I focused on my business and devouring relationship books. I worked on staying grounded. I meditated and listened to my own hypnosis recordings. It was work, it took effort to bring my mind out of the hurt and into my present life. It took work to clear the judgments about John, but also about myself.

Having my business kept me grounded. I felt I had purpose in working with clients and when I was in sessions with them, I could forget about myself and feel I was contributing and making a difference. *I could do this.* It was easy to take people into hypnosis, doing the inner work of transforming the stuck places and accessing wisdom, insight, and intuition. It was a welcome break to focus on my clients' lives, I could forget about my own demise and help them with through their profound transformations. It was somewhat of a contact high to be swimming in hypnosis with them throughout the day.

Reflection: Friends can be life savers in times of crisis. Connecting with others who can offer good advice on the situation can help bring clarity, and insight and keep us more grounded rather than letting our minds ruminate. Who do you know who would be a good fit for getting insight about your current situation? How can you strengthen your positive social support connections?

CHAPTER 30

Support Groups - Battle of Beliefs

As John and I separated trying to figure things out, I realized my social circles had really revolved around him and his family. All the holiday celebrations, birthdays, and social get-togethers were with his family and now all those connections were up in the air. All those relationships where I'd invested time and connection would not be around if John and I split up.

I hadn't created a lot of friendships. I had a lot of community connections. I went to the networking groups, meeting with local business owners where we talked about how to refer business to each other, so I knew a lot of people, but they weren't close friends I could confide in. I had a few friends, but they had kids and partners and lives, so they weren't always available, and I didn't want to bother them. So I realized I needed to expand my social support.

I thought maybe connecting with others who are going through the same thing as I was would be a good idea for support and friendships. So I looked up local support groups for Lupus and found a meeting. The focus of the group was to meet others and make connections with like-minded people. *Okay,* I thought, *I will give this a shot.*

I walked into the noodle house restaurant for the Lupus support group meeting, there was a small group of women gathered around several tables pushed together. They looked middle-aged and older, they seemed pleasant enough.

"Is this the Lupus support group?" I asked.

"Why yes. Welcome, come join us," said a grey-haired woman with glasses and a stout figure. "My name is Betty. We all just get our own meals and then we can sit and chat together."

I went to the line at the counter to fetch my dinner and then took a seat next to a middle-aged woman with dark curly hair, it had a few streaks of grey down the sides and we said hellos.

Betty spoke, "Welcome everyone. We have a new face, so let's go around the table and introduce ourselves."

Around the table, people shared their names: Betty, Maria, Emma, Lisa, Lenore, Katie, Sarah, Sally and myself.

Betty addressed the group, "We are all here to support each other. It's hard living with Lupus and nobody else really understands. We don't look sick, but we don't feel good. People just don't understand that, there's a lot we just don't feel up to doing. And sometimes it's hard to take care of your family and keep friends when you just don't have the energy."

The ladies nodded their heads in agreement around the table. Betty continued, "Sheila is in the hospital again, so you might want to reach out to her and say hello, she's had some kidney problems, but she goes home this week. I know she'd love to hear from any of you. Okay, just chat amongst yourselves, we'll recap with updates at the end."

Maria turned to me and asked, "When were you diagnosed?"

"2006," I said. "What about you?"

"I was diagnosed in 2004," she said. It took two years before I actually got the diagnosis, the doctors didn't know what was wrong with me. They didn't seem to believe me at first, they told me I was imagining it or that it must be hormones. It was really hard not knowing what was wrong with me and the doctors couldn't seem to figure it out."

"How long did it take for you to get the right diagnosis?" She asked.

"I worked with a Naturopath, and she recognized the signs of the butterfly rash and then we did my bloodwork and she said I had the marker for it. So the diagnosis was fairly quick," I said.

"That's lucky. It was so hard for those two years not knowing what was wrong with me. It was actually a relief when I finally got the diagnosis. At least I had an explanation for what was happening," she said.

"I can imagine that would be hard not knowing," I added. "What advice would you have for newcomers?" I asked, I wasn't exactly a newcomer, but I was curious to hear the response.

"Well, just get through each day," she said. "It's going to be tough, it's a hard life, accept you'll have pain your whole life, but just take it one day at a time."

"And be prepared for hospital bills," chimed in Emma, the lady with frizzy strawberry curls from across the table. We all have a bunch of hospital bills that are too big to pay. Your caseworker is your friend, they'll help you navigate all of that."

"Yep, they just add up. I have a shoebox full of hospital bills. Some of them the insurance covers and a lot of them insurance won't pay for and you have to figure it out for yourself," Sarah added matter of factly. Sarah had straight short hair and glasses." The doctors all bill separately, so it's an ongoing string of bills."

"Yes, I've had my own run-in with hospital bills. The last stay cost me about $72,000. I couldn't get insurance because I had a pre-existing condition," I said.

"Yep, most of us can relate." Maria continued, "Lenore over there was just in for the last month, I was surprised to see her here today. Her kidneys were shutting down. She only knew because her legs were swelling. Some of what we think is normal is actually a sign that other things are going wrong, very wrong."

Eek I thought in my mind. My legs had been swelling too.

"And Sally over there, I feel so bad for her, she's got a new baby and just got diagnosed. She hardly has the energy to do anything let alone take care of a newborn," Maria said.

"Katie went into the hospital because Lupus got her lungs, she could hardly breathe and was on a respirator for a month. Glad to see she's doing better." She pointed to a blond woman with grey streaks through her hair, she was wearing oxygen tubes to her nose with the tank by her side.

The woman sitting across from me chimed in, "Talia and Julie usually come too, but Talia just got out of the hospital last week and Julie was just too exhausted to come." Sarah said.

As I looked around the table, I noticed all the ladies there had big bowls of pasta. Although I loved noodles, I had a salad because I knew how wheat affected my system, causing inflammation and more pain.

"Well, I've noticed that if I don't eat wheat I feel better," I said, thinking to share some insight and maybe spare them some pain.

Nobody said a thing. A conversation started up near the end of the table. "Yep, the hospital bills are astronomical," Katie said from the far end of the table. And the conversation started up again about how their last trips to the hospital and the stacks of bills from it and the financial stress on their husbands.

As I looked around me, I noted the irony of the gluten-filled, wheat noodle bowls at every placement. I was doing pretty well with keeping an anti-inflammatory diet. It was easy to stay committed to healthy eating when I knew the direct effects, but it had sure been a process to figure out.

Maybe they didn't hear me, I thought. I said a little louder, "Well I've noticed that for me, wheat makes my symptoms worse, but eating salads and whole foods and staying away from sugar, I just feel better," I offered. "What have you noticed that makes it better?" I asked.

"Oh, I asked my doctor about diet and foods and he said that nothing like that would work. He said that it doesn't matter what you eat because it's your immune system," Maria replied.

I was astounded but held my tongue. Inside my mind screamed, *Whaaaat? Of course, what you eat affects your body and your immune system. Haven't doctors heard of allergies, where the immune system overreacts causing inflammation and even restricting the airway? Didn't doctors know that some foods are inflammatory and others are anti-inflammatory? Didn't doctors know that more inflammation causes more pain?*

Of course, doctors haven't studied nutrition, they only know what's in the medical books and who writes the medical books? Pharmaceutical companies. Of course, medical professionals are well-meaning, but it was disheartening to hear how this poor advice of 'don't even try' was undercutting any efforts on their part, especially for something as simple as experimenting with changing out a few foods.

Sarah added, "Yes, I asked my doctor too about what I ate, he said I could eat whatever I wanted, except when my kidneys started going downhill, then they put me on a kidney care diet."

"What's the kidney care diet? I asked. *Oh so there's a kidney care diet but not anti inflammatory diet? Well at least some areas of medicine were paying attention to foods.*

"You have to eat low protein and not too much potassium and also low salt," Sarah said.

"You just have to accept it and make the best of it, sometimes the body betrays you," Sarah said.

As I looked around the room, it felt surreal to be here. It seemed everyone here was resigned to their fate, not even looking for answers and accepting the misery of the condition. It was as if hope was drifting above us like a boat on the water, but it seemed to be drifting away. As if every conversation was adding another rock to my feet as I sank below the waterline, being smothered by the resignation and the temptation to give up.

I thought wistfully, *How could this be my life? I longed for the days of paddling on the rivers, dodging the rocks through whitewater, and feeling the strength of my muscles as we hauled boats and gear to the trucks. I missed those magical times when I knew myself to be strong. I missed swimming in the Northwest waters, feeling the splashes and thrills of being alive. It had already been years since my 'glory days' but I longed for it still.*

And now I was here, hobbling to the table, swapping hospital stories, and feeling trapped by a body that no longer allowed for diving off cliffs and swimming in turquoise waters on sunlit summer days. Life had taken a dull and lackluster quality, and there was a sense of numbness, sliding toward despair.

It seemed easier to let go of hope; the temptation of giving up was palpable and suffocating. *You must just accept it, you have limits now,* a friend's words rang in my head. But I couldn't give up the vision of healing like all these ladies had done, I had already found things to help me feel better and I was improving, I was managing it at least.

I wouldn't say I had a lot of energy before the meeting, but after hearing their stories, I felt totally drained and more exhausted than I had been in months. I left the support group feeling more disappointed, more discouraged than before. Seeing all these women who were "following doctor's advice" rather than being open to solutions. It was as if the group was a flock of rabbits, going about the business of eating grass in the meadow, knowing the phantom hawk was out hunting. The rabbits wandered around the open meadow, hoping that it wouldn't be their day to be carried off by the phantom hawk that lived inside their own bodies.

The "doctor's advice" seemed to say: *It doesn't matter what you do, you can't affect it, you can't change it. Lupus is coming for you, the hospitals will eat you alive with bills and financial chaos. It will tear your families apart and you'll have a life of pain, but listen to the doctors, you'll suffer less if you don't try and just give in to your demise.*

I could appreciate the idea of supporting each other, but in reality there was no talk of what we could do, only commiserating. I felt surrounded by the mindsets of these ladies, it was a window into an alter reality, what life would be like if I gave up. I didn't want to see my life the same way. I didn't want to see my body the same way or just follow the however well-meaning and misinformed, "doctor's advice."

The more we talked over lunch, the bleaker it felt as the ladies shared their hospital stories like wounded soldiers. There was no hope here, there was no focus on what could make it better, only a sad resolution to awaiting the fates of phantom hawks and hospitals.

And when I mentioned things that worked, well I was dismissed because the doctors had said, *"There is nothing you can do."* Of course, to these women, the doctors would know better than I did, it wouldn't do any good to argue. But it was my body, I got to choose how I cared for it. I could recognize what makes it feel worse and what makes it feel better.

If I were to stay true to my own path and healing, working with a 'solutions focus' and taking action on what helped me feel better, then I couldn't be a part of this group. I could feel the conversations drain away my energy, dragging me down. My suggestions were easily dismissed, it was clear my influence here would be to no avail.

Everyone has a healing path and this group was simply not for me.

I understood the importance of having support, but the downside of it was that without a solutions focus, the talk around the table just reinforced each other's stories and fears. I knew I wanted something different, I needed something different to help me rise above the waterline. I didn't need more rocks on my feet, I wanted someone on the boat to send a line down so I could pull myself out. *There must be more healing possible,* I thought.

As I walked back to my car, I noticed that I limped more walking back across the parking lot than when I had gone in. My joints felt more creaky and achy, and the shadow of a phantom enemy within echoed itself in my movements. This support group wasn't for me and my body was telling me so. I imagined clearing out their thoughts and stories from my mind.

It felt more like a resignation group rather than a support group. I resolved to not go back, what I needed was more hope. What I needed was to surround myself with people who believed in healing and overcoming. What I needed was people who saw me not as the disease, but as my vibrant self. I wanted those reflections of me in my mind in my energy and the space around me.

I noticed as I cleared my thoughts and turned my attention to going to the movies the coming Friday, my legs seemed to feel better. I wasn't as stiff, and I felt flexibility return to my knees and hips.

Reflection: What environments support you in healing and recovering? Which people and social circles are either reinforcing sickness or reinforcing hope and wellness? Where do you feel support in holding the vision of wellness and healing?

CHAPTER 31

Life Upturned Again

One day Rachel came home, "I met someone at the gym today, she has Lupus and she was telling me about all the crazy stuff that went with the disease." Rachel opened a conversation one night. I could tell there was fear at the edges of her eyes.

"What do you mean about the crazy stuff?" I asked.

"She said she goes kind of foggy sometimes and one time she even chased her kids around the house trying to hurt them," her voice cracked as she spoke.

"Wow, that is crazy. I don't know that that's Lupus, it sounds more like a reaction to medications rather than Lupus itself."

"Well, it has me thinking, I have my little boy and I got to look out for him," she said.

"What do you mean?"

"Well, you can't stay here anymore. It's the weekend, I need you to figure something out by Monday," she said flatly.

"You're kidding me, you're kicking me out and giving me three days because of what a stranger said at the gym?" I asked incredulously.

I was floored, I thought we were friends. Didn't she know me at all? Again, the floor seemed to drop out from under me like a gaping chasm.

"Wow, tenants usually get a 30-day notice, I can't believe you'd do this to me." *I was just getting back on my feet, I didn't need this.* Fear corrodes clear judgment and sanity and it evaporated our friendship in a puff of smoke because of something a stranger said. *All our late-night conversations, our collaborations, apparently meant nothing. She didn't know me at all.*

But of course, I would start looking because who wants to stay in an environment where you're not seen, not trusted, not wanted? My business wasn't making enough money to afford something on my own so I started hunting for a room to rent. I found a room for lease in a house with three other tenants who were from India and the house owner lived in the basement. The Indian guys were all working at a tech company and sending money back home to their families. In the evening, they'd each close their room doors, sit in their rooms, and chat with their families online. They were very quiet, keeping to themselves and consequently not very social. I called it the 'boarding house.'

My room was at the end of the hall, it was a warm room with wood floors and although it was small, it felt safe. Maybe I could get my feet back on the ground.

Moving day came, John brought his truck. We had agreed to stay friends, though it was more of his idea. However, it was nice having the help. I had a couple of friends help me move out of Rachel's and into the boarding house. It was doable, I could make this work.

I got settled into the new space, it was pleasant enough. My commute to my office went from 20 minutes from Rachel's place to 5 minutes down the road, my office was less than a mile from the 'boarding house.' I continued to build my practice, working on my business and going to network meetings. I felt I lost not only John but also another best friend, Rachel. She and I had spent our days off together, going to the beach or working on our businesses at the local pub. It was nice feeling the support of friendship, but now I just didn't want to talk to her. Moving out was a shock and I felt betrayed again.

But at least I had my business. Interestingly enough, my business income had just about doubled in the last six months since I had moved out of John's place. It felt like I had new possibilities on the horizon like I could dream again about the future. I started imagining new possibilities for myself. I hired an intern to help me with videos and started a YouTube channel. I even ventured out on a couple of dates.

"I can do this," I told myself. I had more time and more money as clients were starting to find me.

"I can do this" became my mantra. I could get back on my feet.

And yet there was the swelling that started in my legs. I had asked the doctor to give me a prescription for Lasik for the edema, it had worked for a couple weeks, but it obviously wasn't enough. I decided to try another specialist and found him less helpful than the first one. He took 10 minutes to talk with me, charged me $500 for the 10 minutes, and then ordered thousands of dollars in bloodwork and lab tests and all this I had to pay out of pocket because I had no health insurance.

I couldn't get insurance now as I was self-employed and it was a "pre-existing condition" and at the time you couldn't even apply for health insurance if you had a prior condition. I felt so frustrated: frustrated with the system, frustrated with the condition, frustrated with my body.

I'd worked so hard. I had been doing my own personal work, journaling, meditating, and doing the clearings that I knew. I had been clearing out layers of traumas and the mental stress patterns surrounding them. I had been working through negative beliefs, ideas like "you can't trust people" "I can't survive on my own" and betrayal. There had been a lot of upheaval in my life in the last six months, losing John, moving twice, and losing a best friend.

And yes, the curveball with John was a huge stressor, but I was making it on my own.

I came home from work one day. The house was quiet, all the tenants were in their rooms with the doors shut, I could hear the sing-song of Indian chatter through the doors in the hallway.

John's family had been my family for the 10 years we were together. We had done all the holidays together, all the birthdays and now all these relationships were gone. It was more than support, I felt the loss of people who cared. I suppose I could have met with his mom who'd been a huge help for us, but it just felt like too much. I tried going to lunch with her once, but the whole time I was on the edge of tears, seeing her was just a sad reminder of no longer feeling like a part of the family.

Of course, I was no longer friends with Rachel, how can you stay friends with someone who doesn't really see you for you? And my other couple of friends had families and businesses so they didn't have extra time. I didn't want to be a burden. I felt so alone, so isolated. I realized I had let my life become very focused around John, I had buried myself in work and I hadn't reached out to make friends in the community. I knew a lot of people, I had a lot of colleagues in the local chamber and business community, but I didn't have the close connections of people I could rely on, and I didn't want to trouble them with my problems.

I guess I hadn't really focused on building strong personal friendships. I had a few close friends, but they lived elsewhere. Maybe I should just give up and go back to Utah. That's where most of my family was. It felt so defeatist though. It felt like giving up, like failing."

"I can do this," I repeated to myself.

CHAPTER 32

Healing Beliefs Encoded in Spirit

A rash had broken out all over my body. My body felt hot and irritated, there must be something I could do with hypnosis to address this skin rash. I called up a fellow student who had been in my hypnosis training to see about trading sessions and perhaps we could see what was causing the rash.

I met my friend Roselyn at her office, the environment was serene with soothing music that filled the waiting area. It definitely felt like a spa: white, clean lines and serene decor. She led me into the quiet hypnosis room with soft golden lighting.

We got settled into the 2 chairs, she would lead me through a session first. She walked me through the first steps of deep breaths, clearing the mind and getting to that familiar quiet space of hypnosis trance as she wove the words into waves of comfort and relaxation.

Roselyn directed, "As you now feel so deeply, comfortably relaxed, now we want your mind to notice this rash on your skin. Asking the mind, what is this rash all about? What's causing this?" She asked.

"It feels like sadness," I said.

She said, "Let your mind take you back to the first place this sadness began...."

A hazy window opened up in my mind, "I see a small village in Europe. I see stone houses and thatched roofs, like the 1400's. I see the people of the village with angry faces.... They are gathered around me.... yelling for my death. I'm tied to a post, standing on a pile of sticks. They are chanting, 'witch, witch, witch' as if caught in a frenzy of anger as they watch me burn," I said.

I watched wisps of smoke curling up from the pile of sticks where I was tied up in the center of the village. I felt anger, anger coursing through my body, and rage. *How could they turn on me? These people were familiar, I had grown up with them. This was my community and they had turned on me? Didn't they know me? I felt so angry and their hate became my hate.*

As I was dying, I felt my skin flush with heat as I cursed them with my rage from the pile of sticks that would be my funeral.

Roselyn continued, "What needs to be healed here?" Roselyn asked.

I could see myself on the smoking pile of sticks. "I need to let go of the anger and hurt so I can move on. Yes, I felt betrayed, but I don't have to carry the anger forward."

"Take this anger all the way past the end of that lifetime and into the space of between lifetimes. In that space of between lifetimes, just let go of the hate, the anger, the pain, just give it all up to the divine. Allow the positive lessons, learning, and wisdom to come back to you. As you let go of all of that, what do you notice?" She asked.

"It feels like relief, it's lighter, there's ease, there is peace," I said.

"Allow that soothing place, as light and comfort to fill all the hurt places within you," Roselyn said.

"Now, invite the souls of all those who participated in your death to that place between lives, gather up your wisdom and learnings, and share with them the learnings, the light, and wisdom. Asking them to share their wisdom and learnings with all the other characters in this play. Life is learning and growing, as we transform the wounds into wisdom and learning, we can even heal karma. Allowing higher love to heal the hurts so that your mind-body-spirit system is free, free to accept higher wisdom, higher love despite all that's happened," she said.

"What do you notice?" She asked.

"There was so much fear. They were acting from fear, I was caught up in the chaos of fear of the times," I said. "Fear was a cancer that took over the community."

I could see how fear had become a dark cloud over the entire community, swallowing victims as one person was accused and then another and another. I could see it now, fear was the infection and the community was the prey. The fear and anger just perpetuated in the population.

It was fear that was the villain and each person giving in to the fear let it spread like wildfire. In the fear, they forgot to trust love and trust their heart, they couldn't see a higher way. Fear clouded their vision and distorted what they saw. The fear grew like a cancer in the village, in the consciousness, blocking people from their connection to intuition and eroding the community into chaos, destroying the connections, destroying love.

Roselyn continued, "Share the healing with all the souls in those events that affected you until it feels complete. Bring your mind and being back to love. Let me know when all the wisdom and learnings are shared and all the anger and pain is cleared."

After a pause of I don't know how long, I felt it was clear, "Yes it's done," I said.

Roselyn then brought me back through the hypnosis journey back into the soft golden lights of the room where we were sitting.

Roselyn asked me, "So that was interesting. Do you believe in past lives?"

I was really taken aback, "I don't know I said. I believe it could be ancestral memories coming through. I wonder if it's just how the mind is organizing it or even perhaps the mind is using a metaphorical story to reflect an underlying pattern so the unconscious mind can resolve or shift the pattern," I said.

I continued, "It was certainly fascinating, I could see the houses and the people. I could feel the energy of the fear and how everyone was caught up in it," I said. "It was really wild; my skin doesn't seem as hot with the rash as before."

"Well, as you know, it doesn't really matter if you believe in past lives or not, that's what your mind wanted to clear and resolve. We don't need to judge whether it's a past life, ancestral memory, or just a story that your mind wanted you to work through," she said.

"It just felt like a dream, but I could feel aspects of it," I said. "I guess my unconscious mind was getting triggered with fear of standing out, fear of being betrayed in the community. It was like, 'You can't trust people,' and 'people turn on you,' and 'I'm all alone, I'm not safe.' Do you believe in past lives, Roselyn?" I asked.

"I'm open to it, for me I think it helps explain certain people I've met in my life. People you meet where you start talking with them, but it feels like you've known them before. I've had a few people like that show up," she said. "Sometimes I'll even get flashes of other times and places."

"Huh, it's just so interesting," I said. "I've lived my life anonymously, even nomadically. I worked for wilderness programs and moved around from place to place. I never really stayed in touch with people and didn't really keep up with friends. This seems to explain that pattern," I said.

"Well, either way, it's what your inner wisdom wanted to address," she said.

My philosophies of the meaning of life had certainly grown beyond what I was taught by the religion I grew up with. I no longer saw the afterlife as heaven and hell. No matter your religion, whether you are Hindu or Buddhist, Jew or Christian or atheist, we are all souls first; I don't think our religions matter so much on the other side.

It was my understanding that in the place of between lives, we all return to source, to truth, to love. As souls, we are all children of the divine, and unconditional love is the core of who we are. The truth of who we are is peace, love, light, joy, and connection to God.

The experiences of earth life give us the choice to experience what we are not so that we can better realize what we are: peace, love, and joy. The more we choose love, the more we allow wisdom and healing in our minds and our bodies.

It was fascinating to me that even though I had died and transitioned into the world beyond from that life, for some reason I hadn't let go of the pain of that earth life and the betrayal. I had carried the betrayal, anger, and hurt of that time forward. What we don't let go of or don't forgive creates a thread of energy we carry with us. Those hurts we carry are an energy that then affects the energies of our lives even as we move forward from one lifetime to another unless we clear it, forgive it, and finally let it go.

Reflection: What hurts can you let go of and forgive to allow greater healing in mind-body-spirit?

CHAPTER 33

Sabotage with Sunlight

I woke up one morning with all my problems swimming in my head: I felt anger at my ex, I felt anger at my body, I felt anger at my health condition. My legs had been continuing to swell although I was taking the medication for the edema. I just needed a distraction, I needed to clear my mind, to clear my mood. I decided to drive up to a favorite waterfall I knew in the hills not too far from John's place.

It was a brilliant day of clear skies and sunshine in early spring. I drove up the familiar and winding road, I had always loved that drive. It was so green and seeing the spring sunlight scattering through the new leaves, glittering with gold sunshine, reflected off the leaves and into my heart, filling it with tiny sparks of brightness.

I was going to have fun today, I was going to enjoy the sunshine and the water all on my own. *Who needs friends who don't really see you or believe in you anyway?*

I drove across the small bridge of the first waterfall, and it was spectacular. The water was roaring from the spring rush of snowmelt. People were climbing on the rocks by the waterfall, and shouts of laughter bounced off the large boulders at the edges of the riverway. The roar of water echoed off the surrounding trees with a power that was palpable.

I parked the car and climbed down onto the rocks to take advantage of the sunshine. I found a beautiful spot, hearing the roar of the water, sparkles of laughter, and people playing in the river. *Oh, how the sunlight felt warm and bright on my legs. No, I wasn't going to wear sunscreen, I'll just have a little bit of sunshine, just a touch. I'd be okay I thought, I won't stay long.*

I allowed myself to fully slip into the moment, with the sound and spray of the water, the feel of the sunshine, and the sounds of people and dogs occasionally chiming in with yips of happiness, enjoying the early spring blue skies.

Just a moment of bliss. I let myself drink it in, it felt so good to be out in the world.

It felt so good to be outside, to be out in the sun and surrounded by life. What a lovely little break from the chaos of my life. I knew it was irresponsible, but I didn't care. I just wanted a day of sunlight and water. I wanted to feel like there was nothing wrong with me. I wanted to feel a reprieve from all the betrayal, rejection, and defeat. And here it was in just a little moment of bliss, echoes of happiness from the boulders and the water.

I allowed myself to revel in it, the sounds, the sunlight, the sensations, and then I decided I must be responsible and made my way home. On the drive home, I could feel my skin start to itch. I wasn't in the sun long, but my skin was already starting to react. Apparently I had stayed too long. My skin started to crawl, *it would be fine. It would be fine.* I told myself.

The next day I woke up with huge welts the size of golf balls all over my legs. My afternoon of rebellion the day before had cost me a flare-up. My legs felt so itchy, hot and irritated.

Ugh, what have I done? I thought.

I must admit I had been mad: mad at the illness, mad at my condition, mad that I'd lost my home, mad that I'd lost my partner, he was my best friend. I felt the betrayal of someone I called a 'friend' kicking me out of her home and only giving me three days. *Life wasn't kind, it was all so unfair.*

Over the next couple of days, the welts subsided, but the swelling in my legs returned. I was feeling more and more drained of energy, and more exhausted. And there was a pressure in my lungs, they felt restricted. When I went to bed at night, if I laid down flat, it felt like a refrigerator on my chest. I had to start propping myself up with pillows at night to reduce the pressure so I could breathe.

I called my mom in Utah, looking for support.

"Hi Mom," I said.

"Hi honey, how are you doing?" she chimed in a cheery voice.

"Not so good. I still have the swelling in my legs. I'm taking the Lasik, but it's not seeming to make a difference. Rachel kicked me out of her house, and I'm renting a room. I'm just so tired of it all," I said as I started to cry, "it's all just so much, so overwhelming," I said through the tears.

"Well, why stay up there in Portland? Why not just come home?" she asked.

"Home meaning Utah? Utah isn't my home, I've lived up here in the Northwest now for ten years, this is my home. I can make it here, my business is doing well. If I stay I at least have my business. If I move back to Utah, I'll lose it all, I won't have anything. I'd be giving up," I whimpered.

"Well, how is your business going?" She asked.

"The business is good, I'm seeing clients, it's working, I'm just so tired all the time," I said.

"If it's too much, just come home, you can take a break," she said.

"I'm here for now, I'm going to try making it on my own," I said.

"It's hard without support," she commiserated with me. "Just remember you do have family here, we love you," she said.

"Thank you, I love you too," I replied.

I dried my tears, it felt good to just cry and have a friendly voice commiserate with me. We chatted about the weather and other family news.

After I hung up the call, I walked back over to my bed, I heard these words in my mind so clear as if someone was right there with me. *"If you don't leave you will die."*

I was a little taken aback, I believed you could talk with spirit guides, but it had never come through so clearly at least not since I was a kid. In my head I went over the reasons to stay in Portland, I didn't have anywhere to go if I moved back to Utah, I would lose my business. I was established here and it was working. *I could do this, I could make it work.*

That afternoon, my brother David called from Salt Lake City, I answered the call, "Hey Dave, how's it going?"

"Things are good here," he said. "Holly, Mom told me how things are going for you. I talked with my family, and we have an extra room in our house. Just come and stay with us, you'll have a place to stay until you can get back on your feet." David was just a few years younger than me and he and his wife Kari had two small boys.

"I don't know Dave, it feels like giving up," I said.

"It's okay to take a break. I know you're fiercely independent, but it's okay to rely on other people sometimes. Just come take a break and get your health back," Dave said.

"Thanks for the offer Dave, My business is up here. If I move, I'd have to start all over from scratch, let me think about it." I could feel the emotion welling up in my throat.

"You have a place here with us if you want, we love you, we care about you," Dave said.

"I'll give it some thought," I said and we hung up.

All the frustration of the last months welled up within me, my body getting sicker and feeling more exhausted. The doctors were no help. They felt dismissive, too busy to be bothered. Each visit was the same, testing hand strength, measuring weight, and reviewing medications. They actually had no plan for me to heal, the only treatment was immunosuppressant drugs for the rest of my life.

I was just racking up more bills with more testing, even thousands of dollars I had to pay out of pocket as I had no insurance. And the isolation, I didn't have anyone I could rely on.

I hadn't seen my nephews in a couple years, the boys were 5 and 9. I tried to make it back to Utah once a year to visit, but sometimes I just couldn't make the time. But, it would be fun to be a part of their lives, celebrate birthdays and holidays with them and watch them grow up. It would be good to be surrounded by people who cared, people who loved me.

Still, I would lose my business. I wouldn't have a way to pay for anything. The prospect of starting over in a new city, starting from scratch seemed daunting. I'd have to learn a new city, make new connections all over again, I'd have to change my website, and redo all the stuff that went along with setting up in a new location, of course, that was just details.

Still, how long could I keep trying to limp along in Portland on my own? I could do it if my health weren't taking such a turn if only I were feeling better.

Life felt like such a struggle. It felt so hard. After working with clients during the day, I would head to my one little bedroom, there was no one to talk to, just the four walls and the unpacked boxes piled up along the walls. My roommates were all cloistered in their own rooms, chatting online with their families in India. As I walked down the hallway to my room at night, I passed the closed doors and could hear the sing-song chatter of them talking excitedly with their loved ones. I felt on the outside of it all, more than alone, I felt...abandoned.

Sometimes the easy way is the best next step, a random quote echoed in my head.

The words, *If you don't leave, you will die, r*ang in my mind. It would be nice to just take a break. I felt the appeal of relief from trying to make it all work on my own. Relief from the isolation, relief from the loss and upheaval. I could be surrounded by people who cared about me.

The next day, I called my brother back, "Hey Dave, I'm going to take you up on your offer. It's just such a struggle up here with my health and the medical bills and I feel so alone. Is that room still available?"

"Of course Holly, we just want you to come and get better," he said.

I gave my 30-day notice on the room I was renting. I was on a month-to-month contract anyway so that was easy enough. I had packed up most of my stuff at John's place from when I moved out six months ago. Most of it was in storage in his shed until I had a stable place. It meant closing down my practice in Vancouver. I was on a month-to-month contract there as well, renting a small treatment room in the massage clinic where I had been for six years.

I had a friend who was also a Hypnotherapist. She was willing to take the clients who had already bought vouchers from an ad service I had been using. I set about letting clients know I was wrapping up and moving to Salt Lake City, Utah.

The day came, and I loaded up my clothes into the back of my small purple GEO Metro. John had agreed to drive with me to Utah as I was just feeling so exhausted all the time. The swelling had continued, and I was feeling more drained, and more exhausted. I was thankful he'd offered to drive with me so we could keep each other awake on the 12-hour trip. We had made an effort to remain friendly, although it had been hard work. It was nice having his support.

We arrived on a Saturday morning at my brother's red brick two-story house with a car full of clothes and my GEO Metro. It was good seeing Dave, Kari, and the boys. There was excitement in their home and I felt the bustle of it. The boys were excited too, showing me their room with new bunk beds, they had doubled up in one room to make space for me to come, and I was touched by their willingness to make space for me.

John helped me unload my car. Unpacking simply meant wrapping my arms around all the clothes still on hangers stacked in the back of my Geo Metro and hanging them in the closet of the room my brother had cleared out for me. I didn't bring much else, a few personal items, an overnight bag, toiletries but that was about it. All my other stuff, mostly boxes and boxes of books and my outdoor gear was stacked away in John's garage. John then headed to the airport to catch a plane back to Portland. It was nice we'd been able to stay friends but seeing him was still sad.

The room at my brother's place was basic: white walls, an empty closet, and a window. There was a queen bed made up with a soft blue comforter and a couple of pillows.

My brother's house was lovely, his wife Kari was good at keeping clean spaces, uncluttered and decorated in *Home and Garden* magazine style. He also had a couple of dogs, whippets that looked like miniature greyhounds with sleek short fur, Liza and Bella.

It was a new start, a new space and at least I had people who cared about me. I felt the bustle and excitement of movement, the dogs followed me around curiously. Everyone was so accommodating, and I felt relief as I relaxed on the bed.

Well, unpacking was easy enough. Now I just needed to get re-established with a good doctor, rebuild in a new city, recreate a new life with new people, make new friends, and rebuild my business and find my footing again.

It felt like a weight lifted, maybe this is exactly what I needed a fresh start, now if I could only get my health back. It was a new start, a new space and at least I had people who cared about me, people who loved me.

Reflection: We all need social support and love is a basic human need. Love can come from many places, not just a significant other. It can come from your dog, your cat, family and friendships. Where can you recognize love in your life? If there were an easy way or next step what would it be? Where can you rely on others?

CHAPTER 34

Back to the Hospital

My Mom was also living at my brother David's house during the week while she worked as a nurse in a long-term care facility in Salt Lake City. Then during the weekends, she would drive to the four acres of her childhood home that my grandparents had left to her about 2 hours away.

My Mom's cousin Grant was a family doctor just south of Salt Lake City, she made an appointment for me to see him and she accompanied me to the appointment. My energy was still low, I felt exhausted and tired quickly, finding it hard to breathe. The nurses checked me in, took my vital signs, and led me to a treatment room.

Grant was a tall man, clean-shaven with sandy blond hair, wearing a white lab coat and a stethoscope around his neck. He carried a clipboard for paperwork. He listened to my lungs and then took my pulse.

After his quick assessment, he looked at me with seriousness, "You need to check yourself into the hospital right away," he said emphatically. "You're not well and you have multiple things going on."

"Well, I feel tired, but I don't feel that bad, are you sure I need to go to the hospital?" I asked.

"There's not a lot I can do for you, you really need medical attention. When you get back to Salt Lake, just check yourself into the hospital," he said.

"Well, I'm driving back to Salt Lake today, is it okay to go to the hospital tomorrow?" I asked.

"Just don't delay on this. You really need medical help beyond what we can do here, drive back and get yourself checked into the hospital," he emphasized.

I was a little bewildered, he made it sound so serious. "Okay, I'll check into the hospital when I get back to Salt Lake City," I agreed. My Mom and I drove back that afternoon and I made plans to check in at the hospital the next day.

The next day, I arrived at the Intermountain Medical Center with an overnight bag, a simple change of clothes, and of course books to keep me company. I checked in at the desk where the admin lady handed me the paperwork.

"What brings you in today dear?" She asked as I turned the paperwork back in.

"I don't exactly know; I went to see my family doctor and he said I needed to check myself into the hospital right away. So here I am," I said still feeling bewildered.

"What symptoms have you been having?" she asked.

"Well, I'm exhausted, I have swelling in my legs. I can't lie down to sleep at night because it puts too much pressure on my chest, so I have to sleep sitting up. I have achy joints, so some days it's hard to move. I was also diagnosed with Lupus, an autoimmune condition in 2006," I said.

"I'll get your paperwork processed and we'll get someone to see you," she said.

Sometime later, a nurse showed up calling my name. I followed her to a treatment room, I quickly felt out of breath as we walked down the hall. She took my vitals and listened to my lungs.

"The doctors will be with you shortly," she said as she left the room.

The doctor came in to assess and take my vitals. Nurses were in and out, and the doctor left and returned with two more doctors. The room quickly became busier as the white lab coats and blue scrubs started swarming in the small treatment room and whispering together in the corner.

"We're going to give you a blood transfusion because you're so anemic," one doctor said. They set up an IV in my arm and attached the bag of fluids to the pole they wheeled next to my bed. There were now five doctors talking in the background.

About ten minutes into the procedure, suddenly I was gasping for breath. I couldn't breathe, the doctors swirled around in a flurry of activity. Someone handed me an oxygen mask and I gasped into it.

"What's happening?" someone asked.

"She's having a hard time breathing," someone said.

"It must be the blood transfusion, but how would that cause difficulty with breathing?" another doctor asked.

I sat up straight in the hospital breath, gasping from an oxygen mask with short, panicked breaths, trying to slow my breathing down. I just couldn't get the air. A nurse stuck a needle in my arm and the world went fuzzy and dark.

I woke the next morning in the sterile hospital room hooked up to an IV next to my bed.

A woman in her mid-forties with dark hair twisted up into a hair clip and a pleasant disposition wheeled in a machine and set it up next to my bed. She was dressed in regular clothes, no scrubs.

"You gave everyone a scare last night," she said. "You had a lot going on with congestive heart failure and kidney failure. They removed about a pint of liquid from around your heart," she pointed to a bag of yellow fluid hooked to the side of the bed. That fluid bag is draining more from around your heart." She said, "You have five doctors working on your case, so it's good to see you stable."

"What do you mean?" I was confused. "Last thing I remembered was a blood transfusion, an oxygen mask, and a bunch of doctors, what happened?"

"I'm here for your dialysis session," she continued.

"What do you mean dialysis session?" I asked.

"Your kidneys are in failure, they're not cleaning your blood, so the dialysis machine helps your body clean your blood and then gives it back to you," she said.

"Does it hurt?" I asked.

"Oh no, you'll feel a poke with the IV, but that's it. I'll just be here waiting with you while the machine is working," she replied. "You don't have to talk if you don't want to, you can just relax."

She went about setting up the machine and hooking me up to it. I looked around the hospital room, the plain walls, the beep of the machines. *This was not where I wanted to be again. I didn't need this. And now congestive heart failure? What is that exactly? And kidney failure? Why was all this happening?*

How did I not see it coming? I knew the unconscious mind could cause health issues from stress or other unresolved events. I had been telling myself I was okay at the conscious level, I had been using the practice, *'I can do this.'* But I could see now that my health really started going downhill after breaking up with John, six months after the breakup, I noticed the swelling in my ankles.

At the unconscious level, I just probably hadn't recovered from feeling that I had lost everything: I lost my partner of ten years, I lost my business, I lost my home of 5 acres, I lost my dog, I lost my cat. Everything was in John's name. I didn't want to move my cat away from the 5 acres, she loved being outside. I had raised her there and there wasn't a place for my cat at my brother's house. I'd left her in

The Miracle Code

Washington too. All I had was a closet full of clothes and my cheap car.

The dialysis lady, Tiffany came every day for 2 hours to run the dialysis machine for my kidneys. She said I didn't have to talk if I was too tired, and she often read while I slept. The week passed in a haze of sleep and the whirring of the machine cleaning my blood. There was a small window in my treatment room where I could see outside, the sparse cold leafless trees of November.

A week later I was released from the hospital back to Dave's house. With the kidney failure, the doctors didn't know how long it would take for my kidneys to come back to functioning. They said my chances were good because I was only 39. In the meantime, until my kidneys were working better, I had to go to the dialysis center three days a week to have my blood cleaned by the big dialysis machines, which looked somewhat like a washing machine, which I guess was fitting.

I settled into a new routine at my brother's place. Every morning after the kids left for school and after Dave and Kari left for work, I was alone except for the two whippets who would scratch at my bedroom door. I would open the door to let them jump in my bed as they snuggled under the covers, to press their sleek warm bodies against my legs. I'm pretty sure these little naked dogs were using me for my body heat, but it felt comforting to have them snuggled up against me.

When I was ready to get up, I would sit on the edge of the bed and cry for the struggle that was my life. This was not what I wanted, but then there was still the day ahead. The big empty day.

Reflection: Sometimes you just need a good cry, a good outlet to let go of overwhelming emotions. There are many ways to clear out the overwhelm of emotions, how do you clear yours? There are struggles in life, and times we feel low, how are you honoring Your emotions in difficult times?

CHAPTER 35

Gratitude: A Forgotten Medicine

The sound of scratching at the door woke me to yet another morning. I watched the sun streak through the window and across the blue and white comforter. The house was quiet except for the naked dogs scratching, asking to be let in to snuggle. The kids had left for school and my brother and his wife had gone to work.

And I was alone in the big, beautiful house with the bleakness of my life. I had nothing to my name except a closet full of clothes and an old Geo Metro. My little car was great on gas mileage, but certainly nothing to look at.

I let the dogs into the room and raised up the covers to invite them to curl up with my legs. At least Eliza and Bella were with me, although sometimes I wondered if I was just a convenient heater. The blank day spread out in front of me. It was my day off from dialysis, but instead I had to face the nothingness that was my life. The sadness and despair invaded my mind and I let the sobs roll up from my gut to my throat and into my eyes as the tears poured through.

Breathe into it, just breathe into the center. I cried, giving into the thread of the emotion, cried it out all the way down, all the way to the center of it until it was gone. And there at the bottom of it, there was nothing left to cry. There were no more tears, it was just gone. *Well chalk up another round for feeling your emotions,* I thought. Crying was the body's natural outlet to reset itself, a cathartic relief.

I sat up in bed and looked around at the plain white walls.

And still there was the day and at least there were the dogs. I climbed back into the bed and pulled the covers over my head, wishing my life were different. Life had changed so much in the last year. I had had the relationship, the house, the career, and decent money doing something I loved and yet here I was cloistered in a spare room of my brother's house, sick and feeling barely alive. I felt that I had lost everything. I was no longer the wilderness girl, no longer the girlfriend, no longer in Portland, I no longer really had my business even.

The day loomed before me. I tried to close my eyes and go back to sleep.

A part of my mind chimed up, *So you're going to sleep it away?*

Uggh. I felt the reality of it, nothing was going to change unless I did something different.

Okay Holly, what do you want to do with your day? I asked myself.

I felt broken, I had seen amazing results with my clients, and I had watched them heal. Why couldn't I find healing for myself? Why had my journey been so rough?

Ahh shake it off, time to get your day going, it's time for morning prayers.

Saying my morning prayers, "Dear God, please bless my family, please bless me that I will heal that I will," I stopped my prayers midsentence. I'd been praying to God for 10 years for healing, *why aren't you helping me?* I was tired of the repetition of hearing myself ask over and over, please help me heal, please help me to be well. I determined to stop praying. It was futile, nothing was changing over 10 years, nothing had changed. I felt hopeless.

All I could hope for was to make the most of my day. All I could do was go back to the basics.

I unwrapped myself from the blankets and the dogs and started running the water for my morning bath. I couldn't shower because the doctors had surgically placed a dialysis port in my neck which I couldn't get wet because it could get infected. They used the port to hook me up to the dialysis machines. I had to take baths instead. I slid into the warm water as it swirled around and cradled my body.

But as I tried to relax and let my mind go clear, all I felt was bitterness. With all this that was happening to me: the diagnosis, living with autoimmune, the breakup with John, betrayal of friends, I had always been trying the best I could. My best wasn't enough, so yes, I was upset at God.

I was more than upset and frustrated, I was angry at God, "Why aren't you helping me?" I screamed out loud at the bathtub. I also felt torn, I had always considered myself a spiritual person. I was intuitive and had felt angels and spirit guides when I was young, and there was part of me that loved God.

I had seen people shut down from God and in doing so shut the door on possibility and hope. And maybe it wasn't God's fault that I was sick.

Who's fault was it then? Was it my fault? I had always been healthy and I was doing the best I could. Was it John's fault for leaving me and triggering my autoimmune? Was it my parents' fault for bad genetics? Was it the boys who traumatized and tortured me all those years ago, was it their fault? Was it my fault that I had internalized the traumas?

Well, whatever it was, I'm not going to shut down with bitterness, but I couldn't pray anymore asking for healing. It just felt so redundant, like a broken record. I climbed into the bath to soak and wash. *Okay, what CAN I do with my day?*

I could go to the bookstore. I finished my bath, got ready, put on my clothes, and drove to the local bookstore. I couldn't buy anything, I had no income, and no money, but I could read. It felt nice to act like a normal person and be out in the world as if there was nothing wrong with me. I searched for books on happiness in the self-help section. *I had to find a way to pull myself out of this funk of despair. I had never had to work for happiness before, not like this.* I sat in a chair and dove in to find some morsel of wisdom that could uplift my mind and spirits.

Thumbing through I landed on a chapter that talked about the importance of gratitude.

Yes, I could remember the basics. Gratitude, I mused on gratitude. What is gratitude? When do we feel gratitude? *Ahh just have gratitude, that's so overdone in the self-help world,* my inner snark monster thought.

I looked at my life, and the reality of it was I had been focusing on everything that I had lost: my relationship, my business, my money, my status.... and the truth of it was...in all this chaos of change, I was still okay. I was breathing, I was alive, and I was getting the care I needed.

I had a roof over my head. I had family that cared about me. I had time, open time that I hadn't had while running my business. I had time for meditation and hot baths. I had time to read and research. I had thinking time, reading time, and movie time.

And the machines that cleaned my blood three days a week were sort of a miracle. I googled it and found that dialysis machines were invented by Willem Kolff as an "artificial kidney" in 1943. He constructed the first apparatuses using orange juice cans, sausage skins, and old washing machine parts. After years of development, it finally became this amazing machine that could clean my blood while my body recovered. Since 1972 treatments have become available to everyone regardless of their ability to pay.

I was receiving support, medical care, and getting access to services that could help me bridge the gap to health. I was receiving care and services that I couldn't pay for. When I thought about it, it was really mind-boggling to recognize all the people who came together to make dialysis treatments possible. Not just the invention, but the current system: the doctors, the nurses, the dialysis workers, the lab technicians, the machines, all of it. I felt awe for a moment of recognizing the miraculous network that was tangibly supporting me. And there it was, sincere gratitude.

That night as I went to bed, I decided to replace the asking with gratitude in my prayers. I turned my thoughts to God and simply said thank you.

Thank you for my brother and his family. Thank you for the boys being willing to share a room so there was a room for me. Thank you for the four walls around me, thank you for the carpet, the walls, and the comfortable bed. Thank you for running water and hot baths. Thank you for a deeply comfortable pillow. Thank you for the dogs that wake me up in the morning. As I said the thank yous, I felt a wash of relief from all of the mental anguish of my situation. And in all of the upheavals and the hospital stays, my body was still okay. I was still okay. Thank you that I have family who cares about me. Thank you that I am loved.

Thank you for the doctors and nurses who were caring for me. Thank you for the medical expertise passed down through years and years of people dedicating their lives to finding answers and helping people. Thank you for the dialysis machines, thank you for the system allowing me to get medical treatments I couldn't afford, and lifesaving inventions. Thank you for all the people who've supported me, been there for me, and showed up for me. I thought of the many mentors and teachers who had shown up along my journey. Thank you that I've always had help, that I've always been guided with a breadcrumb trail of inspired people.

As I said my thank yous, I felt a light stretch from my heart to the sky and beyond. I could feel a bubble of light around me. I was okay and all these people, machines, and services were showing up for me. I felt awe for all of it. And thank you, whether I healed or not didn't seem to matter so much as I felt caught up in the awe of gratitude and connection in this grand ripple of life, this network of the miraculous, the dialysis machines, the doctors, the nurses, the facilities. I was in awe, it was all showing up for me, like a saving grace.

A heaviness cleared and hope glowed through my body. *All you need is a pocketful of dreams and the resolve to take the steps ahead,* my inner philosopher chimed in. I could see my path, I was okay, I'll just take it one day at a time.

As my energy brightened, I started feeling the inklings of hope again. What if I could rebuild life and my business? Sure, it would take time, but time was what I got. I could do it. I built my business from the ground up once before and maybe this time it would go faster. I just needed to get in and connect with the community and find the resources. I could do this, a day at a time, a step at a time and I had time.

Reflection: When we are feeling bleak, the mind sees everything through that lens. As I had been looking at all I had lost, I was missing out on the bigger picture: that I was being supported and people were showing up for me. I could see the medical treatments for the miracles they were, which started with someone's vision of saving lives and I was reaping all the good intentions. Where have you been feeling lost or hopeless? When you turn your mind to gratitude what do you notice instead?

CHAPTER 36

Awakening to Joy

It was a weekday; I drove to the bookstore to peruse other people's thoughts etched into papers and cardboard. If I was going to rebuild my life, I needed something inspirational, I needed a pick me up, I needed happiness back.

As I looked back, I could see that I had taken happiness for granted. I always had a next adventure, a next big project, or the next thing to do. I was by nature a doer, I was good at jumping in and getting things done. Happiness had been easy for me with each next thing to be accomplished.

But with all the developments over the past 6 months, happiness felt like an elusive mystery suddenly out of reach. Maybe someone else's thoughts could help me make sense of the puzzle of happiness. I drove to the bookstore hoping to find something I could use.

I walked among the self-help books, looking for answers to the happiness question. I found one book in particular, *Awakening to Joy*. I got a coffee at the adjoining coffee shop and settled in to read.

The book talked about how our Western culture has trained people to seek happiness through stuff. We've learned happiness is something we buy through media and consumerism. We've learned happiness is something we acquire, achieve, or accomplish. We then chase one goal to the next searching for happiness. "When I get the new car, then I will be happy. When I get the promotion, then I will be happy. When I get the next relationship, then I will be happy."

Do this thing or buy this stuff and then you will feel happy. But the happiness only lasts until the novelty of the new thing wears off and then we are back to seeking the next thing, in an endless cycle of chasing happiness. I could agree with all of that.

The book proposed: What if happiness isn't something that we hunt down to buy or accomplish, what if happiness isn't achieved when life is perfect? What if happiness is more than the next car or the next vacation? What if happiness is not an event or achievement, but what if it's more like a flow that moves through our lives? What if happiness is actually happening all the time, we just haven't been paying attention to it?

The concept was simple, notice the smallest moments of happiness as they show up: it could be a warm hug of a friend, it could be a wide-eyed moment of wonder of a child, it could even be the smile of a stranger. Count even the smallest glimmers of happiness until it creates a string of lights through your life, a string of all those bright moments.

The book went on to explain there are many flavors of happiness. There is quiet happiness and there is also loud ecstatic happiness and all the shades of happiness in between. Sometimes our expectation of happiness is big loud happiness and so we miss out on noticing the quiet and gentle happiness because it whispers. Every day offers multiple ways to see, notice, and experience happiness, are we paying attention?

Okay, I'll try it I thought. I enrolled my mind. *Can my mind help me recognize and notice even the smallest moments of happiness?* I felt an inner yes. What if every day rather than seeing the black hole of depression, what if life instead was more like a treasure hunt? A treasure hunt of recognizing, and noticing the smallest moments of happiness when they showed up?

I drove back to my brother's house, feeling a buoyancy in my heart. As I walked back to the house and opened the door, there were the dogs, Liza and Bella, tails wagging ecstatically. I bent down to see their little faces, their cold noses touched my cheek as they tried to lick my face, I laughed trying to evade their wet tongues and there it was...happiness.

Yes, it was happiness, a palpable feeling within as I recognized the light in their eyes and their tails wagged when I walked through the door. I let myself revel in the joy of their greeting, the joy of the moment, just a moment, a glimmer of happiness.

I found it, happiness is a cold wet nose and a borrowed dog.

Happiness is just like any other muscle, the more that we practice it, the stronger it gets. Happiness is happening all the time, are we recognizing it? And happiness happens even in the smallest of moments. I loved the concept, happiness is showing itself in many ways every day, are we noticing it when it shows up?

Reflection: Is your mind willing to help you notice the many flavors and whisperings of happiness as you move throughout your day?

CHAPTER 37

Remaking a Life

As I started noticing the small moments of happiness, I felt my spirit uplifted. It was as if an inner reserve that had dried up was now being filled expanding into a reservoir. Along with the happiness also came energy, physical energy to do, to accomplish, to achieve. *I'm ready,* I thought. *I'm ready to get back to work.*

I called a fellow Coach I knew who lived in Salt Lake City and she gave me some phone numbers of people who might rent office space. One of the contacts was a psychologist who had a part-time room to rent, so we set up a tour. It was a professional building, the walls were white and clean, there was a minimalist quality and the room to rent was small but workable. She was only asking for a small monthly fee and month-to-month contract which fit my budget. After saying yes to rent the space, I felt energy with a bunch of tasks in front of me, I was suddenly in the process of reconstructing my life.

I started working on my website, updating it to my new location. I transferred the advertising I had done in Washington to Salt Lake City and within a couple of weeks, I was seeing clients again. My energy was still low, I was only seeing 1-2 clients a day at first. But it gave me something to do, it was something to look forward to and I knew the work. It was familiar and easy as I had done thousands of sessions with clients over the last six years. Starting small was okay, it was a good place to start.

Dialysis was three days a week, I scheduled clients on the days I didn't have dialysis. But as the weeks turned to months, I found my strength and stamina returning. In just a couple of months, my practice was back to part-time hours. It felt good to have purpose, it felt good to contribute. Even though I hadn't healed myself, I could help make a difference for others.

I continued my self-care routine of my morning smoothie and supplements. Most every day I had my bath and morning meditation. I meditated on my body, on my health, and doing the inner change-work I knew how to do with NLP and Hypnosis. I once again started imagining my body well, I imagined doing things that I enjoyed like hiking and sunning myself on the beach in Mexico, the dream was not gone, it was just delayed. There was some comfort in the hope that I wasn't there yet, but maybe there was still a way, a path forward.

With my commitment to helping others with my hypnosis practice, I had purpose and direction. At the office seeing clients, no one knew of my personal life and struggles. I could step into a different role, one where I looked normal.

Sure I had lost some things, but if I focused on what I'd lost, I would only feel the despair of it. If I didn't paint a new picture, I would be stuck in the black hole of depression and numbness.

So I imagined life as an open canvas waiting to be sketched and colored in. I could feel gratitude for what was right here in the moment, I could reconnect and recommit to my purpose, I could do what I knew, and the days were becoming a treasure hunt of small moments of happiness.

I kept up my daily practice. As I was still going to dialysis 3 days a week, it was important that I continued to feed my mind with positive focuses to rebuild my body and health as I waited for my kidneys to get back to work and my body to heal.

Reflection: When we are sick with a diagnosis, we are often receiving care from others. It was therapeutic for me to switch the role I played from being the "sick" person to being the facilitator. As a Coach, I didn't have the answers for others, but I knew the process of connecting people with their own answers. And the magic of NLP processes and Hypnosis of course stood on their own. I could be seen in a different role, which held a positive reflection for me.

If you are feeling low, perhaps with an illness, or perhaps a circumstance in life, in what small way can you reach out to someone else to brighten their day? It can be simple: a heartfelt hug, a compliment, or a word of encouragement to let someone know they matter, that they are seen and valued. Playing the role of giving helps us stretch beyond our limitations and into connections, and the positives we feed into the world create a ripple through our lives.

CHAPTER 38

Kidney Transplant List

After 6 months of going to dialysis three days a week, I was rebuilding my life starting with my business and seeing clients on the days I didn't have dialysis. My kidney doctor, the nephrologist, was regularly at the dialysis center seeing patients and he would check in on me from time to time. He asked me to come into the office for a checkup and we set up the time.

Kevin, my nephrologist, had dark hair touched at the temples with grey, he walked into the clinic office and closed the door. "Holly, I've been looking over your labs, it's been about six months and your kidney function just isn't improving like we'd hoped. I'm going to recommend that you apply to get on the kidney transplant list. At this point, we need to look at the possibility of getting you new kidneys if they don't turn around. It would mean being able to get off of dialysis, but there's a lot to consider, so I recommend you go to an information meeting at the hospital next Thursday."

"Well that sounds serious," I said.

"We just don't know if your kidney function will return. If you go to the meeting you can get all the information and it's a process to get on the kidney transplant list. It can take years to get new kidneys, so you may as well get it started sooner rather than later just in case you need it," he said.

Thursday, I walked into the large conference room, where 6 other people were seated at the table. A woman with short brown hair ushered me in to take a seat and gave me a pen and a pack of papers. "Come in and take a seat, we'll start the video in a minute. My job is to give you all the information about what it means to apply for the kidney transplant list," she said. I took a seat at the conference room table as the others filed in and I set about doing the paperwork in front of me.

"Hi everyone, my name is Karen, hand your paperwork over to me. There's a lot to consider with the kidney transplant list. It can get you back to living life. Many people who've had the transplant procedure can be off of dialysis and getting back to regular activities," she said. "It can mean getting your life back. We're going to watch a short twenty-minute video that explains everything and then we can have time for questions at the end," she said and proceeded to set up and play the video which projected to a screen on the wall.

At the end of the film, Karen turned up the lights and addressed the conference room, "As you saw in the video, getting new kidneys can give you freedom from dialysis to live a normal life. However, there is a lot to consider, it will require you to continue the immunosuppressant medications."

"How long after the transplant does it take for your body to accept your kidneys and normalize so you can get off the immunosuppressant meds?" I asked.

"You can't go off the medications, you'll be on them the rest of your life. As I said, there's a lot to consider in the operation," Karen said. "Sometimes you'll have to wait for several years to get a kidney that's compatible."

"If I would need monthly medications for the rest of my life, how much do the medications cost?" I asked.

"It's just about $2,000 per month," she said flatly.

I was shocked, "How can people afford that?" I asked.

"Well, most people have to drain their accounts down to less than $3,000. Then they can apply for disability and fall under Medicaid services of disability, then the state will help cover medications. You should all have a case worker by now to navigate these services, they can walk you through all the paperwork," she said.

Karen continued to answer questions as people asked about the logistics of the procedure, what percentage of the cost could be covered, and what people would need to pay out of pocket. This path of kidney transplant option was not painting a pretty picture of the future for me. However grateful I was to these modern inventions of dialysis; I knew I didn't want to be enslaved to dialysis machines or medications costing $2,000 each month. It would essentially consign me to a life of poverty. You couldn't even apply to the program unless you had less than $3,000 to your name.

Karen continued to answer questions around the table for another 30 minutes or so, but I sat stunned. I was caught between a rock and a hard place; I didn't like these options. *"What else is possible?"* I thought. It was a phrase from a conscious living group I had run across in Portland.

When the meeting ended, I took my paperwork and set up an appointment with the case worker assigned to me. *Just take each next step, one day at a time,* I thought.

I met with the case worker who walked me through the immense paperwork of applying for disability and assistance with dialysis and treatments. Disability covered medications and a small monthly stipend, but it wasn't enough money to cover rent and food on my own.

With all the hospital bills, dialysis treatments three days a week, and working minimally with clients, I was thankful for the help of disability. But if I was going to believe in more and create a better vision of my future, I needed my kidneys to get back to work. And I needed to expect that receiving disability was temporary.

Reflection: Sometimes we don't have good options, but those are only the options we are aware of. There can be other options we may not have considered or yet been exposed to. Asking, "What else is possible?" can open up the mind to finding and recognizing greater options and greater answers. Sometimes your path forward opens up one step at a time. What else is possible and what's your next step? Open the space for bigger answers and take your practical next step forward.

CHAPTER 39

Asking the Mind-Body for More Answers

I continued my morning self-care routine. One day as I ran the water for my morning bath and meditation, I sat back into the warmth and let my mind tune into my body. I imagined shrinking my awareness smaller and smaller and traveling down through my blood vessels and down into my kidneys, which after 6 months of dialysis were still not responding as they should. *What are my kidneys doing and what do they need?*

Me: "What's this all about?" I asked.
Inner voice: *"Sad,"* The kidney seemed to say.
Me: "What's the sad about?" I asked.
Inner voice: *"Failed."*
Me: "What failed?" I asked.

My thoughts turned to everything I'd lost and what I didn't have. I lost my home and 5 acres. I thought of the beauty of the trees, the grass, the meadow that was no longer mine. I'd lost my best friend, my partner John. We'd managed to stay friendly, but of course, it would never be the same. I'd lost my cat and my dog. I felt the loss of it all.

The judgments of my religious upbringing came to mind as if part of my mind were judging me for not living up to the standards of having "the one eternal companion." I was taught you find your mate in this life and it's forever. Of course, I no longer believed this rhetoric at the conscious level, but I could feel the pull of a part of my mind, my unconscious mind, holding onto the old ideas. I failed the relationship and in so doing, I had failed God. That somehow, if I was unpartnered, unmarried, I didn't have God's approval.

I was a single woman, unwanted, and unloved. I felt the shame of it. *I could tell this probably also had generational threads to it, the judgments and shame of being a single woman.* For centuries women were second-class citizens, not being able to own property or have jobs or make money, fully dependent on the good graces of a husband or the men in her life.

Inner voice: *"I failed, sad."*

I started to talk back to that part of my mind, "I'm still here. I'm still alive." I drew from the many client sessions about the idea of "failure."

I told the parts of my mind, "Life is a process, like riding a bicycle. We don't get it all at once, it's a process of figuring it out. Even when we fall off the bicycle, we are learning coordination, balance, momentum, movement, and putting it all together. So the next time we get on the bicycle, we are even more prepared to be more successful. In fact, we become more and more capable with every try."

I gave each of my kidneys the image of a bicycle. "There is no failure, there is only the process of learning and growing and figuring it out. Can you just keep going? We aren't done living, I need you to keep going."

At first, when I added the image of the bicycle, it seemed like the gears were rusty, so I imagined oiling them and turning the wheels 'til they turned smoothly.

"Wonderful kidneys, you are so important to me. You have a very important job of cleaning my blood, clearing out the toxins of the past, and letting go. I love you kidneys, I need you to just keep going. Thank you for all you do for me. Thank you for all you have done for me over the years, I need you to just keep going."

I turned my attention to the right kidney, "Are you willing and able to just keep going?" I asked.

Inner voice: *"I'll try,"* whispered through my mind.

I turned my attention to the left kidney, it felt slower, "Are you willing and able to just keep going?" I asked.

Inner voice: *"I'll try,"* said another whisper.

Me: "I love you and appreciate you, you are important to me. Thank you for working for me. I love you."

Inner voice: *"But sad, not loved."* It felt it was from my left kidney.

I felt my kidney needed something to focus on, "We need a new vision, my life is now like an open canvas, clean and white. And we have a whole paint set of every color. I get a new canvas, a new beginning, we can paint whatever we want. We can create a new vision, a new future."

These parts of my mind had been focusing on what was lost, I needed to get it to switch to the appreciation of the here and now and the possibilities of what could be.

Me: "Yes loved," I said back. "On this new canvas, I would paint my family who loves and supports me. I added the faces of my mom, my brother Dave, Kari, and their two boys. I imagined heart lights shining from me to each of them and back again. I added in other family members who weren't physically in my life: my brother in Arizona along with his family, my dad, my sister and her family and each of her kids, and my younger brother in Fillmore where my mom lived on weeks off from work. I would add the nice home where I stayed and my soft pillows and blankets. I would add a restart of my NLP & Hypnotherapy business, helping others get past the inner blocks," I painted all these onto the open canvas in my mind as I narrated the process to my kidneys.

I directed my attention to the left kidney, "Now with the bicycle and half-filled canvas, and knowing love is everywhere, how do you feel now?"

I felt the energy of a sigh of relief and hope radiated through.

Inner voice: *"Better, I'll try,"* it seemed to whisper.

Me: *"Just flow the wheels, day by day, step by step while we are alive, is that okay?"* I imagined the wheels of a bicycle turning and turning.

Inner voice: *"I'll do what I can,"* it seemed to say.

I kept up my meditation routine, checking in on my kidneys and telling them that I loved them and valued them. Someone had gifted me a book of meditations. They were simple, they were easy and I started each day with the quiet hours when the family had left: a bath of hot water, checking in with myself then going through one of the meditations from *Soul Mind Body Medicine by Dr. Zhi Gang Sha.*

A couple of months later, my nephrologist Dr. Kevin met with me to review my bloodwork.

"Holly your bloodwork came back and your kidney filtration rates have improved. I believe they are on the mend. We'll keep an eye on them, but if this trend continues, you'll be off dialysis within a couple of months," he beamed.

I appreciated his warm-hearted sincerity. He certainly was making a difference in this field with more than just his expertise, but with the care and compassion he brought to his patients. I could truly appreciate all the help I was receiving from all the people involved: Dr. Kevin, the staff of the dialysis center. the lab techs, and all the professionals doing their part in the grand machine of Western Medicine.

The good news spurred me to continue my daily meditation practice. I believed the meditations were working, but it was nice to see the results and have proof of it. As my kidneys continued to improve, I went from dialysis 3 days a week to 2 days a week, to one day a week and finally, I was weaned off of dialysis completely.

The psychologist whom I had been renting space from decided to let her office go and move in with a wellness center, a community of massage therapists, healers, and practitioners. I was invited to join as well and we collectively moved into a suite of a larger building. In the move, I found a whole host of kind-hearted sincere professionals and lightworkers. The new space had multiple treatment rooms for sessions and a larger room which was perfect for teaching classes and holding community events. There was energy and motion with all the people and friendships abounded. Life was on an upswing.

My home life at my brother David's house was pretty quiet during the week, but he and his wife had made friends with many of the neighbors. On the weekends, there were large gatherings, laughter, and good conversations. Mostly my energy was so low, I just watched as an observer. It took months for me to get back to a semblance of myself, the self that could engage, participate and laugh again.

And the years passed as I continued my self-care, building my strength and my practice back into full-time.

Reflection: What's your daily practice? Especially when there's a health issue or a health crisis, it's the body's way of getting our attention. With meditation states, we can practice listening deeper to our bodies, which are reflecting energies and beliefs from the unconscious mind. When we address these inner messages, we can clear the mind, and resolve the inner issues so we can tune into harmony of the mind-body-spirit system to rebalance, harmonize, and heal.

What's the message from your body or the symptom? We can update the unconscious levels of mind faster by using its language; symbolism, imagery, story, metaphors and feelings. What can you include in talking with your mind-body-spirit system?

CHAPTER 40

I Hate You Tango

"I hate you! I hate you!" I was screaming at my ex as I was cleaning out my stuff from his house. His mom started coming up the walkway, "I hate you too for making me love your family and making me leave." I woke up from the dream. It was surprising because my ex and I were still friendly, and we checked in from time to time. I thought I had cleared out the anger and feelings of betrayal, but apparently not.

It had been four years since we split up. I imagined that time heals the wounds, that all you need is time and the hurt and pain naturally fades away, but not so. And there certainly are levels to how deep the wounds of the heart go and what the unconscious mind hangs on to.

This whole dream was very surprising to me, I don't do anger very often, let alone hate. Anger wasn't acceptable as a child and certainly not hate. When we argued as kids we were told, "contention is of the devil" so I was taught it was better to give up rather than to fight.

But I knew from my NLP-Hypnosis training and experience, that rather than avoid it or cover it up, it's better to face it and go through the emotions so you can let it go. So I dove into it. I let myself feel the hate. I scanned through my body and asked, "What part of me is feeling hate?"

I felt a twisted knot in my stomach, raw, red, and pulsating.

Me: "What is hate?" I asked myself.

Inner voice: *He hurt me. He betrayed me. He rejected me.*

Me: "What does the hate want?" I asked.

Inner voice: *Revenge. I want to make him hurt, I want to cause him pain.*

Me: "And what would that get for you?"

Inner voice: *Fight back my mind said.*

Me: "And what would that get for you?" I asked my mind.

Inner voice: *Justice, we'd be even. Then he could know how he hurt me.*

Me: And what would that get for you?

Inner voice: *Understanding.*

Me: And what would that get for you?

Inner voice: *Then I could have peace.*

Me: Interesting, if you get caught up in the fight and getting even, it doesn't really create peace does it? What does revenge and getting even create?

Inner voice: *More hurt, more fight.*

Me: Hate comes from blame, blaming someone for causing harm, for causing hurt or pain. The positive intention of blame is to identify who or what is responsible. As we live in a world of cause and effect, assigning blame tries to determine who or what caused the pain, in some sense the mind is trying to problem-solve for the future, so it can avoid pain, but gets caught up in recreating what it doesn't want.

The problem with blame is that it renders us powerless. If someone else is to blame, the other person caused the harm, we are absolved of responsibility but also left without any capability to avoid it or change it. We've left the power in the hands of the other person.

In the words of Eleanor Roosevelt, "No one can hurt you without your consent," is the idea that if we allow what others do or say to hurt us, it's because we've given our power over to them. In emotional pain, we buy into another's thoughts or ideas and accept their opinion about who we are or what's possible for us over our own. If another person is responsible for hurting us, we are allowing them to have power over us.

Responsibility gives us power. When we can see what patterns, we can be responsible for, then we can change them. In taking responsibility, we learn, we can change, and we have the power to improve and make better choices, which then lead to better outcomes.

Relationships are an interplay of actions and reactions, of cause and effect. What is the other party responsible for and what are you responsible for? This will help you see your patterns. Ask your mind to tease apart the tangle of it and you'll find elements within a negative situation that you could accept responsibility for, learn from, and do differently.

If you're not getting what you want in a relationship, whether a significant other or family member or friendship, can recognize what's your part in the dance?

When you can recognize the part you are playing, then you can own it and then you can do something different, you can change the dance. Maybe I didn't ask for what I wanted or maybe I wasn't clear about what I wanted or needed?

Rather than fight myself over anger and deny and bury my emotions, it's better to listen to your emotions and go through them. What are they telling me?

Me: So what is this about? *Anger.* Angry because...

Inner voice: I am angry at my ex for: *he left me, he rejected me, he betrayed me, he replaced me, he hurt me, he kicked me out of my home, he kicked me out of his family, he kicked me out of his life, he broke my heart.*

Me: Okay self, that sounds really broken. I understand your pain, but you are more than someone else's opinion, you are more than someone else's ideas of value and beauty. Yes, it hurts to leave a relationship, but how did you energetically leave the relationship before he betrayed you?

Inner voice: *I desired someone else who could share my path, I wished for a partner who could understand my world, I wished for someone who could grow with me and who could share my inner world.*

As I looked back at the relationship with John, I could see I got caught up in the routines of life and work. Working hard during the week and weekends became a blur of laundry dishes and housework. I felt fulfilled with my work life, but I wasn't doing things that nourished me in my personal time. I made excuses: I didn't have time, I didn't have money, I didn't have freedom. I numbed myself to adventure and I shut myself down.

The things that John and I had loved to do together: hiking, being in the mountains or paddling on the lake, we rarely did anymore. I recognized I had shut down energetically and as a reaction, he found someone else. And at the time, I got caught up in the hurt and the pain of it and I couldn't see that he was really setting me free.

Yes, it hurt to be betrayed, to be replaced, to feel devalued....

But it also set me free. Free from the routines I had created with him, free from the patterns of stifling myself to adopt his wishes, free to dream a new dream and imagine something new, free to find the joy of life and living again, free to live with adventure, free to find someone that could match me better and who is open to seeing and enjoying the goodness of life, rather than bogged down in stress.

I remember the year before my life in Washington all blew up, I went to see a psychic friend and I got a reading from her. She told me, "Oh I see that you will change everything in your life this next year, you change your relationship, you change where you live, you change who your friends are, I see a lot of change for you."

I wasn't interested in all that change, I remember thinking, though I didn't say it out loud, *"You're a bad psychic, you don't even know what I want!"* Sometimes other people can see things for us that we refuse to see for ourselves.

So why blame him? He gave me a gift in disguise. Did he leave me or did we both grow apart? Did he betray me or did he just change his mind? Because of my loyalty, I probably never would have left without the external bump. I would have continued my patterns, and he would have continued his and we would have both continued to feel trapped in our routines, in our malcontent, in our criticisms, and stuck in our ways.

It wasn't a bad life. He wasn't abusive, we never fought, I wasn't unhappy. Somehow, we just got lost in the routines. Adventure, a key value for me, was ignored and put off for maintaining the day-to-day. My zest for life outside of work just faded. I felt totally fulfilled in my work, but I was alone...we were alone, two people sharing a house and we ended up more like roommates rather than lovers.

And so we parted. And I moved out and we dated other people. And he found a new girlfriend and he replaced me. And it hurt and it crippled me for a while. And it was hard to get back on my feet. And I did struggle. I ended up with a flare up because of my stubbornness that put me back in the hospital, but even that was temporary. I had continued to do my inner work, clearing my stress patterns, rebuilding my confidence, and it took time. But more than time, it took effort and it took a mind-shift. The most profound changes we can make are within our own mind and our inner perspectives.

But life got better, so much better. I got to reinvent the habits and patterns we had created that had become the default. I wasn't watching television shows that weren't uplifting for me. I was using my time for reading, researching, and directing my mind in positive ways.

And over time, I got my sparkle back. I got clear with myself, recognizing new visions of the future, and new possibilities. And I have hopes and dreams again, I have hope, I found secrets of joy. I learned to believe in myself more.

Heartbreak is about looking back, looking to the past and what you have lost. To truly heal, you need hope to look to the future, what is next for you and to imagine something better. And it will be better, I told myself. I have taken the time to recognize my patterns and heal the patterns. I have opened up to see new possibilities and what's next for me will be better because I'm more clear with me.

Relationships are like the tango, it takes two. It's action and reactions. Even our thoughts, opinions, and attitudes color how we show up and how we are received or not received. And my next relationships will be even better because I've learned through the process. I know what I need. I know that I need adventure. I know that I need to dream without limits, we weren't doing that together. We had created habits of logistics and frustrations with each other.

A colleague of mine had taught me the Huna process with me, the Hawaiian process of releasing. The Huna process was simple, think of a person in your mind, visualize them, and repeat. "I'm sorry, please forgive me, thank you, I love you."

I know when someone has done you wrong, it feels weird to say I'm sorry. But we can understand it as: I'm sorry for your pain, I'm sorry for any way I have wronged you knowingly or unknowingly. Please forgive me for any pain or injustice I caused you in this life or any other. Thank you for the lessons and learnings. I love you refers to the idea we all come from love, at a foundational level we are all made from love and to love we will return, which employs the higher truth of who we are.

I expanded the process to go more in-depth, in my journal I elaborated on each of the phrases. I am sorry for not speaking up for what I wanted. I'm sorry for not standing up for myself and my dreams. I'm sorry for adopting your wishes and losing myself. I'm sorry for not demanding more of you because it would have asked you to invest in the relationship and grow with me. I'm sorry for not asking for my own needs. I'm sorry for not knowing how to share more with you. I'm sorry for changing. I'm sorry we grew apart.

Please forgive me for being complacent in the relationship, for not fighting for us sooner. Please forgive me for getting caught up in the day-to-day routines. Please forgive me for not challenging your patterns. Please forgive me for wanting something different. Please forgive me for complaining about us to my friends. Please forgive me for not sparking joy in you. Please forgive me for leaving you behind.

Thank you for the years we spent together. Thank you for the good memories we shared.

Thank you for the support and care you gave me along the way. Thank you for sitting by me at the hospital for the weeks that I was there. Thank you for what we learned together. Thank you for the experience of living on a beautiful 5 acres in Washington with trees and meadow and deer. Thank you for letting me go so I could find someone who wanted to share my dreams. Thank you for making me leave so I can grow. Thank you for playing a role in my grand play of life.

And finally, I love you. I love you and release you to your highest good and learning. I hope you find everything that you are looking for. I hope your life is all that you want it to be.

As I wrote it, I realized it wasn't just him. We had both grown apart, we had disconnected. Our separation had been happening for a while. We had 10 years together and out of the 10 years, about 9 of them were actually pretty darn good. As my neighbor said at the time, "You guys had a good run." I could see it now, we did really well for a lot of years.

The problem in blaming the other person is that we end up unconsciously blaming ourselves in a deeper more destructive way. If he is a wrong and a bad person, I picked him. He was my choice, why then did I choose a bad guy, what does that mean about me? Then we go down a destructive spiral of self-blame and self-doubt, " I don't make good choices, I can't trust myself, I can't trust my intuition," etc. etc.

This self-blame and self-doubt can be crippling and bleed into other areas of life. We have a better time moving forward if we translate the wounds into learning and growth. In learning from it, we are then empowered to move forward in better ways.

By releasing with the Huna process, you needn't shut yourself down in bitterness, self-blame, doubt, and fears. You can let go and 'recycle' the negative emotions and clear the slate. Clear the slate to move forward.

What is letting go? Letting go, we may try to let go through using hate and anger. We blame the other person for causing us pain. We blame them for leaving us. We blame them for giving up on us. And when we blame and use anger, it can give us strength to leave and venture out, it can give us energy...for a while. But blame, anger and hate can leave a blight on your heart.

If your ex was a *bad* person, what does that mean about you that you chose this bad person? How can you trust yourself to make a good choice when the last choice was bad?

One client, Burt came to work with me after 2 "failed marriages." He was feeling beaten down from life. I asked him, "So the first marriage, how long did that last?"

"Well it lasted 20 years," Burt said.

"How many of those years were good?" I asked.

"Well, they were all pretty good up until the last two years," Burt said.

"So you had 18 years of a successful marriage and then you divorced and changed the relationship," I said.

"Well, yes I suppose. I hadn't thought of it that way," he replied.

When a relationship ends, we tend to make it black and white. If it ends, we say it "failed" when it could have been very good for many years. We have these expectations from our culture that 'successful' relationships should last forever. But there are many reasons for relationships and many things to learn along the way to relationships that are more fulfilling and enriching for us.

And what does it mean if it 'failed'? If we say, "I failed," then the mind takes it on at the identity level and the unconscious mind generalizes. I failed this, I failed that and even I'm a failure (which is a recipe for depression).

Blame of other and blame of the self just gives away our power and keeps us stuck. If we recognize what we learned through the experience, then we can begin to process and heal the heartbreak.

Relationships are about patterns. I have my patterns, you have your patterns, and then the relationship is the interplay of those patterns. There are many reasons to be in a relationship and just as many reasons to end a relationship. We don't have to limit it, judge it, or judge ourselves for changing our minds.

When we fall in love, we see the other person almost as their highest self. We believe in the best of them, they can do no wrong and their good traits outshine all their faults. When we "lose love" we then feel ourselves crash down from seeing all the good in the other person and instead of the good we see, we see their faults, their shortcomings. As the relationship turns sour, we focus more on the shortcomings and the hurts until that's all we see about the other person.

I believe we choose our relationships at a soul level for what we want to learn rather than for how long the relationship will last. We are all on our journey as souls, learning and growing through the experiences of life. Our souls are more interested in what we are learning along the way.

And so part of letting go is listening to our own selves, recognizing what there is to resolve, allowing ourselves to carry the positive lessons and learnings forward, and letting go of the old stories of judgment and blame, but rather creating clarity with understanding and wisdom.

What can I appreciate about the time I had with John?

I can appreciate that we had a house together and I was able to live in a beautiful place on 5 acres for many years. I can appreciate that we had a window of partnership and that we were best friends for a time. I can appreciate that it felt good to rely on someone, that it felt good to share a home and have someone who wanted the best for me, and who was invested in my life. I can appreciate all the dinners we cooked together, all the good times and soft moments. I can appreciate that we shared our lives together for a window of time. I can appreciate all the starry nights we shared with a glass of wine in the hot tub looking out across the night sky with the crisp air. I can appreciate the little homestead we created together with chickens and the dog and the cat. There was so much that was idyllic, and I got to enjoy it all along the way.

And I got to "play house for 10 years," because that's what we're all doing as adults, playing house.

I could see it now, the reason for congestive heart failure, sure I was aware of the metaphor. The heart is the center of love, where we feel our connections, and our relationships. When it ended with John, I did the processing along the way of the intellectual releasing of John and the splitting up of life, relocating, and untangling our lives. Although I had addressed the unconscious mind in the change, it hadn't fully updated the layers of my mind which still held the anger and bitterness. I looked through my body into my heart, there was some residual there that was dark, it hadn't updated.

To the parts of me doing anger and hate, "I see you I'm sorry, please forgive me, thank you, I love you." As I directed the Huna process to my heart, I felt a heaviness clear, I felt a shift even a shift of energy.

Perhaps these unconscious parts of the mind hadn't updated because I was too quick to forgive. Perhaps it was because we tried to be friends after the breakup. Or perhaps it was a part of my mind that had been hiding out because anger and hate aren't pretty. As we accept our humanness and bring compassion to ourselves, we can recognize even the hidden layers of old wounds and update the layers of the mind doing the old thinking. We can engage the many aspects and layers of self in moving forward whole-heartedly, clearly, and aligned with higher wisdom.

Nobody is only one thing, there is no villain 100% bad and no hero 100% good. As humans, we are all on the scale of good, bad, and every degree in between. We are humans, we are learning and in learning we make mistakes. An intuitive life doesn't mean it will save you from the bumps of life, it means it will guide your steps through the storms that you came to grow through and overcome. Have compassion for yourself in the journey, it's a process and be willing to own your whole self.

So for the time and who I was, what I believed, and what I knew, John was the right guy for the time. As I look back through time, it wasn't time that healed the wounds, it was perspectives. What if it was meant to be just as it was? What if it's all a coordinated dance? What if our breakups, separations, or divorces are coordinated by our souls to stretch our hearts and challenge us to grow our love bigger?

Could I have recognized the patterns sooner? Perhaps. But it evolved in whatever way it did by thousands of choices, it couldn't have been predicted by my 28-year-old self. My life was better for the relationship, I experienced more, I learned more, it doesn't so much matter the outcome of it, I am okay where I am.

Reflection: Where might you be holding an old grudge or a negative attitude about someone from one of your stories? The negatives we hold onto block our own life force energies and create a layer of stress within our minds and our bodies.

CHAPTER 41

Process: The Wishing Well Meditation

The concept of this process is simple yet emotionally it can take some practice. Releasing the negative grudges, attitudes, and judgments we carry about others creates unnecessary stress in the mind-body-spirit system.

To start with, think of a person that you have a minor conflict with, perhaps a misunderstanding or miscommunication. As you think of that person, what thoughts and feelings come to mind? Pause to notice, perhaps even write it down.

And then notice, as you think of this person, how does your body feel? Where are you holding tension or tightness? This tightness is communicating to you the stress you carry because of what you carry in your mind about this person, the negative thoughts, attitudes, and judgments.

Give yourself some quiet space and perhaps 10 minutes or more to just be uninterrupted and relax in the process. I like to set a timer because when we start tapping into meditative states, we also tap into timelessness or flow states.

Start with 3 Clearing Breaths: Take in a deep clearing breath, hold the breath, package up stress and frustration, and release it. Taking in another deep and clearing breath, filling your lungs and holding that breath, let the tension build in your body and then release the breath as if you're letting go of the cares of the day, letting go of the outside world. And one more deep clearing breath, filling your lungs, and gather out stress and difficulty and focus it into your lungs and release the breath all the way down as you exhale, letting go and relaxing into your own inner world.

The Healing Light Sequence: While you continue to notice that easy flow of breath, now notice, imagine a healing light flowing down through the top of your head, washing through your face, your head, your neck, and into your shoulders. Letting the healing light pour through your head, through your shoulders, down to your elbows, washing through your arms to your fingertips. Notice as that healing light pours through your chest, your back, notice it feel it as it washes through your body, through your stomach, through your pelvis, through your thighs to your knees, letting it wash through your shins, your calves to your ankles to the bottoms of your feet.

And everywhere that healing light flows, you can feel that clarity and lightness soaking into your body, with that clarity and lightness soaking into your muscles, let it soak into your tissues and to the bottoms of your feet.

And now in your mind's eye, imagine that person standing in front of you, see their face, their posture, just imagine the sense of this person. And now, in your mind just repeat:

"I wish you well on your journey" and notice how you feel as you allow yourself to just wish them well.

"We are all learning and growing in this adventure of life, I wish you well."

"Thank you for the learnings, mistakes are part of learning and I wish you well on your journey."

You can just continue repeating, "I wish you well" or you can add your own words. Continue repeating until it feels clear for you. You can then bring another person to mind, going through the same process and on and on going through all the people you've had conflicts with or until the alarm you set brings you back to everyday life.

Notice how you feel and notice how your body feels. This gentle process can release the stress that your mind and body system is holding onto about this person as well as clearing out negative attachments we may carry with other people. As you continue to practice this process, you can add more difficult people or situations that you want to let go of.

Reflection: What negative judgments and attitudes are you willing to let go of so your mind-body-spirit can embody more inner peace? Who are you willing to "Wish them Well"?

CHAPTER 42

Recovery Meditations

Creating daily self-care and daily reflection meditations was an important part of my process and I drew on many fields of study for my inner work. Each morning I woke up, I started with my gratitudes. Thanking and appreciating what was in my life currently. Then I would pour a bath, choose a meditation theme for the day, and settle into the inner world of quiet to listen more deeply to my mind-body-spirit system. Here's another meditation that truly helped me understand the bigger question of why this condition happened to me. Keep in mind these responses were more like feelings rather than a voice.

I got quiet in my morning bath and let my awareness go internal. What are the parts of the mind creating Lupus? I imagined pulling all of Lupus out of my body, packaging it out in front of me, what would it look like?

I held a cloud-like mist in my hands, somewhat formless and ghostlike.

Me: "Lupus, what do you want?" I asked.

The Mist: *"I want to hurt people,"* it said.

Me: "Why do you want to hurt people?" I asked.

The Mist:" *"To keep them down."* I knew from my work that often our symptoms have a positive intention behind the action or behavior, you can find the positive intention by asking without judgment.

Me: "What would that get for you, to keep people down?"

The Mist:" *"Then they would be quiet and look for the hurt,"* it said.

Me: "What do you mean look for the hurt?" I asked.

The Mist:" *"The hurt on the outside is a reflection of the hurt within,"* It said.

Me: "And if people could see the hurt within, what would that get for you?" I asked.

The Mist: *"Then I would have done my job,"* it said.

Me: "What does that mean, doing your job?" I asked.

The Mist:" *"Helping people see the hurt and reclaim the self,"* it said.

Me: "What does that mean reclaim the self?" I asked.

The Mist *"Healing the past, letting go of the hurt,"* it said.

Me: "And if you could do all that: help people see the hurts they carry, so they could let go of the past and heal the hurt what would that get?"

The Mist:" *"Clarity."*

Me: "Clarity about what?" I asked.

The Mist:" *"Clarity with self. Recognize the truth of who you are,"* it said.

Me: "And what would that get?" I asked.

The Mist:" *"Healing."*

Me: "So to get back to the truth of you is healing?" I asked.

The Mist:" *"Yes."*

I sat with the conversation, soaking it in. I looked at my own life and the series of healings of the past hurts, healing the traumas, the meditations, the forgiveness processes. I certainly was a different person than the person who was diagnosed in 2006. I had certainly gone through my inner fires, digging out places of pain I had held onto, even the hidden ones that I didn't know were there, the buried ones, especially the buried ones.

And I recognized that through all of it, in healing my experiences, I had sorted through ideas and beliefs that had infected my mind. It was the healing processes that I took myself through that helped me recognize that it was the untruths that caused the pain. The healing process had really been a battle, a battle of perceptions. And bit by bit as I had cleaned up my perceptions of myself and life, I had come to a greater clarity. I had cleaned up my ideas about self, my identity was not based on the hurts of the past, but now forged from the greater experience of my profound self, my expansive self, even more informed by my divine self.

I looked back over the definitions and roles I had grown through. I saw myself through many phases and expressions of me. I had to sort through what was me and what was not me. I had come to new definitions of myself. I had come to a greater clarity of myself, a greater belief of myself.

Many of my definitions of myself had been from the things that I did and the roles that I played. I had been the adventurer. I had been an herbalist. I had been the wilderness girl. I had been a world traveler. I had been a backpacker. I had been a white water guide. I had been the student. I had been my own case study. I had been the victim. I had been the healer. I had been through all these journeys and these faces of me.

I recognized what I had learned by working through the condition of Lupus, I learned forgiveness. I learned deeper compassion for others who suffer. I learned to judge less and support more when people are in pain. I learned compassion for the state of humanity and so many who suffer from some form of illness or chronic condition or the emotional pain of traumas. I learned that the untruths we carry create interference in our systems which can then lead to physical symptoms over time.

I learned that the answers we are looking for are often dynamic with many threads. I learned to be committed to my own vision of healing even though others didn't believe it, discounted it, or tried to persuade me from it.

I learned hope is a valuable commodity. I learned to have patience with my body, to truly value and care for my body, and to treat it with respect. I learned to see and relate to my body in a more compassionate and caring way. I learned to recognize the beliefs that either hold you back or propel you forward in creating what you want in life. I learned to prioritize myself and choose beliefs that support my vision. I learned I was dynamic, evolving, changeable, and flexible and I could grow in wisdom.

Through the course of my self-study, through the practice of listening to my body, decoding the symptoms, and working through the layers of mind-body-spirit systems, I learned. I learned we can clear out the mind traps and open up to new possibilities, even find pathways forward to experience what we thought was impossible.

Even the impossible is just a series of steps and processes along the way. The path to the impossible is a series of perceptions aligning you to your greater truth. You are greater than any of the roles you have played or choose to play now. In our little human lives, we forget our greater truth. The truth of you is your expansive self, your dynamic self, your divine self, and ultimately you are love.

The nature of healing is letting the light of love clear the darkness. The nature of healing is to shine the light of love with ourselves and with others.

CHAPTER 43

Resolving Sabotage of the Mind

Although I was getting back to health, I still felt the symptoms of achiness and exhaustion when I exercised. I had done so much inner work on shifting Lupus, I felt like I was close to finally tipping the scales, but I didn't know what was left to help my mind shift.

I called one of my friends and colleagues, Chris who was also trained in NLP & Hypnosis, to see if he wanted to do a trade, we could help each other clean up some of our inner beliefs and patterns. We agreed to meet by phone.

"Hi Chris, thank you for working with me on this. As you know, I've been going through this whole medical, kidney thing. Even though my kidneys are getting better and I was able to come off of dialysis, I really want to heal Lupus. I really want to be able to be out in the sunshine, I want to be able to hike and climb mountains again, I want to enjoy life again and get my energy and vitality back."

"So you've had this medical thing, this trouble with your kidneys, but the reason you had kidney problems was from Lupus, is that right?

"Yes, and although my health and energy are improving, I still feel some of the symptoms of achiness in my joints, or my skin begins to crawl if I'm out in the sunlight. I'd really like to just change this inner pattern of Lupus," I said.

"Sometimes it's not just one thing, it's an interplay of many things, so let's see what we can figure out negotiate with your mind about what's going on internally that's causing the Lupus," he said.

"Okay let's see what we can negotiate with your body. Clear your mind, take a couple of deep breaths, and take your awareness into your body, what systems of your body need support?" he asked.

"The kidneys, even though they are better, I need them to keep getting better," I said.

"If there were a metaphor of kidneys and what they do, what would that be?" Chris asked.

"They clean the blood, the blood cleans the cells and tissues and transports nutrients, so they filter out the garbage and keep the blood healthy and flowing. Blood is the flow of life, they keep life flowing."

"So they filter the blood to keep it healthy and to flow life through your body? Great, ask what do the kidneys need?" Chris asked.

"They need support. They need to be able to do their job and not be attacked," I said.

"Who or what is attacking them?" asked Chris.

"Well, they got attacked by my immune system, so there's a fear they'll be attacked and they need support," I said.

"The body is meant to work in harmony and every part of the body has a job. When one part isn't doing its job it creates imbalance which then affects all the other systems as well. So, what system needs to support the kidneys?" he asked.

"Immune system," I said. "The immune system needs to stop attacking me and stop attacking my body. I've tried talking to the immune system, but I don't know how to update it. It just seems so nebulous, when I ask where is my immune system, I can't really pinpoint a location."

"Well you know, if you look at what the body is doing as a metaphor, we can see a bigger picture, let's break it down. What does your immune system do?"

"The immune system protects the body from viruses and foreign invaders," I said. "And it creates antibodies to attack what is not self. But in the autoimmune condition, it's turning against the body and attacking my own tissues."

"Well let's look at that, it's attacking your own body. What's the metaphor of that?"

"Well, I thought the metaphor was that I must be attacking myself, like being too hard on myself or blaming myself, which I guess was true in the past. But I've cleared everything there that I could think of, I don't have negative self-talk anymore," I said.

"So if the immune system is supposed to distinguish between what is you and what is not you, why do you think it's not recognizing you and attacking your tissues?"

"Well, somebody said, "the body betrays you, but I don't think that's it. I think it's the unconscious mind is trying to help, but it gets confused. So, I would say it's about confusion."

"Confused. So what is the confusion about? Get quiet and go internal what is the confusion in the immune system?" Chris asked.

"I took a couple of breaths and focused internally, I don't know, I can't tell," I said.

"So let's imagine a stage in your mind, this stage represents this play of Lupus and the actors of this play are the parts of the mind doing this old habit of Lupus," he said.

"Okay yes, I didn't have the condition before but my body picked it up. I wasn't born with it, so I must have "learned" it along the way. And then my body must have created a habit, a habit of functioning improperly or a habit of Lupus," I echoed.

"So what are the actors in this play of Lupus?" he asked.

"The immune system, it's like an army general, it has troops to protect the body," I said. "It's somehow giving orders that are confused," I said.

"How many parts are being represented that have some confusion of who you are?"

"It feels like three, three actors on the stage," I said.

"Go to the first part, how is that actor of your mind represented?" Chris asked.

"It's young like it's about three," I said.

"What is it saying?" Chris asked.

"It's feeling bad, no it's saying *"I'm bad,"* I said.

"If this represents a part of your mind that took on that idea, *I'm bad,* what is it *trying* to do by holding that belief?" Chris asked.

"It doesn't want to get in trouble, it wants to stop making mistakes," I said.

"And if it weren't in trouble and it wasn't making mistakes, what would it have then?" Chris asked.

"It would be okay, it would be acceptable," I said.

"If it could be accepted or acceptable, what would it have then?" Chris asked.

"It wants to be accepted, it wants to be acceptable.... oh, it wants to be acceptable to God," I said. An inner lightbulb in my mind lit up.

"And what does that get?" Chris asked.

"Love, it wants to be loved by God," I said.

"So it wants to be loved by God, but how does it feel about God now?" Chris asked.

"It says you have to be perfect to be loved by God," I said.

"So the next actor in this play, what does it look like?" Chris asked.

"It's older, maybe 5, it's shadowy and feeling shame," I said.

"This shadowy figure doing shame, what does it want?" Chris asked.

"It wants to be acceptable, no it's more than that, it wants to be perfect," I said.

"And if it were perfect, what would it have then?" Chris asked.

"If it were perfect, it could be loved .....and loved by God," I said.

"Okay so we recognize this part also wants to be loved by God, but it thinks it has to be perfect. Are there other actors here?" Chris asked.

"Yes, there's a punisher, it's kind of scary and big and dark," I said.

"What is this "punisher" saying, what does it want?" Chris asked.

"It wants to punish me. It's saying, if you're bad you must be punished," I said.

"And what does this punisher want?" Chris asked.

"It wants me to be perfect so it will save me from being punished by God. So if I'm punished then God won't have to, it's trying to save me," I said. "Oooh

I didn't know these beliefs were in there, these are icky."

"What would you tell a child about being punished to make him or her perfect?" Chris asked.

"Well, that's an outdated idea, punishment doesn't teach, it only creates resentment. If you punish or hurt a dog for wrongdoing, it just learns it can't trust you and if it continues, the dog learns to fear you and then hate you," I said. "And with people, when we are doing fear, it corrodes trust and so if someone fears you, there's no trust," I said. "I don't believe God works that way."

"Is there any other part that's important here?" Chris asked.

"Yes, it seems there's one hiding in the corner. She's dressed in a grey tattered dress and smudges all over her face," I said.

"And what does that part say?"

"It's saying it's my fault, I must be bad, God must be punishing me. I think it's from the abuse." I said.

"It's common for children who go through abuse to think it's their fault. Would you tell a child that had been abused it was their fault?" Chris asked.

"No, I'd tell her that the people who hurt her were sick and twisted, confused and out of alignment with love," I said. "I would tell her, she is brave for surviving," I said.

"Does she need anything else to know it's not her fault and she is okay?" Chris asked.

"Yes, I would give her a hug, and tell her she is okay. And I give her a star telling her she is loved and precious. And I can have the parts of me that have already healed from this surround her and tell her she is okay and loved."

"Now see all these actors in the play, and have the kidneys look over to see the immune system, the army of generals, and see they are getting orders from who?"

"It seems from the punisher," I said.

"So if the punisher now knows that punishment doesn't teach, it just hurts and causes resentment, ask the punisher if it's willing to take on a new job for Holly? What would be a better job that would help Holly improve, not through pain but through awareness and learning?" Chris asked.

"Well instead of focusing on mistakes and what I'm doing wrong, if it could focus on what I'm doing well or what I am learning, it could help me improve and feel better. Awareness teaches, and learning causes us to improve, I would love for that part to be an encourager instead," I said.

"Ask the part that has been doing punishment, would it be okay for that part to be an encourager instead of a punisher so that Holly could learn faster through awareness and encouragement?" Chris asked.

"Yes, it says it will try," I said.

"It just has to be willing and that's wonderful. And now what would the encourager do differently?" Chris asked.

"Well it could relax and appreciate what's working," I said.

"And how does that change what orders the immune system is getting?" Chris asked.

"Well if that part could relax, the immune system could relax and do its job," I said.

"And what does the immune system need to know to not be confused, to be clear about what to attack and what to not attack?" Chris asked.

"It needs to know that there is no perfect, no one is perfect, but that I am learning and improving," I said. "It needs to know mistakes are part of learning, mistakes don't make us bad."

"So seeing the part over there in the grey dress feeling bad, thinking it's bad, what do you tell her?" Chris asked.

"I'm going to give her a rainbow wand and a magnifying glass and tell her she is learning and it's okay, mistakes are part of learning. It's like falling when you are learning to walk or dropping something when you are learning to catch, it's all part of learning," I said.

"Wonderful, giving those images and messages to the part, how does that part feel now?" Chris asked.

"She has brightened up with the wand and the magnifying glass, she looks happy and curiously excited to learn," I said.

"So now that the punisher has become the encourager, and now that the immune system is not confused, but it's clear, and now that the five-year-old knows mistakes are part of learning, there is no perfect, there is only learning and growing. And the three-year-old knows it's not her fault, that she is loved and okay and acceptable to God, any other part that needs to work together in this play?" Chris asked.

"There's a steel box in the play," I said.

"And what does that steel box represent?" Chris asked.

"It's harsh and strong. Oh, I see, I feel it represents ideas of God, God is a punisher," I said. "It might be old sayings from church."

"So if God isn't a punisher, would it be okay to check in with God about that? So would it be okay to include a representation of God to see what God says about all this? And how would God be represented?" Chris asked.

"I see God as inspiration and light so I can see a shower of light in the play now," I said.

"Great, go to the shower of light, let yourself step into that, and what does God say about punishment, is God punishing Holly through Lupus?" Chris asked.

I imagined standing in the space of the shower of light and replied, "No, God is allowing...but allows us to learn through choices and actions, the results and consequences of those actions are part of the learning. God allows the consequences of our actions so that we learn. That feels clear, the confusion of the immune system causing the condition was from old ideas, beliefs, energies that are not in alignment with higher love and wisdom," I said, it was all coming clear to me.

"What would you like to do now?" Chris asked.

"I'd like to clean up the steel box," I said.

"Very good, go ahead and clean up the steel box, how would you do that?" Chris asked.

"I'm sending that shower of light over to the steel box, and I'm seeing it transform into light," I said.

"Wonderful," Chris said.

"So go ahead and tell the little girl and all these parts that God isn't a punisher, then what do you want her to know about God?" Chris asked.

"God is love, unconditional love. God is the expansiveness, the oneness, the connectedness of all things, the divine unconditional love. I would tell her she's loved and send all of these parts of the mind love, they are loved," I said.

"Wonderful, was there a time you felt that oneness, that divine love?" Chris asked.

"Yes, I was sitting by a river in the sunlight, sad about a lost love, and just got this golden feeling that I was okay, that it's all okay. I'm okay, I just felt connected to the divine, I felt the oneness," I said.

"Wonderful, letting that love and okayness flow through you and sending it out to each of these parts of the mind, giving them all the higher wisdom and insight they need, what's happening now in this play?" Chris asked.

"Well the encourager is now telling the girl in the grey dress he's sorry and the little girl with the magic wand is changing the grey dress into a sparkly pink one. And the soldiers in the background are keeping watch and now they are tossing a ball, and playing a new game," I said.

"If you could give a word to this new game, what would it be?" Chris asked.

"It would be harmony. They can all play and work together, they are all important even though a couple of them were confused about the job they were doing," I said.

"Wonderful and now checking in with yourself, letting the updates radiate through all the places of you, how do you feel now?" Chris asked.

"There's a sense of relief, like harmony is possible, it's a new habit a habit of inner harmony," I said.

"Is there anything else that is needed?" Chris asked.

"Yes, the immune system, it needs an update, I'm just not sure exactly how that would work or what that would be," I said.

CHAPTER 44

The Grand Intelligence of Mind-Body-Spirit

"Going internal and have your mind just connect with the sense of your body's grand intelligence. There's a part of your mind that knows how to heal and we could even call it, the inner healer. The part of your mind that can see the bigger picture of your mind-body-spirit system and how all these work together. Can you get a sense of that now?" Chris asked.

"Yes, I feel an expansiveness all around me," I said.

"Wonderful and notice that expansiveness. So now, just go internal and access your immune system, what do you notice? If it had a location in your body, where would it be?" he asked.

I couldn't pinpoint it, it was grand, it was like a cloud, "Oh it's everywhere, I just feel it's all over, it's in the cells in the blood, in the skin, the immune system cells in the marrow of the bones, the immune cells are everywhere," I said, no wonder I couldn't pinpoint it.

Good to recognize, now asking the immune system as you recognize it all over using a scale like a radio dial 1 to 10, 10 being on overdrive, 1 being not engaged and 5 being just right, where has it been operating on that scale?"

"Oh it's been set to 8, close to overdrive, it's been overworking, overreacting," I said.

"Okay and now asking the immune system, now that all parts of the mind are agreeing to work together and the old ideas and reasons for punishing Holly were not valid, is it willing to reset itself to the midpoint: not overworking, not underworking, but just right?" Chris asked.

"All alone," I said. *"It feels all alone, I can't trust people,"* I said.

"I see, I can certainly understand the idea of alone, but as you know you are not alone, you are connected, we just addressed the divine and oneness didn't we?" Chris asked.

"Yes, yes I feel the divine with me sometimes, I like calling it divine better than God, it fits better for me," I said.

"Right so at the higher levels of awareness, you are never alone. So now would the immune system be willing to notice this divine love, this oneness, to recognize you're not alone? Do you believe in ancestors watching over you and angels working with you?" Chris asked.

"Why yes I do, I believe I am guided. I've felt my grandma check in on me a time or two and I do believe angels help us out and spirit guides give us nudges in our choices," I said.

"So go ahead and imagine your ancestors or grandparents with you and now imagine the angels also with you now, and adding in your spirit guides," Chris said.

"Okay, yes I can imagine my grandparents and the angels all around me," I said.

"And now asking your immune system to recognize that you are guided, that your ancestors are watching over you and the angels are with you," Chris said.

"Wow, that feels better. I feel a sudden relief, like an inner buzzing just quieted down. Wow, I feel that energy, like I can relax, I don't have to be on hyper-alert, I'm not all alone, I'm connected," I said.

"Wonderful, so now that your immune system knows you're not alone, where is it able to reset the operating dial now?" Chris asked.

"It feels like it was able to go down to a , but there's still a high alert, it's on high alert, it's a fear," I said.

"So what would it need to be able to reset to the 5, which means working just the right amount, not overworking or underworking, but able to respond to foreign invaders and able to protect you?" Chris asked.

"It needs to know I'm safe," I said.

"And how or what keeps you safe?" Chris asked.

"Intuition, it needs to be informed by intuition. The parts that have been doing the fear have been causing the immune system to run on overdrive. But we don't want to shut fear down completely, we still want to be able to respond if we need to. But what if the part doing the fear could send an alert signal, or what if the fear itself was an alert signal cueing the mind to pay attention, but then have intuition inform those parts about whether it's a real threat or not a threat? Yes, so if the intuition could inform the fear, then the immune system could relax and reset," I said.

"Okay so go ahead and do that now, ask the fear part to signal the intuition, that it can raise the alert if it needs to. But recognize intuition is the part of you connected to the divine, it sees a much bigger picture, and it can know if you need to be in fear mode or if you can just relax," Chris said.

I imagined running telephone wires from intuition down to the parts of the mind doing the fears.

"So now ask Intuition, is it willing to inform the parts of mind and body doing fears if and when fear sends a signal about something?" Chris asked.

"Yes, that's a really good fit. I still want fear to be heard, but I don't want fear to be in charge. I want intuition to be in charge and tell fear that it's either okay or that we need to take action," I said.

"Wonderful, go ahead and make those connections now and tell me when it's complete," Chris said.

I continued focusing internally for a couple of minutes as I imagined setting up the internal communication so that the fears could be informed by intuition. "Yes, it feels complete," I said.

"Great, so now that fear is being informed appropriately, but you're still able to respond as needed, now asking the immune system if is it willing to reset to 5, working just the right amount? and go ahead and do that now," Chris said.

"Yes, that really feels good," I said. I felt a static energy through my body quiet down and neutralize, an inner relief.

"Okay, now with the immune system reset, with all these beliefs reset to a better perception of reality and with knowing that you're not alone and you don't have to go through life all alone. And knowing you are guided, with all these adjustments, now let's explore each of the scenarios where you want your body to behave differently, how do you want your body to respond differently now?" Chris asked.

"With the sun, I want my body to feel good in the sun and not break out into hives. I want to let the sun shine on my skin, feeling good, enjoying the sun. I want harmony with the sun, like when I was a kid," I said.

"Okay, imagine sitting in the sun on a beautiful day, you can feel the warmth on your skin, and ask your body, how does it feel about the sun now with all these adjustments?" Chris asked.

"It's good, it's really good, I can relax and enjoy it. I can harmonize with it. I am harmonizing with sunlight, sunlight is good for me," I said, I could feel a shift in my mind.

"Great and now that it can do that, how else would you like your body to respond differently?" Chris asked.

"Feeling good with exercise, not getting exhausted, just loving to run again. I was the fastest runner in Elementary school all the way through 3rd grade, I loved to run," I said. "And I love to hike, I love to work my body and feel the muscles."

"Okay so imagine doing that, hiking miles and miles and feeling great in your body, how does your body feel about that now?" Chris asked.

"It feels possible, maybe I'll work up to it, but yes it feels good," I said.

"Now taking all these changes into the future, feeling good in the sunshine, hiking miles and miles, feeling good in your body, plenty of energy and able to really work your body, feeling your muscles. Taking it through the next week, two weeks as if living with these new settings and this new energy of harmony. Then take it forward, feeling good into six weeks and six months into the future with all these adjustments, then 1 year into the future and 2 years into the positive future as your body is working in just the right ways that keep inner harmony, feeling good in your body with all the health, all the strength and energy and from that positive future self. Turn around and look back at yourself and give yourself some good advice from that positive future, what advice do you give yourself?" Chris asked.

"You got this, it's okay to start with small steps, and pay attention to your body and intuition, but you got this," I said.

"Bring that positive future self all the way back through the years, back into your body as your unconscious mind makes those updates in all the places, levels, and ages of you. How does that feel to you now?" Chris asked.

"So good, I think that's it, I can feel an energy shift," I said.

"Now asking your unconscious mind, the Grand Intelligence informed by the Divine, have all the reasons for Lupus been resolved?" Chris asked.

"Yes," I said.

"Are there any other reasons to continue the old habit of Lupus?" Chris asked.

"No it can reset, the whole mind-body-spirit system has reset," I said.

"Is there some way the body or intuition can communicate with Holly in the future if it needs to get her attention or bring awareness to the body or other parts of the mind before it creates a symptom?" Chris asked.

"Yes, intuition can ping me to pay attention," I said.

"Wonderful, integrating all these updates into all the places, levels ages of you now, how does that feel now?" Chris asked.

"It feels complete," I said. "Thank you, Chris, for working with me, I feel really clear and more open. Now I want to go journal and write everything down," I said.

"You're so welcome Holly, we are all here to help each other out on our soul's journeys," Chris said.

Sometimes we think the unconscious mind is a singular entity, but it operates more like a jar of many marbles and there can be multiple "parts" of the mind involved with a condition. This format of actors in a play allowed me to see the multiple parts and how they were interacting in a metaphorical model showing the interplay of mind and body.

Sometimes we blame our body or our mind for bad behavior. NLP Principle: Every part of the mind and body is trying to do something positive for us, even if the behavior is not appropriate. When you look for the positive intention, you can clarify what the part of the mind was trying to do and give it a new job more in line with what it actually wants. This can also be done through the ART to Love process as well, see the Resources section.

It wasn't long after this process that my body finally rebalanced and normalized. I'm happy to say that I haven't had symptoms of Lupus since 2016. I noticed more energy at first and then started taking steps to see how my body handled exercise and sunshine. I continued my healthy eating plan and my self-care routine of journaling and meditation.

There were so many people along the way who showed up for me and worked with me. I am so deeply grateful for all the professionals who helped me through the many layers of healing past traumas and the multiple layers of the mind affected by these traumas. These trusted professionals have dedicated their lives to this work. I feel profound gratitude to be able to learn from them, work with them, and also to play a role in other's journeys of healing. I am so deeply grateful for the awareness and ah-ha moments along the journey. Each little moment built to the next one and the next.

I am so grateful for the friends and family that helped me through my process, who showed up for me when I needed people to rely on. I'm so thankful for my brother and his family who all welcomed me in and gave me a place to stay while I rebuilt my life.

I am so grateful for the community of friends I found in Salt Lake City with the wellness center, their support, their willingness to believe in my ability to overcome and heal the illness. I'm so grateful to the doctors and medical staff who saved my life and the grand miraculous machine that is Western Medicine.

And I'm so grateful to the handful of medical doctors who helped me find natural ways to truly support my body in its healing processes while I figured out the layers of the mind to unravel and update so my mind and body could express new habits of harmony.

As I built my strength and stamina, I started offering local classes at the wellness center to share the tools and skills that had been so powerful and helpful to me along the way. I went on to partner with a friend to create The Life Harmony Wellness Center in Salt Lake City, Utah.

The profound transformation I experienced with these tools and skills inspired me to teach classes and workshops and continue working in these fields of NLP, Hypnosis & Thought Pattern Management.

CHAPTER 45

Full Circle at The River's Edge

Standing on the shore of the Green River in Dinosaur National Park, I watched my retreat attendees floating next to the boats while we were waiting to be called for lunch. The river guide staff were busy preparing the food, slicing and dicing for the sandwich buffet.

Feeling the warmth of the sunlight on my skin, hearing the sound of the rolling water as it lapped by and the bumping of the rafts as they gently swung back and forth with the rhythm of the river, I was struck with a moment of awe and gratitude for the journey. As I felt better and better in my body, as my energy increased, I had added more fitness back into my life and I committed to more adventures. And here I was back on the river, finally.

I'd come a long way over the past years. I'd come to Utah with a car full of clothes and a pocket full of dreams of healing and rebuilding my life. I felt so thankful for all the synchronicities and all the help along the way. I felt so thankful that my brother Dave extended the offer to stay with him and his family when I was having such a rough time. I realized they made adjustments, having their two boys share a room so there was a space for me.

I felt thankful for the doctors and nurses who patched me back together when I was in crisis. I felt thankful for the dialysis machines that did for my body what my kidneys couldn't do for a time. They truly were miracle machines which began as orange juice cans, a washing machine, and sausage skins, they had come a long way to becoming this life-saving technology.

In a few short years, I'd re-established my business, and working with my massage therapist friend, we opened the Life Harmony Wellness Center together. I felt thankful for Angela as a business partner and a confidante and thankful for the fellow practitioners who were renting space within the center. Having a wellness center had been a dream for so long and now it had become a reality.

And I had friends and family in my life. When I thought of the contrast of what I had been living in Vancouver, I didn't think I was unhappy, but I had really small social circles. Most of my social support was John's family. I realized how isolated I had been only focusing on work and the small social circles. In changing my beliefs of being alone, I opened up to new community connections and friendships in Salt Lake City.

Life was better in so many ways, I got my independence back, and I had overcome so many obstacles. I felt like I was finally living on my own two feet and I would be signing on my own home soon. I felt deeply thankful for the skills and capabilities I had learned to help clients untangle the mass of inner habits and develop new patterns of thoughts and feelings. I felt so thankful for all my mentors and teachers and practitioners of this field who dedicated their lives to this deeper knowledge.

I felt awe as I thought about the synchronicities that showed up for me. I felt awe for all the people who played a part in my story, for the people who played a part in my learning, my growth, and my recovery and healing. I felt awe for the many practitioners of healing modalities I worked with along the way, each sharing their unique gifts. I could even say I was thankful to John for being a support and a partner for the ten years I was in the Northwest, even though it ended traumatically for me I could see the many gifts of our relationship now.

My deep gratitude was highlighted by the laughter of the students floating and splashing in the water and the sunshine as I felt the sand under my feet. It felt good to have the confidence to allow the sun on my skin, to feel the wind and the air and water under a blue sky again.

The journey of life is a river with twists and turns. There are slow spaces, there are swirling eddies, and there are rapids. Even though you can't see around the bend of the river, you can trust the river to carry you.

You can trust life to carry you to new experiences, new shores, new learnings, new friendships, new wisdoms, and even new possibilities. You can trust the river of life to support you in learning and growing through the ages of you.

You can fight the current or you can surrender to the flow and trust in the journey. It's the fighting of the current, the struggle of fighting reality that leaves us feeling exhausted.

As long as you keep your hope buckled up like a life jacket, the hope and love we carry allow us to keep afloat even when you think you can't swim. We can trust the river and rely on hope and love to keep your head above water.

As long as you can hope, you can direct yourself towards new horizons and possibilities. As long as you can love and let your heart be open to the journey of it all, the ups and downs, the twists and turns, life will carry you to where you need to go. Trust life is working for you, even when you don't see it. Life is a process of learning and adjusting, learning and adjusting.

We may not see all the reasons why we struggle, no life is perfect and there are many twists and turns. We all have things we are learning and growing through in life and life is a process. If we can see our challenges in life as a grand puzzle, we can play the detective recognizing what we are learning and how the pieces all fit together. We can have wonder and curiosity with the grand design that is unfolding bit by bit. We then can see the grander wisdom of this three-dimensional, choose your own adventure, virtual reality tour as souls in the human experience.

I had multiple sessions of speeded healing, unraveling the tangles of the mind, changing the stress habits of the brain, shifting the automatic emotional patterns, and applying mind-body-spirit principles with great results, and even sometimes dramatic results. The nature of healing is transforming the wounds into wisdom.

I continued to work with clients on all kinds of health issues, addressing the mind-body-spirit interactions, and over time, I began to notice certain patterns. As I sought out advanced training in the field of NLP as a Master Practitioner and then as NLP Health Certified Practitioner, I developed a systematic approach to recognizing the brain habits that keep clients stuck and applying the change work of the mind which engages the body's ability to heal and repair itself. I developed a system and a process to piece together the puzzle of health.

And I worked with a lot of weight loss issues. Hypnosis is very popular for weight loss. I taught classes for creating healthy habits, and changing over your eating habits to healthier food options as I was an avid supporter of natural health. I started to recognize that in some ways health issues were very similar to the work I was teaching with weight loss. It's not a one-size-fits-all all approach. I address each client individually, recognizing that the reasons for the extra weight can range from simple to complicated.

Through the work, I recognized that when we deal with the mind-body-spirit interactions, there are no simple answers, but we must address the issues and resolve the mind-body interference in each case as a unique individual. From working through my condition and seeing thousands of clients over the years, I found there are similar threads or similarities in understanding the mind-body-spirit interactions.

And finally through my own determination, applying, testing, experimenting, and working with others in my field, I found relief. Relief for me came by degrees, noticing what worked in small ways and then building on that. And I developed self-care routines to care for my mind-body-spirit system daily. And I not only found results in applying the small steps, but I also found big wins in healing from the allergy to the sunlight, recovering my strength and stamina, finding greater energy and aliveness.

At this point, I'm happy to say I no longer have any symptoms of Lupus, I am medication-free. If you don't have the symptoms, do you really have the disease? I'm doing the things that Western Medicine said I wouldn't be able to do and I've been ticking things off of my bucket list: swimming with dolphins in Mexico, traveling with friends to tropical places, riding the mountain lakes and rivers, getting sunburns again and it feels amazing!

Illness is simply a condition of health that needs to be resolved in order to achieve our next level of wellness. But it wasn't a straight road, it took twists and turns with ups and downs with many little ah-ha moments along the way. There have also been many wonderful people, synchronicities, and healing perspectives along the way and it has been a wild ride.

May you find the courage to believe in more, listen and work with your intuition, and find your own healing path to health, recovery, and even vitality. May we all heal, and may we leave behind old doubts, fears, and misperceptions that cause interference in mind and body. The emotional baggage we carry is the accumulation of the thinking errors we've taken on about life, about ourselves, and about the nature of the world around us.

May we all find peace, joy, love, and purpose beyond self. May we release the negative thinking errors and uplevel to the greater truths that life itself is a grand miracle unfolding and we are all part of a grand design.

May we all heal through the multiple levels of self and consciousness to embrace our higher possibilities in this grand adventure of life. May we all heal and allow others the grace to heal as well, even when they haven't been their best.

Check Resources section for free tools visit: ==>TheBrainTrainerllc.com/book

About the Author
Holly Stokes

Holly Stokes, Master NLP Coach Trainer & National Guild of Hypnotists Trainer, 4-time Author, and Speaker, began working professionally as a Master NLP Coach & Hypnosis Professional in 2006. She has since worked with thousands of clients in 'rewiring' the brain out of old habits, fears, stress, and self-sabotage that steals health and vitality. Through Neuro-Linguistic Programming (NLP), Hypnosis, Thought Pattern Management, and Coaching, she loves teaching and rewiring brains out of the hard stuff and into leading healthier, happier lives of purpose and achievement.

She loves teaching and training students in NLP & Hypnosis skills and offers advanced training workshops for clearing anxiety, recoding and releasing traumas, creating healthy lifestyles, mind-body-spirit healing strategies, and more. She regularly speaks at NLP and Hypnosis Conferences. She has been quoted by Shape Magazine, Active Times, and Chicago Tribune.

She appears on podcasts, radio shows, and local TV in Salt Lake City, where she keeps a full-time practice and co-owns The Life Harmony Wellness Center. She says, "Life, health, happiness, achievement - all gets easier with your brain onboard."

In her free time, she loves being outdoors and can be found skiing and snowboarding or out on the mountain lakes and rivers paddleboarding and kayaking near Salt Lake City, Utah.

Get the 16 Key Principles of Self-Healing: ==>www.TheBrainTrainerllc.com/book

Books by Holly Stokes:

- A Lighter You Train Your Brain to Slim Your Body
- A Lighter You Healthy Eating Made Easy
- Visioneering Your Business: Startup Growth & Profitability

Summary of Mind-Body-Spirit Resources:

There are many tools and resources available for your healing journey. Each person's path is unique and one modality may work better than others or be more useful at different windows of time. If you are experiencing a health issue, please continue to seek proper medical care and you can also augment your healing with the Complementary and Alternative Medicine practices and modalities. The most important tool you can acquire during recovery is your own awareness and intuition.

In cases of a health condition or diagnosis it's important to support the body with healthy foods, regular meals and an Anti-inflammatory Diet and whole foods can be foundational to your health. While this can make a huge difference for many people, it may not be enough. Understanding food allergies and clearing out allergens and food sensitivities can take the extra burden of stress off your system as you recover. Other resources for the body may include natural supplements, herbal formulas, and natural health practices, etc. A Naturopathic doctor or other holistic health practitioners may also have more answers and resources to this effect of supporting the body through natural health practices.

Supporting the mind: We know the body responds to the mind and what we think about. This is shown through the stress response. We can limit the stress in our lives, and make time for stress-relieving activities like yoga, journaling, and meditation. Meditation has been shown to have amazing effects on depression, loneliness, and isolation and can increase areas of compassion and connection as well as it actually changes your brain! See resource articles.

We can get even more traction with the mind by addressing the inner stress habits at the internal level, the brain habits of the mind causing stress. By addressing these inner stress habits, we can curtail stress at its source and then replace stress habits with habits for the relaxation response. Understanding and clearing out old ideas, negative thinking and recurring negative thought patterns can go a long way in creating your inner state of peace, clarity, and harmony. As the mind and body have the resources needed for inner clarity and harmony, the body can normalize and rebalance, creating outer harmony and well-being.

The language of the unconscious mind is story, imagery, symbolism, metaphor, and feelings. Working with levels of spirit, you may be addressing your spiritual beliefs, cleaning up old ideas about God or the Divine, and adopting new insights, learning, and wisdom. Some of these beliefs are simply transferred through generations, from one generation to the next. Whether you believe in past lives or not, we can recognize these as healing metaphors, there is typically something to resolve or clear out allowing us to be more in alignment with Divine Love, Higher Self, and our higher healing potentials.

Getting clear with your Intuition and inner knowing can help carry you through the process of updating your mind-body-spirit system and moving into greater harmony. There is much to learn through the healing process, however, the principles are the same, coming into alignment with the health and healing means letting go of old ideas and beliefs and up-leveling your mind to operate with higher wisdom and insight.

The nature of all healing is turning our wounds into wisdom. May we all heal in the many levels of mind-body-spirit.

References & Resources

Websites:

Aydelott, Rich. 2024. "Enjoy Living the Best of Your Life! – Restore Health, Find Your Passion and Reason for Being...." AmazingLifeWellness.com. 2024. https://amazinglifewellness.com.

==>Get 16 Keys to Self-Healing & Discover the Power of the Mind through Placebo Effect Research, Self Hypnosis Exercises and more. Visit: ==>TheBrainTrainerLLC.com/book

Grey Goose Graphics. "Research || Research & Recognition." *Randrproject.org*, 2015, randrproject.org/research.html. Accessed 23 Aug. 2024.

Books:

Black, Jessica K, N.D. The Anti-Inflammation Diet and Recipe Book, Second Edition: Protect Yourself and Your Family from Heart Disease, Arthritis, Diabetes, Allergies, and More, Aug 18, 2015

Benson, Herbert, and Miriam Z Klipper. 2001. *The Relaxation Response*. New York: Quill.

Christopher, John R. 1982. *Regenerative Diet*. Nutri Books Corporation.

Lieberman, Shari, Ph.D. 2006. *The Gluten Connection*. Rodale.

Lieberman, Shari, Ph.D., and Nancy Pauling Bruning. 2003. *Dare to Lose: 4 Simple Steps to a Better Body*. Avery.

Ready, Romilla, and Kate Burton. 2010. *Neuro-Linguistic Programming Workbook for Dummies*. John Wiley & Sons.

Zhi Gang Sha. *Soul Communication : Opening Your Spiritual Channels for Success and Fulfillment*. New York, Atria Books, 2008.

Articles:

"Glyphosate General Fact Sheet." 2019. Orst.edu. 2019. http://npic.orst.edu/factshcets/glyphogen.html#whati.

"How Does Gut Directed Hypnotherapy for IBS Work?" *CAM Therapies*, 14 Apr. 2023, cam-therapies.co.uk/ibs/ibs-hypnotherapy/.

Miller, Frederick W. 2023. "The Increasing Prevalence of Autoimmunity and Autoimmune Diseases: An Urgent Call to Action for Improved Understanding, Diagnosis, Treatment, and Prevention." *Current Opinion in Immunology* 80 (102266): 102266. https://doi.org/10.1016/j.coi.2022.102266.

Samsel, Anthony, and Stephanie Seneff. 2013. "Glyphosate, Pathways to Modern Diseases II: Celiac Sprue and Gluten Intolerance." *Interdisciplinary Toxicology* 6 (4): 159–84. https://doi.org/10.2478/intox-2013-0026.

Senefelt, Philip, and Alfred Barrios. n.d. "Understanding Hypnosis: Theory, Scope, and Potential. American Journal of Clinical Hypnosis - AMER J CLIN HYPN. 53. 134-136. 10.1080/00029157.2010.10404336. ." Hauppauge, NY: Nova Science Publishers.

Seppälä, Emma Ph.D. 2013. "20 Scientific Reasons to Start Meditating Today | Psychology Today." Www.psychologytoday.com. September 11, 2013. https://www.psychologytoday.com/us/blog/feeling-it/201309/20-scientific-reasons-to-start-meditating-today.

Slomski, Anita. 2019. "Hypnotherapy Provides IBS Relief." *JAMA* 321 (4): 335. https://doi.org/10.1001/jama.2018.22028.

futur 2 zusammengeflossen sind, das werde ich doch nicht sagen, und dass das mein letzter satz gewesen ist. (ab, 52–53)

Das abschließende Bild, in dem mehrere Zeitebenen aufeinanderprallen, ist die einmalige und unwiederholbare Zeit der vorausgesagten Katastrophe – es ist die gewaltsame Manifestation eines immer wieder beschworenen „Jetzt, Jetzt, Jetzt!" (Röggla 2015, 53), das sich nur einmalig realisiert.

4.6.3 Nachrichten vom Weltuntergang

Im Hinblick auf die bisherige Analyse hat sich herausgestellt, dass Röggla in *die alarmbereiten* nicht die Kommunikation kritisch inszeniert, wie bspw. im Fall von *wir schlafen nicht*, sondern ihre Übertragungsmechanismen. Die Sprechinstanzen werden als Stimmen ohne Körper in einem medialisierten Kommunikationsakt dargestellt. Sie sind also keinem direkten Kontakt mit der Wirklichkeit und das schlägt sich textuell radikal in der konjunktivischen Sprache nieder. Dafür steht die letzte Kurzgeschichte, *deutschlandfunk*, emblematisch.

Zunächst spielt sie im Raum des Radios, dem symbolischsten Ort der Kommunikationsübertragung, weil dort die konkreten Kontexte der Wirklichkeit zusammenkommen, um durch eine körperlose Stimme in die immaterielle Dimension des Äthers gestrahlt zu werden. Per Radio vollzieht sich also die physische Abstraktion des Realen in Form einer mündlichen Erzählung, die das letztendliche Ziel des formalen Experimentierens von Kathrin Röggla in diesem Werk ist.

Darüber hinaus haben die Stimmen, die in *deutschlandfunk* zum Wort kommen, keine menschlichen Züge. Sie sind „radiostimmen" (Röggla 2010, 177), sprechende Geräte, die wiederholen, was in der Welt geschehen ist. Diese körperlose Charakterisierung wird zunächst durch die Illustration von Grajewski (Röggla 2010, 176) angedeutet, die eine leere Radiokabine zeigt, auf der in von Schallschwingungen erschütterter Schrift „on air" geschrieben steht, während im Vordergrund ein weibliches Gesicht einsam zuhört.

In diesem Prosastück gründet sich die Erzähltechnik auf das rückwärts-Prinzip: Die Katastrophenchronist:innen gehen, mit kurzen Unterbrechungen der Zuhörer:innen, die zentralen Themen der Sammlung durch. Ist also der mystische Auftakt der *zuseher* als Prolog der Sammlung anzusehen, bildet *deutschlandfunk* hingegen ihren Epilog. In den ersten Zeilen der Prosa wird die rückwärts-Frage implizit aufgegriffen:

- die ganz schnelle antwort, die hätten sie nicht parat, hat der pressesprecher gesagt. aber wer hat die schon? es gilt jetzt abzuwarten, bis eine normalisierung eintritt. es gilt zurückzukehren zu einem alltag, den man übereilt verlassen hat.

> – retrospektiv nehmen die dinge gerne eine andere farbe an, das darf man nicht vergessen. sie haben dann eine andere temperatur, sie sind dabei abzukühlen und sehen dann anders aus. (Röggla 2010, 177)

Aus dem ersten Austausch zwischen diesen anonymen Radiostimmen kann man die politische Funktion des rückwärtsgewandten Erzählens entnehmen: Es bietet sich als retrospektive Beobachtung an, die einer Gegenwart, die „immer am laufen" (Röggla 2010, 177) ist, „eine andere farbe […], eine andere temperatur" verleiht. Kathrin Röggla selbst unterstreicht diesen Aspekt im Rahmen der Poetikvorlesungen an der Universität Bamberg 2018:

> Die Welt scheint rückwärts zu laufen. Ein rewind ist angesagt, eine ständige Rückspulnummer, als müsste man nur zu einem gewissen Punkt zurückkehren, um dann in eine Zeitlosigkeit eintauchen, die uns errettet aus der sich ständig anbahnenden und dabei sich selbst überholenden Katastrophe, die wir Geschichte nennen. (Röggla 2019b, 19)

In Rahmen dieser Forschungsarbeit wurde die Zentralität der rückwärtsgewandten Erzählweise schon in Bezug auf das Frühwerk Rögglas mehrmals betont. Nun lässt sich feststellen, dass die letzten Seiten von *die alarmbereiten* den Endpunkt der fortschreitenden Verfeinerung dieser Idee auf der literarischen Ebene freilegen. Einen weiteren Hinweis dazu findet man in den später im Text angesprochenen Szenarien, die eine starke metaliterarische Valenz aufweisen. Sie fassen nicht nur die Themen der Sammlung zusammen, sondern auch die Kerne von Rögglas Gesamtwerk. Die Passage „eine form vom alltag zusammenzubringen" (Röggla 2010, 179) ruft unmittelbar die Prekarisierung des Lebens auf, die in einem Kontext des medialen Drucks „das phänomen der zuseher" (Röggla 2010, 184) erzeugt.

Der Entwicklung des rückwärts-Prinzips folgend, zeigt sich eine gewisse Kohärenz in Kathrin Rögglas Konzeption des Schreibens, die seit 1995 darauf abzielt, die passende Form zu finden, um einen soziopolitischen Wandel zu repräsentieren, der sich auf der Zerstückelung, Trennung und Auflösung des Individuums angesichts der wirtschaftlichen Produktion von Arbeit, Profit und, letztendlich, Panik gründet.

4.7 *Nachtsendung. Unheimliche Geschichten* (2016)

Die Kurzgeschichtensammlung *Nachtsendung. Unheimliche Geschichte* weist mehrere Kontinuitätspunkte mit *die alarmbereiten* auf, vor allem auf thematischer Ebene. Schon das Bild der Sendung deutet sowohl auf die Reflexion von Übertragungsmechanismen der Kommunikation hin, als auch auf das Szenarium des Radios, das im Zentrum von *deutschlandfunk* stand. Es handelt sich jedoch um eine Nachtsendung, d. h. eine nächtliche Sendung, in der das Gefühl des Unheimlichen, das im Untertitel verkündet wird, zum Tragen kommt. Dementsprechend hebt Schöll den intertextuellen Bezug zu den *Nachtstücken* von E.T.A. Hoffmann hervor (2019, 110), denn die Sammlung ist als eine Kette flüchtiger Manifestationen des Unheimlichen in der zeitgenössischen Welt aufgebaut. Die einzelnen Geschichten werden von einem narrativen Rahmen zusammengehalten, der auch eine intertextuelle Beziehung zu Boccaccios *Decameron* herstellt, da der Erzählzyklus aufgrund einer Katastrophenbedrohung entsteht (vgl. Krauthausen 2019, Pontzen 2019). Das erste und das letzte Prosastück tragen denselben Titel, *Starter*, und spielen sich am selben Ort, einem Flugzeug ab. Insofern bilden sie die Rahmenstruktur.

Die Sammlung beginnt im Zeichen eines doppelten Notfalls: einem materiellen eines Flugzeugs, das aufgrund unbestimmter technischer Probleme nicht abfliegen kann, und einem mentalen der Passagiere, die, im Flugzeug festsitzend, ihre Angst durch das gegenseitigen Erzählen von Geschichten vertreiben, genauso wie im *Decameron*:

> Nach der Durchsage herrscht erst einmal Stille. Alle Passagiere warten ab, was geschieht. Niemand scheint Auskunft geben zu können. [...] Mit ewig Wartenden lässt sich doch das meiste Geld verdienen, das wissen alle. [...] Sie würden Kühlschrankmagnete betasten und sich einem lustigen Tassendesign gegenüberfinden, das als hiesige Botschaft an die vorbeireisende Welt gedacht war, die niemals ankommen kann. [...] Es wäre alles besser, als hier drinnen in der Maschine weiter zu warten. [...] Dann könnte auch der Augenblick entstanden sein, in dem man anfangen würde, miteinander zu reden. Ja, man würde aus den riesigen Fensterfronten auf die dunkel werdende Stadtlandschaft da draußen schauen und sich Dinge fragen. Wann das erste Haus zu brennen beginnt beispielsweise, [...]. Man würde anfangen, miteinander zu reden, und ganz automatisch bei den Geschichten ankommen, die man sich eben erwartet von solchen Situationen. Geschichten, die einem noch übrig bleiben und die man sich etwas fahrig zu erzählen beginnt, als wäre das ein Ritus. [...] Eine Erzählung nach der anderen würde man auspacken. (Röggla 2016b, 5–7)

Die Handlung findet in einer stationären Verkehrsanlage statt, im Bauch des Flughafens, des Nicht-Ortes *par excellence*. Die Ursache dieser Latenzzeit wird nicht genannt, so dass offenbleibt, ob die Passagiere, deren Anonymität durch die Verwendung der Form „man" suggeriert wird, am Rande einer Katastrophe stehen.

So vertraut wie den Röggla-Leser:innen die Themen auch vorkommen, die hier angesprochen werden, so wenig lässt sich über den Stil sagen. Der zitierte Auszug zeigt eine deutliche Veränderung in Rögglas Schreiben, das hier auf der Verwendung von Großbuchstaben und auf einer neuen Spannung zwischen dem Indikativ und dem Konjunktiv II fußt. Diese stilistische Lösung ist von besonderem Interesse. Man beachte, dass die Darstellung der konkreten Notlage, und zwar des technischen Problems, in der faktischen Dimension des Indikativs erfolgt: „Alle Passagiere warten ab, was geschieht." Die Geschichte entwickelt sich jedoch „in der Klammer des ‚Würde'" (Paß 2019, 137) weiter, also in der hypothetischen Dimension des Konjunktivs II. Die formale Entfaltung des Motivs des Unheimlichen liegt also in der spannungsvollen Gegenüberstellung dieser Modi. Dadurch stellt Röggla die Wahrhaftigkeit des Erzählten programmatisch in Frage. In diesem zeitlosen Moment des Wartens schafft der Konjunktiv II eine leichte Verzerrung des durch den Indikativ ausgedrückten Alltags und gerade darin manifestiert sich das Gefühl des Unheimlichen. Daher arbeitet die Autorin auch noch in *Nachtsendung*, wenn auch mit anderen Stilmitteln, am „Derealisierungsgefühl" (Röggla 2013b, 14), das der Zeitgeist der Gegenwart ist. Dieser Aspekt verdeutlicht sich im letzten Prosatext der Sammlung, der symbolisch wie der erste beginnt:

> Seit der Durchsage herrscht erst einmal Stille. Alle warten ab, was geschieht. Noch ist nichts gesichert, hat man immer wiederholt, doch was da nicht gesichert ist, erzählen sie einem nicht. [...] Dann verkünden sie die alles erlösende Ansage: Man werde jetzt doch starten. Einfach losfliegen, als wäre nichts gewesen. [...] Es wird ein heller Tag, ist anzunehmen, ja, man hat jetzt schon den Eindruck, als werde es immer heller. Und so ist es dann auch. Sie fahren los, starten, und es ist eigentlich so wie immer. (Röggla 2016b, 281–283)

Die Dauer der Flugverspätung wird nicht erwähnt, so dass alles, was im Eröffnungstext im Konjunktiv II steht, vielleicht nie passiert ist. Im Gegensatz zum ersten gleichnamigen Text ist der abschließende *Starter* ausschließlich im Indikativ geschrieben. Die Düsternis, die in der ersten Szene herrschte (vgl. „die dunkel werdende Stadtlandschaft da draußen"), ist durch die freudige Erwartung der Zukunft ersetzt, welche die bevorstehende Abreise ankündigt: „Es wird ein heller Tag".

Mit *Nachtsendung* stellt Kathrin Röggla noch eine Facette des „spätkapitalistische[n] Psycho-Szenario[s]" (Pontzen 2019, 154) der Gegenwart dar und durchquert dabei ihre symbolischen, materiellen und immateriellen Orte. Diesbezüglich liefert Pontzen eine genaue Kartierung der Settings in der Sammlung:

> Diese Grundqualität nutzt Röggla thematisch-motivisch für institutionelle Räume (Versicherungen, Bürgerinitiativen), soziale Orte und Rituale (Tagungshotels, Klassentreffen, Karneval) und schichtspezifischen Ambientes (Selbsthilfegruppen, Kitas, Cafès, Ressorts), alltags-, arbeitsweltliche und sozio-ökonomischen Themen (Gentrifizierung, Entmietung, Entlassung) sowie Leiden und Krankheitserscheinungen (von Erschöpfung über Burnout, Depression, regretting motherhood bis zu Krebsangst), deren Verbreitung, Verknüpfung, Verstärkung und Verdichtung von zahlreichen (meist digitalen) Medien geleistet wird. Es handelt sich um Rundmails (N, S. 107), Anrufe (N, S. 15lff.), Musik im Drogeriemarkt (N, S. 160 ff.), Gerüchte (N, S. 169 ff.), Radiosendungen (N, S. 213 ff.), Navigationsgeräte und Städteapps (N, S. 237 ff.), Big Data Fahndung (N, S. 244 ff.), Ministerielle Richtlinien/Listen des Bundesministeriums für Bevölkerungsschutz (N, S. 264), Protokolle von Meetings usf. (Pontzen 2019, 152)

Daraus folgt, dass in der Sammlung neben dem Sendungsbild auch eine nur scheinbar unterschiedliche, dabei aber immer gleiche menschliche und soziale Geografie wiederkehrt. Diese Konstatierung hebt die Serialität der Entfremdungsprozesse hervor, die schon in den vorangegangenen Werken dargestellt wurde, aber hier die Gestalt der Wirklichkeit und nicht ihrer Verschiebung annimmt. Deshalb sollte der Stilwandel in *Nachtsendung* aus dem folgenden Blickwinkel betrachtet werden: Die zunehmende ‚Stabilität' der Krise, in der Rögglas Werk sich entwickelte, hat die Autorin dazu gezwungen, die *human-specific* Perspektive, die in ihrem Frühwerk eine zentrale Rolle einnimmt, zu überwinden, da sie nicht mehr angemessen ist, um die räumliche und sprachliche Homologisierung darzustellen, die unsere Zeit kennzeichnet. An ihre Stelle tritt eine Vielfalt von Figuren, Geschichten, Orten und Dynamiken, die jedoch immer demselben sprachlichen Diktat unterliegen. In *Nachtsendung* bringt Röggla also den zeitgenössischen Zustand der Welt „von Nicht-Leben, Nicht-Identität, Nicht-Sprache, Nicht-Wissen, Nicht-Information, Nicht-Kommunikation" (Szczepaniak 2022, 211) neuartig zum Ausdruck. Ihre bewusste Rückkehr zum normativen Schreiben legt somit den Akzent auf die sprachliche Identitätslosigkeit der Gegenwart und gilt damit als Katalysator eines dynamischen Realismus.

4.7.1 Das Unheimliche im verbalen Spannungsfeld

Ein Leitmotiv im gesamten Prosawerk Rögglas ist die Charakterisierung der Sprechfiguren als körperlose Diskursprojektionen. In *niemand lacht rückwärts* findet man das Paradigma des „strohmannes", d. h. der von den Marktgesetzen manipulierten Marionette, in *Irres Wetter* verwandelt er sich in den „sendermann", den menschlichen Lautsprecher des herrschenden Diskurses, bis die Körperlichkeit in *wir schlafen nicht* den Gespenstern des Neoliberalismus weicht. Diese drei Figurationen gehören bereits *in nuce* zur Sphäre des Unheimlichen, wie es von Sigmund Freud[12] entwickelt wurde.

In seinem berühmten Aufsatz geht Freud genau von der Sprache aus und definiert das Unheimliche als eine mögliche, dabei aber unterschiedlich nuancierte Erscheinung des Gewöhnlichen: „Unheimlich ist irgendwie eine Art von heimlich" (Freud 2015, 155). Der Übergang vom „Heimlichen" zum „Unheimlichen" vollzieht sich also im Zeichen einer Perspektivenverschiebung, bzw. einer Entfremdung, die das Verdrängte in einem „Wiederholungszwang" (Freud 2015, 163) enthüllt. Das Unheimliche ist also tief in der Wirklichkeit verwurzelt und genau diesen Aspekt erforscht Röggla in *Nachtsendung*. Auch über die Manifestationen des Unheimlichen in der Sammlung zieht Pontzen ein äußerst umfassendes Resümee.

---

12 Es sei auch kurz darauf hingewiesen, dass der Name Freuds schon flüchtig in *Irres Wetter* auftaucht (vgl. Röggla 2000, 103).

> Die Verfahren rekurrieren auf traditionelle Motive und Konstellationen des Unheimlichen in Literatur, bildender Kunst und Film wie Doppelgänger (Kein Kontakt zu den Toten (N, S. 219 ff.), Klassentreffen (N, S. 66) oder Verdopplungen von Orten (Lanzarote (N, S. 228 ff.), Im Bauch des Wals (N, S. 217)) und Dingen (N, S. 217), Puppen, künstliche Menschen, Olympia, Spuk- und Nachtgestalten, Untote (N, S. 227), unheimliche Geräusche (Sex in Tüten), Sinnestäuschungen (»Dinge hören, die es gar nicht gab« (N, S. 172)), verschwindende Menschen, Dinge, Wochentage (Off the Record), Erinnerungen (Klassentreffen), Masken, Verkleidungen (N, S. 237) resp. deren Ausbleiben, Verfolgung (N, S. 244), Nahtoderfahrung (N, S. 252) und Jenseits (N, S. 224), künstliche Welten mit Eigenrecht (Investitionsfiktion (N, S. 261) oder Katastrophenvorsorge (N, S. 264 ff.) (Pontzen 2019, 152)

Obwohl Pontzens Analyse zahlreiche Impulse für weitere Forschungsbeiträge liefern würde, wird an dieser Stelle das Feld auf diejenigen formalen Aspekte eingegrenzt, welche die Rezeption der Freud'schen Lehre in Kathrin Rögglas letztem Prosaband zeigen, und zwar auf das Verhältnis von Indikativ und Konjunktiv in *Die Fortsetzung*. Der Protagonist ist Peter Herrfurth, ein Firmenangestellter, der seine Routine plötzlich als ungewöhnlich empfindet. Die Distanzierung von seinem Alltag beginnt mit der Unfähigkeit des Protagonisten, telefonisch zu kommunizieren:

> Die Leute reagierten wieder, hatte es auch in Peter Herrfurths Büro geheißen. Sie atmeten ein, sie atmeten aus und sagten dann etwas. Sie hörten beispielsweise am Telefon zu, und danach komme auch gleich was. So etwas wie eine Antwort. Herrfurth bekam aber keine Antwort. (Röggla 2016b, 8)

Wie in Bezug auf *wir schlafen nicht* erwähnt wurde, beruht die Unternehmensarbeit auf der kommunikativen Promptheit, die in der zunehmenden Geschwindigkeit ihre kommunikative Funktion verliert. Deshalb bedeutet für Peter Herrfurth, plötzlich nicht mehr ‚reagieren' zu können, in eine fremde und nutzlose Position am Arbeitsplatz zu rutschen. Diese leichte Entfremdung lässt den Protagonisten die Arbeitsdynamiken in seinem Büro aus einer anderen Perspektive wahrnehmen, als würde er sie zum ersten Mal sehen: die Reinigungsfirma taucht „aus dem Nichts" (Röggla 2016b, 9) auf, fast wie eine übernatürliche Kraft, die „erstaunlich" (Röggla 2016b, 9) ihre Arbeit durchführt. Der Indikativ verleiht der Erzählung einen ironischen Ton und unterstreicht dadurch den unheimlichen Kurzschluss in der Wahrnehmung des Protagonisten.

Ein erster expliziter Verweis auf das Unheimliche findet man im Text, wenn Herrfurth sich, in Panik geraten, in den Fahrstuhl stürzt, um „den Riss [...], der alles durchgezogen hatte" (Röggla 2016b, 11) zu finden. Dieses Bild ist von zentraler Bedeutung in der Geschichte. Zum einen ist der Riss in Bezug zum Titel *Die Fortsetzung* zu setzen und insofern als Bruch einer unhaltbaren Arbeitskontinuität zu interpretieren: „Ihm war klar, wie wichtig diese Kontinuität für das Überleben des Unternehmens war, er sollte vermutlich auch weitermachen, nur fiel ihm schlicht nichts mehr *dazu* ein." (Röggla 2016b, 10). Dieser Riss in der linearen Wahrnehmung des Alltags ist also der Übergang zum Unheimlichen, das Kathrin Röggla als kritisches Werkzeug gegen den unternehmerischen Imperativ des „Weitermachens" verwendet. Die Neurose des Protagonisten dehnt sich auch auf seine persönlichen Gegenstände und Orte aus. Zu beachten ist dementsprechend, dass die erwähnten Orte Parkplätze, Bahnhöfe und Flughäfen sind, und damit die wiederkehrenden Nicht-Orte im Spätwerk Rögglas (vgl. Szczepaniak 2022):

> Oben würde die Putzkolonne inzwischen näher gekommen sein, Herrfurth ärgerte sich, dass er sich nicht die Zeit genommen hatte, seinen persönlichen Kram zu packen, er war sicher, sie würden ihn mitnehmen. Oder noch schlimmer: Sein persönlicher Kram würde nun wie der Kram aller anderen zum Weitermachen verdammt, wenn auch erst mal in den Schuhbladen, nur er stand da unten auf dem Parkplatz und konnte einen Wechsel einläuten, indem er ging. [...] Vielleicht aber, spekulierte jetzt Herrfurth, hatte es Verdoppelungen gegeben, und vielleicht war er eine dieser Verdoppelungen und saß noch in einer zweiten Version oben im Büro? Endlich stand er vor seinem Auto. Ihm war nicht klar, wie das passiert war, aber er musste jetzt einfach wissen, ob die Straßen da draußen wirklich weitermachten, die Flughäfen, zu denen man ganz einfach gelangen konnte, und die Bahnhöfe. Ja, die Züge würden vermutlich losfahren, die Flüge würden stattfinden, als wäre nichts. (Röggla 2016b, 12–13)

Der Wechsel zwischen Indikativ und Konjunktiv spiegelt den Wechseln zwischen Handeln und Denken wider und stellt somit einen halluzinatorischen Zustand dar, in dem die Verbindung zwischen Spekulation und Wirklichkeit der erzählten Ereignisse aufgelöst wird. Diese Wahrnehmungsspaltung wird vom Protagonisten selbst thematisiert, der die Anwesenheit einer „zweiten Version" von sich vermutet, was noch einen Bezug zur Motivik des Unheimlichen herstellt.

Unbewusst vor seinem Auto angekommen, flieht Herrfurth aus dem Tempel des Weitermachens, um zu „einen Ort des Nichtweitermachens" (Röggla 2016b, 15) zu gelangen. Nach der technokratischen Logik der Arbeitsoptimierung, über die sich Röggla hier mokiert, ist das Krankenhaus das Spiegelbild des Büros.

Von diesem Punkt an wird die Erzählstruktur durch die Aneinanderreihung unzusammenhängender Sequenzen charakterisiert, die Herrfurths zunehmende Halluzinationen wiedergeben. Zuerst überrascht die Tatsache, dass der Pförtner ihn erkennt. Dadurch stellt sich heraus, dass Herrfurth ein regelmäßiger Besucher des Krankenhauses ist:

> Er musste jetzt unbedingt überprüfen, ob sein Bett noch leer war oder schon wieder belegt. [...] Er sah sofort, dass jemand nicht mehr weitergemacht hatte. Der Patient sei nicht mehr da, habe man ihn nicht informiert? [...] Er habe nur kurz ausgesetzt, sein Atem, informierte ihn ungerührt der Zimmernachbar, jetzt sei er wieder da. Peter Herrfurth wusste nicht, ob der sich selbst meinte oder seinen ehemaligen Nachbarn, ein Nichtwissen, in das eine ganze Weile das Gefühl einer sich ankündigen Panik hineinlief. [...] Es schien ihm, als wäre er in

einer Art Kälteraum angekommen, oder dort, wo sie die Toten aufbewahren. Zumindest befand sich in diesem Raum, wo er jetzt war, kein Rest Leben. Wie er dorthin gelangt war, würde er später nicht mehr sagen können. (Röggla 2016b, 16–17)

Der Rückkehr des Konjunktiv I in der Darstellung des Dialogs mit dem „Zimmernachbarn" verstärkt die absurde Dimension der Geschichte und stellt die im Indikativ erzählte Version der Ereignisse infrage. Es kann nicht festgestellt werden, ob Herrfurth im Krankenhauszimmer jemanden getroffen hat oder ob er mit sich selbst gesprochen hat. In diesem Spiel zwischen dem Geschehen und seiner Vorstellung, dem Alltäglichen und seiner Entfremdung bleibt das Ende der Geschichte offen: „Nichts zeigte den Riss an, hatte er verstanden, in dem sie alle tatsächlich verschwunden waren, und so würde es auch für alle Zeiten bleiben." (Röggla 2016b, 17).

Die Kurzgeschichte *Die Fortsetzung* bietet sich somit als Symbol für die Sammlung an, in der Röggla verschiedene Ereignisse auswählt, die zusammen eine *Psychopathologie des Alltagslebens* im Zeitalter des Neoliberalismus bilden. Die Manifestationen des Unheimlichen symbolisieren auch sprachlich die ultimative Verschärfung der alltäglichen Neurosen, die tatsächlich die „genuine Basis" (Schöll 2019, 121) der Gegenwart sind.

5 Vorläufiger Epilog – Der Elefant im Raum

Der hier eingeschlagene analytische Weg ist als Versuch gedacht, ein aktuelles Porträt von Kathrin Rögglas Ästhetik zu liefern, indem ihre Entwicklung im Bereich der Prosa als Synthese eines äußerst artikulierten und vor allem noch im Entstehen begriffenen künstlerischen Projekts betrachtet wird.

Die Poetik der Autorin ist tief in einer sowohl gesellschaftlichen als auch theatralen Wahrnehmung der Sprache verwurzelt, die sie zwischen Individuen und Situationen verortet. Diese ‚Zwischen-Stelle' der Sprache spiegelt sich in ihrem Werk in der vielschichtigen Arbeit an Abstraktionsmechanismen wider, die die gegenwärtigen Strukturen der medialisierten bzw. inszenierten Kommunikations- und Machtdynamiken durch ihre Ästhetisierung enthüllen will, um mit den eigenen Mitteln der Sprache eine zeitgenössische Sprachkritik zu üben. Anhand des Nachweises der Zentralität des ‚Dazwischen' wurde zunächst aufgezeigt, inwiefern das Dialogische den Ausgangspunkt von Kathrin Rögglas dokumentarischer Forschungsmethode – und letztendlich ihres Realismus – darstellt.

Gerade aufgrund dieser Konstatierung wurde hervorgehoben, wie die Sprache Rögglas explizit einen performativen Wert aufweist, da die Schriftstellerin durch Verfahren der Mündlichkeitsumschreibung das „kollektive Gefüge" (Deleuze und Guattari 1992) des neoliberalen Sprachdenkens gesellschaftskritisch in Szene setzt. Davon ausgehend wurde Rögglas Prosawerk als Sammlung von „Szeno-Graphien" der Gegenwart definiert, und zwar als Reihe von Alltagsdarstellungen, in denen die Sprache die Instanz der sozialen und kulturellen Szene schreibt und diese gerade dadurch kritisch umschreibt. Auch im Hinblick auf die theoretischen Grundlagen der Autorin eignete sich der Begriff „Szeno-Graphie" (Neumann 2000) als umfangreiches Konzept für die Schilderung der programmatischen Duplizität von Kathrin Rögglas Poetik, denn er legt den Akzent auf die formalen Verfahren, aus denen Rögglas Deklination des Realismus besteht. Vor diesem Hintergrund wurde ihr Prosawerk aus dem Zeitraum 1995–2016 anhand der progressiven Entwicklung von drei Schreibmerkmalen, die ihren Stil deutlich kennzeichnen, qualitativ analysiert: die Montage, die indirekte Rede und die Modellierung der Erzählinstanz. Dadurch wurde versucht, nicht nur die Bearbeitungsstrategien des dokumentarischen Materials, sondern auch die ästhetischen Ereignisse dieser Operation an der Wirklichkeit zum Vorschein zu bringen, um sie letztendlich in Zusammenhang mit den dargestellten Kontexten und Szenarien kritisch zu hinterfragen.

Daher wurde eine Kontextualisierung von Rögglas Poetik im Rahmen der spätmodernen deutschsprachigen Literatur vorgelegt, die vier eminente Vorbilder der Autorin in Betracht zieht: Elfriede Jelinek, Ernst Jandl, Hubert Fichte und Alexander Kluge. Die vergleichende Analyse dieser Ästhetiken, Methoden und Poetologien zeigt, inwiefern Kathrin Röggla sich bewusst in eine Tradition einfügt, die das transformative Potential der Sprache auf die Wirklichkeit betont.

Eine synthetische Bilanz der qualitativen Analyse der Formfindungsprozesse Kathrin Rögglas findet man bereits in der vorgeschlagenen Periodisierung ihres Werkes, in der die progressive Verfeinerung ihres Stils in Kontinuität mit der zunehmenden Entmaterialisierung der Körper-Symbolik gelesen wurde. Betrachtet man die Verwandlung der ‚Strohmänner' des neoliberalen Diskurses aus den ersten Erzählsammlungen in die ‚Sendermänner' der Globalisierung, so verschwindet jede körperliche Eigenschaft im Gespenst-Motiv, der – *bis dato* – jüngsten Figuration der Sprechinstanzen Kathrin Rögglas. Diese Parabel entspricht auch den Orten, die diese Sprechfiguren bewohnen: Der ‚Strohmann' lebt im Metropolen-Modell vor der Globalisierung, während der ‚Sendermann' eine:n ideale:n Bewohner:in einer *global-city* symbolisiert. Letztendlich durchquert das Gespenst zuerst die transitorische Architektur der Messe, um dann im immateriellen Raum der medialen Kommunikation zu landen.

Diese Phänomenologie des menschlichen und räumlichen Verschwindens fällt mit der steigenden Konzeptualisierung der Sprachmechanismen zusammen und es ist eben in diesem Sinn, dass Kathrin Rögglas Schreiben als Ausdruck eines szeno-graphischen Realismus bezeichnet wurde. Im Verlauf ihrer ästhetischen Formfindung machen der filmische Alogismus der Montage, der hier als „rückwärts-Prinzip" definiert wurde, und die wacklige Stelle des Ichs (vgl. Röggla 2013b, 30) zunehmend der indirekten Darstellung sprachlicher Strukturen Platz. Mit anderen Worten: Kathrin Rögglas Prosawerk weist stilistisch eine Radikalisierung der indirekten Rede auf. Dient der Konjunktiv im Frühwerk zur Markierung der Distanz der Sprecher:innen von jeglicher Intentionalität der sprachlichen Übung aufgrund der medialen Aufdringlichkeit des neoliberalen Diskurses, so wird dieses Stilmittel in den jüngsten Prosastücken selbst zu einer konzeptuellen Darstellung der Sprache, vor allem in *wir schlafen nicht* (2004) und *die alarmbereiten* (2010).

In *Nachtsendung. Unheimliche Geschichten* (2016) lässt sich die Rückkehr zu einem bewusst normativen Sprachgebrauch beobachten, indem das Fehlen des Konjunktivs zugunsten anderer verbaler Experimente mit dem Indikativ im Zentrum der Sammlung steht. Diese Tatsache signalisiert eine ästhetische Neuorientierung der Autorin im Rahmen der Sprachforschung und ermöglicht es dieser Studie somit, sich auf eine bestimmte Phase ihres Schreibens zu konzentrieren, die vorerst als abgeschlossen betrachtet werden kann.

Obwohl die programmatische Inter- und Transmedialität ihrer Poetik des ‚Zwischen' die zukünftige Richtung von Kathrin Röggla nicht genau vorhersehen lässt, scheint die Autorin jedoch stets einer Annahme treu geblieben zu sein: Es ist die Sprache, die das Reale konstruiert. Von den Spaziergängen in den ehemaligen Berliner Kleingartenkolonien bis hin zu den körperlosen Räumen der gegenwärtigen Arbeitswelt nimmt die ästhetische Operation des rückwärtsgewandten Umschreibens der Wirklichkeit die Züge einer dialogischen Simulation an, bei der die Prototypen jedes einzelnen Kontextes *gesprochen werden*. Dementsprechend wurde die vielfältige Darstellung der Spannung zwischen mentalen Schemata und abstrakten Sprechfiguren des herrschenden Diskurses hier als eine Reihe von präzisen „Szeno-Graphien" der Gegenwart definiert, die, als Ganzes betrachtet, einen allmählichen Prozess der Identitätsauflösung anprangern.

Emblematisch dafür steht die Performance-Installation *Der Elefant im Raum* (2019), die sich als Synthese der sprachlichen Konstellation Kathrin Rögglas zeigt, der in dieser Arbeit nachgegangen wurde „Alle im Raum wissen von einer dringend zu begegnenden Sache, die einfach nicht anzusprechen ist. Diesem Phänomen kann man auf privater, medialer oder politischer Ebene begegnen" (Röggla 2019b, 3). So leitet Kathrin Röggla die Frage nach dem Elefanten im Ausstellungsheft ein. Liest man diese Definition rückwärts, so kann man den „Elefant im Raum" gleichzeitig als Ziel und als Objekt der ganzen künstlerischen Recherche von Kathrin Röggla ansehen. Die aus dem Englischen entlehnte Metapher ist tief im Feld des Diskurses verwurzelt, und genau das ist, wie die Analysen zeigen, der primäre Stoff der Umdeutungsprozesse der Wirklichkeit, wie in Rögglas Werk auftreten.

Für das Projekt hat die Schriftstellerin dieses Konzept in Zusammenarbeit mit Mark Lammert und Eran Schaerf aufgegriffen, um eine performative Untersuchung der diskursiven Tabus und der kommunikativen Störungen der zeitgenössischen Welt in der Akademie der Künste Berlin darzustellen. Der Eröffnung der Ausstellung ging ein Zyklus von Treffen und Debatten eines Forschungslabors voraus, der unter dem vielsagenden Titel „wo kommen wir hin" präsentiert wurde. Auch in diesem Fall zeichnet die Ausgangsfrage die unsichere Projektion in die unmittelbare und trotzdem prekäre Zukunft, die leitmotivisch in Rögglas Werk wiederkehrt. Im Verlauf von „wo kommen wir hin" brachte Kathrin Röggla in Dialog Personen aus dem künstlerischen Bereich, wie den Musiker Manos Tsangaris und die bildende Künstlerin Karin Sanders, mit Expert:innen aus dem politisch-institutionellen Bereich, wie Thomas R. Henschel, Mediator in internationalen Konflikten, oder die Psychologin Gemina Picht.[1] Das Konzept dieser Gespräche spiegelt die programmatische Inter- und Transmedialität wider, welche die untersuchten Werke deutlich zum Ausdruck bringen, und führt sie in den institutionellen und öffentlichen Räumen der Akademie der Künste konkret auf.

---

1 Der vollständige Zeitplan der Sitzungen findet sich unter https://www.adk.de/de/projekte/2019/wo-kommen-wir-hin/ [27.06.2024].

Darüber hinaus tradiert die Komposition der Installationen von *Der Elefant im Raum* auf räumlicher Ebene die oben erwähnte These dieser Forschungsarbeit, die das Werk der Autorin als eine Phänomenologie der fortschreitenden Entmaterialisierung von Menschen und Szenarien interpretiert. Mehr als fünfzig audiovisuelle Materialien bilden diese von Kathrin Röggla und Leopold von Verschuer konzipierte „mehrstündige Hörinstallation" (Röggla 2019b). Darunter gab es sowohl Neuproduktionen der Autorin als auch Adaptionen von Repertoirestücken wie *Herzstück* (1983) von Heiner Müller oder *Manuel* (2003) von Alvaro García de Zúñiga. Die Räume, die die Besucher:innen durchquerten, d. h. die Halle 1, das Studio für Elektroakustische Musik, das Beckett-Atelier, das Foyer und den Gräsergarten, sind jedoch weiße, leere Zimmer, die nur von körperlosen, sich überlagernden, Stimmen bewohnt werden.

Einige Hörstücke weisen bedeutende Leitmotive auf, wie das der Missverständnisse oder des Witzes. Zentral bleibt jedoch das Motiv des Elefanten: Röggla stellt ihn „im" und „aus dem Raum" dar, sowie „im Gericht". Letztendlich segmentiert sie ihn als „Halbelefant". Die Positionen, in denen die Autorin den Elefanten porträtiert, sind von großem Interesse, wenn man sie in Beziehung zu ihrer ästhetischen Laufbahn setzt, denn sie beschreiben und betonen genau die Zwischenstellung, in die Röggla nicht nur den Diskurs und seine Re-Inszenierung, sondern auch sich selbst setzt.

Im Anschluss daran ist hervorzuheben, dass die Prozesse der Selbstinszenierung den Kern eines weiteren Teils des Projekts bilden. Im Verlauf der Ausstellung fanden fünf Happenings unter dem Titel *Der Elefant aus dem Raum* statt, die Kathrin Röggla und ihre Schreibpraxis im Zentrum hatten. Die Performances hatten jeweils die gleiche Struktur: Röggla interviewt Figuren aus verschiedenen Bereichen,[2] wie im Fall von „wo kommen wir hin"; anschließend bearbeitet sie das Gespräch in einem Raum, in den die Besucher:innen hineinschauen können. Zum Schluss präsentiert sie dem Publikum die Ergebnisse ihrer Umschreibung und lässt somit die ausgesprochenen Elefanten aus dem Raum flüchten. Durch diesen Performance-Zyklus setzt die Autorin ihre Forschungspraxis in Szene und verdoppelt ihren performativen Wert. Daher lässt sich das Projekt *Der Elefant im Raum* als – soweit – zusammenfassendes Werk der szeno-graphischen Poetik Kathrin Rögglas definieren.

---

[2] Die vollständige Liste finden Sie unter https://www.adk.de/de/programm/?we_objectID=59648#gespraeche [27.06.2024].

6 Literaturverzeichnis

6.1 Primärliteratur

Röggla, Kathrin. *niemand lacht rückwärts*. Frankfurt a. M.: Fischer Verlag, 1995.
Röggla, Kathrin. *Abrauschen*, Frankfurt a.M.: Fischer Verlag, 1997.
Röggla, Kathrin. *Irres Wetter*, Frankfurt a. M.: Fischer Verlag, 2000.
Röggla, Kathrin. *really ground zero: 11 september und folgendes*, Frankfurt a. M.: Fischer Verlag, 2000.
Röggla, Kathrin. *eine stimme mit eigensinn*. 2002a. https://www.kathrin-roeggla.de/meta/eine-stimme-mit-eigensinn. Personalseite (21.05.2024).
Röggla, Kathrin. *der akustischen fichte*. 2002b. https://www.kathrin-roeggla.de/meta/der-akustische-fichte. Personalseite (21.05.2024).
Röggla, Kathrin. *die furchtbaren längen*. 2003. https://www.kathrin-roeggla.de/meta/die-furchtbaren-laengen. Personalseite (21.05.2024).
Röggla, Kathrin. *wir schlafen nicht*, Frankfurt a.M.: Fischer Verlag, 2004.
Röggla, Kathrin. *ich habe dir gesagt du solltest nicht wiederkommen*, 2003, https://www.kathrin-roeggla.de/meta/ich-habe-dir-gesagt-du-sollst-nicht-wiederkommen. Personalseite (21.05.2024).
Röggla, Kathrin. „stottern, stolpern, und nachstolpern – zu einer ästhetik des literarischen gesprächs". *Kultur und Gespenster* 2 (2006): 98–107.
Röggla, Kathrin und Grajewski, Oliver. *tokio, rückwärtstagebuch*. Wien: Verlag für Moderne Kunst, 2009.
Röggla, Kathrin. *die alarmbereiten*, Frankfurt a. M.: Fischer Verlag, 2010.
Röggla, Kathrin. „Finanz-Punk". *Jelinek[Jahr]Buch* 2 (2011): 15–30.
Röggla, Kathrin. „Stottern und Stolpern. Strategie einer literarischen Gesprächsführung". *besser wäre: keine. essays und theater*. Frankfurt a. M.: Fischer Verlag, 2013a. 307–332.
Röggla, Kathrin. „Die Rückkehr der Körperfresser". *besser wäre: keine essays und theater*. Frankfurt a. M.: Fischer Verlag, 2013b, 23–38.
Röggla, Kathrin. „Gespensterarbeit und Weltmarkfiktion". *besser wäre: keine. essays und theater*. Frankfurt a. M.: Fischer Verlag, 2013c, 209–233.
Röggla, Kathrin. „Geisterstädte, Geisterfilme". *besser wäre: keine. essays und theater*. Frankfurt a. M.: Fischer Verlag, 2013d, 7–22.
Röggla, Kathrin. *Die Falsche Frage. Theater, Politik und die Kunst, das Fürchten nicht zu verlernen*. Berlin: Theater der Zeit, 2015a.
Röggla, Kathrin. *Essenpoetik*. 2015b. http://roeggla.net/von-roeggla/ Das digitale Röggla-Archiv (21.05.2024).
Röggla, Kathrin. *Zürich 2016*. 2016a. https://www.kathrin-roeggla.de/meta. Personalseite (21.05.2024).
Röggla, Kathrin. *Nachtsendung. Unheimliche Geschichten*, Frankfurt a. M.: Fischer Verlag, 2016b.
Röggla, Kathrin. „Fichte zu Fuß". *Sprache im technischen Zeitalter* 6 (2016c). 321–328.
Röggla, Kathrin. „Die Bamberger Poetikvorlesungen". *Literatur im Ausnahmezustand. Beiträge zum Werk Kathrin Rögglas*. Hg. Friedrich Marx und Julia Schöll. Würzburg: Königshausen & Neumann, 2019a. 19–82.
Röggla, Kathrin. „Der Elefant im Raum". Köln: Verlag der Buchhandlung Klaus Bittner, 2019b. 18–51.
Röggla, Kathrin. „Deckerzählung." *Make in Real! Für einen strukturalen Realismus*. Hg. Stephan Kammer und Karin Krauthausen. Zürich: diaphanes, 2020a. 229–242.
Röggla, Kathrin. *Bauernkriegspanorama*. Berlin: Verbrecher Verlag, 2020b.
Röggla, Kathrin. *Ausreden*. Graz: Literaturverlag Droschl, 2022.

6.2 Sekundärliteratur

6.2.1 Zum Werk Kathrin Rögglas

Allkemper, Alo. „Kathrin Röggla: ‚stottern'". *Poetologisch-poetische Interventionen: Gegenwartsliteratur schreiben*. Hg. Alo Allkemper, München: Wilhelm Fink Verlag, 2012. 417–430.

Balint, Iuditha et. al. (Hg.). *Kathrin Röggla*. München: edition text+kritik, 2017.

Bähr, Christine. „Atemlos. Arbeit und Zeit in Kathrin Rögglas *wir schlafen nicht*". *Ökonomie und Theater der Gegenwart: Ästhetik, Produktion, Institution*. Hg. Franziska Schlößler und Christine Bähr. Bielefeld: transcript verlag, 2009. 225–244. (Hg.) Balint, Iuditha et. al. *Kathrin Röggla*. München: edition text+kritik, 2017.

Canaris, Johanna. „Kathrin Rögglas diskursiver Realismus" *Gegenwartsliteratur: ein germanistisches Jahrbuch* 16 (2017). 233–255.

Clarke, David, „The Capitalist Uncanny in Kathrin Röggla's *wir schlafen nicht*: Ghosts in the Machine". *Angermion: Yearbook for Anglo-German Literary Criticism, Intellectual History and Cultural Transfers / Jahrbuch für britisch-deutsche Kulturbeziehungen* 4 (2011). 147–163.

Coppola, Rosa. „‚alles lässt sich zweimal erzählen'. Zu Kathrin Rögglas Poetik des ‚rückwärts'". *Europe's Crises and Cultural Resources of Resilience: Conceptual Explorations and Literary Negotiations*. Hg. Michael Basseler et al. Trier: WVT, 2020. 199–212.

Coppola, Rosa. „Vor dem Gespenst. Anmerkungen zur Sendermannfigur in Kathrin Rögglas *Irres Wetter* (2000)". *Gespenstischer Realismus. Texte von und zu Kathrin Röggla*. Hg. Uta Degner und Christa Gürtler. Wien: Sonderzahl, 2022a. 181–196.

Coppola, Rosa. „Hörreste, Phonographie, Polyphonie. Akustische Dispositive der Gesellschaftskritik in Kathrin Rögglas Prosawerk". *Wiener Digitale Revue* 5 (2022b).

Degner, Uta, Gürtler, Christa (Hg.). *Gespenstischer Realismus. Texte von und zu Kathrin Röggla*. Wien: Sonderzahl 2022.

Feiereisen, Florian, „Eternal Interns: Kathrin Röggla's Literary Treatment of Gendered Capitalism". *Studies in 20th & 21st Century Literature* 35 (1), 2011;

Glasenapp, Nicolai. „Körper-Raum-Relationen. Status und Dynamik in Prosatexten Kathrin Rögglas". *Kathrin Röggla*. Hg. Iuditha Balint et al. München: edition text+kritik, 2017. 107–123.

Gröbel, Ute. „'short-sleeping, quick-eating and all that stuff'. Kathrin Rögglas novel *we never sleep* and Deconstructive Documentarism". *Fictions/Realities: New forms and interactions*. Hg. Jörg von Brincken et al. München: Peter Lang Verlag, 2011. 101–116.

Gröschner, Annett. „Im Moment durchkreuze ich den Feldbegriff mit meiner Arbeit – Kathrin Röggla im Gespräch mit Annett Gröschner". *Poetik des Faktischen*. Hg. Annett Gröschner und Stephan Porombka. Essen: Klartext Verlag, 2009. 165–188.

Gruber, Carola. „‚Ein „haufen am authetizität?' Kathrin Rögglas *really ground zero*". *Zeitwende: österreichische Literatur seit dem Millenium 2000–2010*. Hg. Michael Boehringer und Susanne Hochreiter. Wien: praesens verlag, 2011. 323–337.

Gürtler, Christa. „Kathrin Röggla auf der Suche nach den Gespenstern der Gegenwart". *Gespenstischer Realismus. Texte von und zu Kathrin Röggla*. Hg. Uta Degner und Christa Gürtler Wien: Sonderzahl, 2022. 159–180.

Hnlica, Ingrid. „‚im berühmten eigenen ton'. Kathrin Rögglas und Elfriede Jelineks Bearbeitungen der Kampusch-Entführung". *Kathrin Röggla*. Hg. Iuditha Balint et al. München: edition text+kritik, 2017. 41–53.

Höppner, Stefan. „Geheimamerika — Daheim-Amerika? Zu Kathrin Rögglas USA Bild in *really ground zero* und *fake reports*." *Kathrin Röggla*. Hg. Iuditha Balint et al. München: edition text+kritik, 2017. 319–338.

Ivanovic, Christine, „Bewegliche Katastrophe, stagnierende Bilder. Mediale Verschiebungen in Kathrin Rögglas *really ground zero*". *Kultur & Gespenster* 2 (2006). 108–117.

Kammer, Stephan, Krauthausen, Karin. „Für einen strukturalen Realismus. Einleitung". *Make in Real! Für einen strukturalen Realismus*. Hg. Stephan Kammer und Karin Krauthausen. Zürich: diaphanes, 2020. 7–80.

Kormann, Eva. „Jelineks Tochter und das Medienspiel. Zu Kathrin Rögglas *wir schlafen wir nicht*". *Zwischen Inszenierung und Botschaft: zur Literatur deutschsprachiger Autorinnen ab Ende des 20. Jahrhunderts*. Hg. Ilse Nagelschmidt et al. Berlin: Franck & Timme Verlag, 2006. 229–245.

Kormann, Eva. „Risiko Schreiben in der flüchtigen Moderne: Kathrin Rögglas Variante einer *littérature engagée*". *Gegenwartsliteratur: ein germanistisches Jahrbuch* 14 (2015). 171–195.

Kormann, Eva. „Wer spricht? Zur ‚wackeligen' Sprechposition bei Kathrin Röggla". *Kathrin Röggla*. Hg. Iuditha Balint et al. München: edition text+kritik, 2017. 124–142.

Krauthausen, Karin. „Gespräche mit Untoten. Das konjunktivische Interview in Kathrin Rögglas Roman *wir schlafen nicht*", *Kultur und Gespenster* 2 (2006). 118–135.

Krauthausen, Karin. „Wette auf die Wirklichkeit. Erzählkalkül in *die ansprechbare* und *Der Wiedereintritt in die Geschichte I* von Kathrin Röggla". *Literatur im Ausnahmezustand. Beiträge zum Werk Kathrin Rögglas*. Hg. Friedhelm Marx und Julia Schöll. Würzburg: Königshausen & Neumann, 2019. 157–184.

Krauthausen, Karin. „Die Dringlichkeit der Form. Zu Rögglas strukturalem Realismus". *Gespenstischer Realismus. Texte von und zu Kathrin Röggla*. Hg. Uta Degner und Christa Gürtler Wien: Sonderzahl, 2022. 81–102.

Kremer, Christian. *Milieu und Performativität. Deutsche Gegenwartsprosa von John von Düfferl, Georg M. Oswald und Kathrin Röggla*. Marburg: Tectum Verlag, 2008.

Lewandowski, Sonja. „Wi(e)der eine Grammatik der Ausnahme. Kathrin Rögglas *die alarmbereiten*." *Kathrin Röggla*. Hg. Iuditha Balint et al. München: edition text+kritik, 2017. 54–78.

Martin, Elaine. „New Economy zombies: Kathrin Röggla's *wir schlafen nicht*". *German Monitor* 76 (2013). 131–148.

Marx, Friedhelm, Scholl Julia (Hg.). *Literatur im Ausnahmezustand. Beiträge zum Werk Kathrin Rögglas*. Würzburg: Königshausen & Neumann, 2019.

Meyer, Franziska. „‚und dabei heißt es aufbruchstimmung'. Das Verschwinden einer Metropolen in ihren Texten". *German Monitor: Pushing at the Boundaries: Approaches to Contemporary German Women Writers from Karen Duve to Jenny Erpenbeck* 64 (2006). 167–188.

Michler, Werner. „‚oder gar die Gattungsfrage noch?' Gattungsarbeit in Kathrin Rögglas *Normalverdiener*". *Gespenstischer Realismus. Texte von und zu Kathrin Röggla*. Hg. Uta Degner und Christa Gürtler. Wien: Sonderzahl, 2022. 103–120.

Morgenroth, Claas. *Erinnerungspolitik und Gegenwartliteratur*. Berlin: Schmidt Verlag, 2014.

Moser, Natalie. „Echtzeit-Fiktion. Zur Funktion des Protokolls und der Übung in Kathrin Rögglas *die zuseher* (2010)". *Kathrin Röggla*. Hg. Iuditha Balint et al. München: edition text+kritik, 2017. 161–180.

Navratil, Michael. *Kontrafaktik der Gegenwart. Politisches Schreiben als Realitätsvariation bei Christian Kracht, Kathrin Röggla, Juli Zeh und Leif Randt*. Berlin/Boston: De Gruyter, 2022.

Nusser, Tanja, „'Realismus beginnt eigentlich immer, und das von allen Seiten, er ist eine permanente Aufforderung'. Über Kathrin Rögglas Texte". *Neue Realismen in der Gegenwartsliteratur*. Hg. Rolf Parr und Søren R. Fauth. Padeborn: Wilhelm Fink Verlag, 2016. 213–225.

Palberg, Kyra. „'short sleeping, quick eating' — Produktivität und Sprechen bei Kathrin Röggla". *Kathrin Röggla*. Hg. Iuditha Balint et al. München: edition text+kritik, 2017. 278–297.

Parr, Rolf. „Das Spiel mit Texten, Fotos und Realismus-Effekten in Kathrin Rögglas *really ground zero*". *Kathrin Röggla*. Hg. Iuditha Balint et al. München: edition text+kritik, 2017. 181–195.

Parr, Rolf. „Souveränitäts- und Realismusgewinne. Kathrin Röggla mit Carl Schmitt oder normalismustheoretisch lesen?". *Literatur im Ausnahmezustand. Beiträge zum Werk Kathrin Rögglas*. Hg. Friedhelm Marx und Julia Schöll. Würzburg: Königshausen & Neumann, 2019. 251–264.

Paß, Manuel. „Rögglas Gespenster. Das ‚Gespenstische' als Reflexionsfigur in Kathrin Rögglas *Normalverdiener*". *Literatur im Ausnahmezustand. Beiträge zum Werk Kathrin Rögglas*. Hg. Friedhelm Marx und Julia Schöll. Würzburg: Königshausen & Neumann, 2019. 123–140.

Pontzen, Alexandra. „Unheimlich vertraut. Kapitalismuskritik und Ressentimentpoetik in Kathrin Rögglas *Nachtsendung. Unheimliche Geschichten*". *Literatur im Ausnahmezustand. Beiträge zum Werk Kathrin Rögglas*. Hg. Friedhelm Marx und Julia Schöll. Würzburg: Königshausen & Neumann, 2019. 141–156.

Rutka, Anna. „Zeitgenössische Gesellschaft und ihre Ängste. Zur sprachlichen Re-Inszenierung des Katastrophischen in Kathrin Rögglas Prosaband *die alarmbereiten*". *Kategorien und Konzepte* 139 (2014). 99–112

Schaffner, Anna Katharina. „'Catastrophe Sociology' and the Metaphors We Live By: On Kathrin Röggla's *wir schlafen nicht*". *The Modern Language Review* 112.1 (2017). 205–222.

Schininà, Alessandra. „A little Alien in New York: *really ground zero* di Kathrin Röggla tra cronaca e realtà". *Immagini e identità urbane tra modernità e postmodernità*. Hg. Alessandra Schininà. Roma: Artemide, 2018. 109–118.

Schininà, Alessandra. „Alienated and Evanescent Identities in the Contemporary World of Austrian Author Kathrin Röggla". *Exploring Identity in Literature and Life Stories: The Elusive Self*. Hg. Guri E. Batsad et al. Newcastle: Cambridge Scholar Publishing, 2019. 228–240.

Schöll, Julia. „Dead or alive. Räume des Unheimlichen bei Kathrin Röggla". *Literatur im Ausnahmezustand. Beiträge zum Werk Kathrin Rögglas*. Hg. Friedhelm Marx und Julia Schöll. Würzburg: Königshausen & Neumann, 2019. 107–122.

Sieg, Christian. „Latenzzeiten und Diskursgewitter. Die Abwesenheit der Katastrophe und die Präsenz des Risikos in Kathrin Rögglas *die alarmbereiten*". *Kathrin Röggla*. Hg. Iuditha Balint et al. München: edition text+kritik, 2017. 236–255.

Szczepaniak, Monika. „Elfriede Jelinek und Kathrin Röggla ‚in Mediengewittern'". *Neue Stimmen aus Österreich: 11 Einblicke in die Literatur der Jahrtausendwende*. Hg. Joanna Drynda und Martin Wimmer. Frankfurt a. M.: Peter Lang Verlag, 2013. 25–35.

Szczepaniak, Monika. „Rögglas unheimliche Nicht-Orte". *Gespenstischer Realismus. Texte von und zu Kathrin Röggla*. Hg. Uta Degner und Christa Gürtler. Wien: Sonderzahl, 2022. 197–216.

Vilar, Maria Loreto. „Decoding images: Top-dog-jobs für Frauen in Kathrin Rögglas *wir schlafen nicht*". *Die gläserne Decke: Fakt oder Fiktion? Eine literarische Spurensuche in deutschsprachigen Werken von Autorinnen*. Hg. Dolores Sabaté Planes und Marion Schulz. Frankfurt a. M.: INTERLIT, 2010. 129–142

Vilar, Maria Loreto. „Gegen die mediale Krisendramaturgie. Zur Performativität des Katastrophischen im Theater von Hilling, Röggla und Jelinek". *Literatur als Performance: literaturwissenschaftliche*

Studien zum Thema Performance. Hg. Ana R. Calero Valera. Würzburg: Königshausen & Neumann, 2013. 109–123

von Bernstoff, Wiebke. „Die Macht der Bilder. Terror statt Toleranz. Theaterstücke von Kathrin Röggla, Elfriede Jelinek, Aly Jalaly". *Aufgeklärte Zeiten? Religiöse Toleranz und Literatur.* Hg. Romana Weierhausen. Berlin: Erich Schmidt Verlag, 2011. 157–174.

Wojno-Owczarska, Ewa. „Der Typus der ‚modernen Frau' in Kathrin Rögglas Drama *wir schlafen nicht*". *Studia niemcoznawcze/Studien zur Deutschkunde* 33 (2006). 391–408.

Wojno-Owczarska, Ewa. „Beziehungen zwischen Literatur und Film am Beispiel des Schaffens von Kathrin Röggla". *Zeitschrift des Verbandes polnischer Germanisten* 2 (2013). 349–368.

Wojno-Owczarska, Ewa. „Zu Kathrin Rögglas Kritik am Rechtspopulismus". *Gespenstischer Realismus. Texte von und zu Kathrin Röggla.* Hg. Uta Degner und Christa Gürtler. Wien: Sonderzahl, 2022. 53–76.

6.2.2 Zu den Vorbilder Kathrin Rögglas

6.2.2.1 Von und zu Elfriede Jelinek, Ernst Jandl und der Sprachskepsis

Gutjahr, Ortrud. „Im Echoraum der Stimmen. Elfriede Jelineks ‚Ulrike Maria Stuart'". *text und kritik* 117 (2007). 19–31.

Haag, Ingrid und Wiecha, Eduard. „Konversation auf Abwegen – zu Ernst Jandls Bühnensatire *Die Humanisten*". *Moderne österreichische Literatur* 15/1 (1982). 115–126.

Hoffman, Yasmin. *Elfriede Jelinek. Sprach- und Kulturkritik im Erzählwerk*, Opladen/Wiesbaden: Westdeutscher Verlag, 1999.

Jandl, Ernst. *laut und luise*. Olten: Walter, 1966.

Jandl, Ernst. „Voraussetzungen Beispiele und Ziele einer poetischen Arbeitsweise". *Protokolle* 70/2 (1970a).

Jandl, Ernst. *der künstliche baum*. Darmstadt/Neuwied: Luchterhand, [1970b] 2008.

Jandl, Ernst. *Aus der Fremde. Sprechoper in 7 Szenen*. Darmstadt/Neuwied: Luchterhand, 1980. Jandl, Ernst. *Das Öffnen und Schließen des Mundes. Frankfurter Poetikvorlesung*. Darmstadt/Neuwied Luchterhand, 1985.

Jelinek, Elfriede. *Die Kinder der Toten*. Reinbeck bei Hamburg: Rowohlt Verlag, 1995.

Jelinek, Elfriede. *Sinn egal, Körper zwecklos*. 1997. https://original.elfriedejelinek.com/. Personalseite (21.05.2024)

Jelinek, Elfriede. *Winterreise*, Reinbeck bei Hamburg: Rowohlt Verlag, 2011.

Löffler, Siegrid. „Die Masken der Elfriede Jelinek". *text und kritik* 117 (2007). 3–15.

Musil, Robert. *Gesammelte Werke in Einzelausgabe*. Hg. Adolf Frisé. Hamburg: Rowohlt, 1957.

Schmidt-Dengler, Wendelin. „Geschichten gegen die Geschichte. Gibt es das Österreichische in der österreichischen Literatur?". *Modern Austrian Literature* 17/3 (1984). 149–157.

Hofmannsthal, Hugo von. „Ein Brief". *Hugo von Hofmannsthal: Sämtliche Werke.* XXXI. Hg. Ellen Ritter. Frankfurt am M.: Fischer, 1991. 45–55.

Wilke, Sabine. *Dialektik und Geschlecht: feministische Schreibpraxis in der Gegenwartsliteratur.* Tübingen: Stauffenburg Verlag, 1996.

Wittgenstein, Ludwig. *Philosophische Untersuchungen*. Frankfurt a. M. Suhrkamp, 1971 [1957].

Wittgenstein, Ludwig. *Tractatus logico-philosophicus*, Frankfurt a. M. Suhrkamp 1999 [1921].

6.2.2.2 Von und zu Hubert Fichte

Bandel, Jan Frederik. „Das fünfte und das sechste Ohr". *Kultur und Gespenster* 2 (2006). 72–81.
Bekes, Peter. „Poetische Erfahrungen des Fremden. Fichtes Romane vor dem Hintergrund der Romanpoetik in den sechziger und siebziger Jahren" *text + kritik* 72 (1981). 86–101.
Dischner, Gisela. „Das poetische Auge des Ethnographen". *text + kritik* 72 (1981). 30–47.
Fichte, Hubert. *Die Palette*. Frankfurt a.M.: Fischer Verlag, 1968.
Fichte, Hubert. „Ketzerischen Bemerkungen für eine neue Wissenschaft vom Menschen". *Petersilie. Die afroamerikanische Religionen. Santo Domingo, Venezuela, Miami, Grenada.* Frankfurt a. M.: Fischer Verlag 1980. 359–365.
Fichte, Hubert. *Versuch über die Pubertät*. Frankfurt a.M.: Fischer Verlag, 1982 [1974].
Fichte, Hubert. *Der Kleine Hauptbahnhof oder Lob des Strichs*. Frankfurt a.M.: Fischer Verlag, 1988.
Fichte, Hubert. *Forschungsbericht*. Frankfurt a. M.: Fischer Verlag, 1989.
Heinrichs, Hans-Jürgen. „Dichtung und Ethnologie". *text + kritik* 72 (1981). 48–61.
Krauthausen Karin. „Fiktionen der Rede. Fichtes Annäherung an Afrika". *Hubert Fichtes Medien*. Hg. Stephan Kammer und Karin Krauthausen. Zürich/Berlin: diaphanes, 2014. 163–189.
Krauthausen Karin. „Messenger Service: Hubert Fichte Writes History". *Colloquia Germanica* 55 (3–4) 2023. 239–266.
Rieger, Michael. *Die Welt durch sich hindurch lassen – Hubert Fichtes Werk als Medium ästhetischer Erkenntnis*. Frankfurt a.M.: Peter Lang Verlag, 2009.
Trzaskalik, Tim. „Geklebte, gelebte Blätter. Notizen zur Gentre des Interviews bei Hubert Fichte". *Kultur und Gespenster* 2 (2006). 82–97.
Wangenheim, Wolfgang von. „Zum Stil Hubert Fichtes". *text + kritik* 72 (1981). 23–29.
Winkler, Willi. *Lokstedt war nicht meine Welt,* Süddeutsche Zeitung 17.08. 2016. https://www.sueddeutsche.de/kultur/deutsche-literatur-lokstedt-war-nicht-meine-welt-1.3124805 (21.05.2024).
Wischenbart, Rüdiger. „,Ich schreibe, was mir die Wahrheit zu sein scheint'. Ein Gespräch mit Hubert Fichte". *text + kritik* 72 (1981). 67–85.

6.2.2.3 Von und zu Alexander Kluge

Cheon, Hyun. *Intermedialität von Text und Bild bei Alexander Kluge*. Würzburg: Königshausen & Neumann, 2007.
Heißenbüttel, Helmut. „Der Text ist die Wahrheit". *text + kritik* 85–86. 2–8.
Kluge, Alexander und Negt, Oskar. *Geschichte und Eigensinn*. Frankfurt. M.: Suhrkamp Verlag [1981] 1993.
Kluge, Alexander und Negt, Oskar. *Maßverhältnisse der Politischen*. Frankfurt. M.: Suhrkamp Verlag 1992.
Kluge, Alexander und Negt, Oskar. *Öffentlichkeit und Erfahrung – Zur Organisationsanalyse von bürgerlicher und proletarischer Öffentlichkeit*. Frankfurt a. M.: Suhrkamp Verlag 1972.
Kluge, Alexander et al. *Industrialisierung des Bewusstseins. Eine kritische Auseinandersetzung mit den neuen Medien*. München: Piper Verlag, 1985.
Kluge, Alexander. *Chronik der Gefühle*. Frankfurt a. M.: Suhrkamp Verlag, 2000.
Kluge, Alexander. *Die Kunst, Unterschiede zu machen*. Frankfurt a. M.: Suhrkamp Verlag, 2003.
Kluge, Alexander. *Die Macht der Gefühle*. Frankfurt a. M.: Suhrkamp Verlag 1984.
Kluge, Alexander. *Gelegensarbeit einer Sklavin – Zur realistischen Methode*. Frankfurt a.M.: Suhrkamp Verlag, 1975.
Kluge, Alexander. *Lebensläufe*. Frankfurt a. M.: Suhrkamp Verlag, 1962.

Kluge, Alexander. *Schlachtbeschreibung*. Frankfurt a.M.: Suhrkamp Verlag, 1968.
Kluge, Alexander. *Tür an Tür mit einem anderen Leben*. Frankfurt a. M.: Suhrkamp Verlag, 2006.
Schulte, Christian. *Fernsehen des Autors. Die Kulturmagazine der DCDP*. 2002. https://www.kluge-alexander.de/zur-person/texte-ueber/details/artikel/fernsehen-der-autoren-die-kulturmagazine-der-dctp.html (21.05.2024)
Sombroek Alexander. *Eine Poetik des Dazwischen. Intermedialität und Intertextualität bei Alexander Kluge*. Bielefeld: transcript, 2005.

6.2.3 Theorie und Methode

Bachtin, Michail. *Sprechgattungen*. Berlin: Matthes & Seitz Berlin.
Barthes, Roland. „Lust/Schrift/Lektüre. Jean Ristat, *Les Lettres françaises*, 9. Februar 1972". *Die Körnung der Stimme: Interviews 1962–1980*. Frankfurt a. M.: Suhrkamp, 2002. 173–191.
Beck, Ulrich. *Risikogesellschaft*. Frankfurt a.M.: Suhrkamp, 1986.
Beck, Ulrich. *Weltrisikogesellschaft. Auf der Suche nach einer verlorenen Sicherheit*. Frankfurt a.M.: Suhrkamp, 2008.
Bröckling, Ulrich. *Das unternehmerische Selbst. Soziologie einer Subjektivierungsform*. Frankfurt a. M.: Suhrkamp, 2013.
Burns, Elizabeth. *Theatricality. A Study in Convention in Theatre and Every-Day Life*. London: Prentice Hall Press, 1972.
Craig, Edward Gordon, *Die Kunst des Theaters*. Berlin: gerhardt verlag, 1969.
Debord, Guy. *Die Gesellschaft des Spektakles*. Berlin: Tiamat 2006.
Deleuze, Gilles und Guattari, Félix. *Tausend Plateaus. Kapitalismus und Schizophrenie*. Berlin: Merve, 1992 [1982].
Deleuze, Gilles. *Kritik und Klinik*. Frankfurt a. M.: Suhrkamp, 2015 [1993].
Ernst, Thomas. *Literatur und Subversion*. Bielefeld: transcript Verlag, 2013.
Fischer-Lichte, Erika. „Grenzgänge und Tauschhandel. Auf dem Wege zu einer performativen Kultur". *Performanz. Zwischen Sprachphilosophie und Kulturwissenschaften*. Hg. Uwe Wirth. Frankfurt a. M.: Suhrkamp 2002. 277–300.
Fischer-Lichte, Erika. *Ästhetik des Performativen*. Frankfurt a.M.: Suhrkamp, 2004.
Fischer-Lichte, Erika. „Theatralität und Inszenierung". *Inszenierung von Authentizität*. Hg. Erika Fischer-Lichte et al. Tübingen/Basel: Francke Verlag, 2007. 9–30.
Flusser, Vilém. *Kommunikologie*. Frankfurt a. M.: Fischer Verlag 2007 [1998].
Freud, Sigmund. „Das Unheimliche". *Gesammelte Werke*, Bd. I. Altenmünster: Jazzybee Verlag 2015. 150–176.
Jäger, Siegfried. „Zu Gebrauch und Leistung des Konjunktiv in der deutschen Sprache der Gegenwart". *Colloquia Germanica* 4 (1970). 268–288.
Kittler, Friedrich. *Philosophien der Literatur. Berliner Vorlesung 2002*. Berlin: Merve, 2013.
Koolhaas, Rem. *The Generic City*. New York: The Monacelli Press, 1995.
Koolhaas, Rem. „junk-space". *Obsolescence* 100 (2002). 175–190.
Krämer, Sybille. „Sprache – Stimme — Schrift: Sieben Gedanken über Performativität als Medialität". *Performanz. Zwischen Sprachphilosophie und Kulturwissenschaften*. Hg. Uwe Wirth. Frankfurt a. M.: Suhrkamp 2002. 323–346.
Le Corbusier. *Ausblick auf eine Architektur.*, Gütersloh: Bertelsman Fachverlag, 2001 [1921].
Milner, Jean-Claude. *Le périple structural. Figures et paradigme*. Paris: Seuil, 2002.

Neumann, Gerhard. „Einleitung". *Szenographien. Theatralität als Kategorie der Literaturwissenschaft*. Hg. Gerhard Neumann et al. Freiburg im Breisgau: Rombach Litterae, 2000. 11–34.

Niehaus, Michael und Schmidt-Hannisa, Hans-Walter. „Textsorte Protokoll. Ein Aufriß". *Das Protokoll. Kulturelle Funktionen einer Textsorte*. Hg. Michael Niehaus und Hans-Walter Schmidt-Hannisa. Frankfurt a.M.: Suhrkamp, 2005. 7–26.

Rajewsky, Irina. *Intermedialität*. Tübingen/Basel: Francke Verlag 2002.

Schnell, Dieter. *Le Corbusiers Wohnmaschine*. 2007. http://bauforschungonline.ch/aufsatz/le-corbusiers-wohnmaschine.html [25.06.2024].

Wildgruber, Gerald. „Die Instanz der Szene im Denken der Sprache". *Szenographien. Theatralität als Kategorie der Literaturwissenschaft*. Hg. Gerhard Neumann et al. Freiburg im Breisgau: Rombach Litterae, 2000. 35–64.

Wirth, Uwe. „Der Performanzbegriff im Spannungsfeld von Illokution, Iteration und Indexikalität". *Performanz. Zwischen Sprachphilosophie und Kulturwissenschaften*. Hg. Uwe Wirth. Frankfurt a. M.: Suhrkamp 2002. 9–62.

Danksagung

Dieses Buch war vor einigen Jahren und diversen Bearbeitungen meine italienischsprachige Dissertation, die ich 2020 an der Universität „L'Orientale" Neapel verteidigt habe. Daher mochte ich mich zuerst bei Valentina Di Rosa bedanken, die diese Arbeit sorgfältig und äußerst kritisch betreut hat. Uta Degner und Matteo Galli danke ich auch sehr herzlich für ihre wertvolle Begutachtung und für das Schaffen anregender Forschungsumfelder in Salzburg und Ferrara. Entscheidend für die Ausarbeitung meiner These war der DAAD-Forschungsaufenthalt an der FU Berlin, wo Matthias Warstat mich als Gastwissenschaftlerin empfangen hat. Zwischen Berlin und Salzburg hatte ich die Gelegenheit, mit Karin Krauthausen in Kontakt zu treten, der ich für die interessanten Gespräche danke. Das alles ist auch dem Einfluss zu verdanken, den Giusi Zanasi auf mein Germanistikstudium hatte.

Für die konzeptuellen Anregungen, die sprachlichen Verbesserungen und für die Geduld, meine Hypothesen immer angehört zu haben, danke ich Beatrice Occhini, Daniela Allocca, Micol Vicidomini, Fabrizio Maria Spinelli, Helene Kraus, Andreas Dittrich, Tina Werner und Marilisa Reisert.

Schließlich möchte ich meiner Familie, Angelo Annarita e Vincenzo, zusammen mit Andrea Bolognino, Vicky Solli, Ilaria Garzillo, Giovanni Passariello, Antonio Arte, Luca Ronchetti, Marzia Romano, Enzo Fallarino, Andrea Magliocchi, Marco Michele Acquafredda, Andrea Avellino, Magda Bellé, Valerio Middione, Rossella Della Corte, Anna Gesualdi, Giovanni Trono, Loretta Mesiti und Luigi Giuliani für alles danken, das nur dem Anschein nach nichts mit der Forschung zu tun hat.

Register

Abstraktion 1, 7–8, 14–16, 37, 121–123, 131
Akustik 34–35, 56, 83

Dialog 3, 20, 73–75, 104–106, 112, 122, 133
– dialogisches 14, 28–30, 35, 71–72, 99, 106, 133
Dokumentarismus 4, 18–19
– dokumentarisch 8–9, 31–40, 46, 65, 67, 71, 82–85, 92, 95–96, 101–103, 131

Engagement 2, 8, 18, 22, 24, 37–38, 87, 111–112
Entmaterialisierung 14–15, 18, 22–23, 66, 77, 108, 132, 134
Ethnopoesie 1, 71
– ethnopoetisch 5, 33–34, 68, 82, 88, 90, 92–93

Feldforschung 2, 18, 65, 71, 86

Gattung 2, 8, 18, 32
– Sprechgattung 12–13, 22, 89, 122
– Genre 2, 8, 13, 18, 88–90, 109, 115
Gesellschaftskritik 26–27, 37, 85, 93
Globalisierung 4, 19, 56–57, 64, 132

Ideologie 8, 9, 11, 19–20, 66, 80, 98, 110
Inszenierung 9–12, 14, 19, 33, 40, 47–48, 60, 98

Katastrophe 8, 51, 76, 80–86, 88, 96–97, 109, 113–124, 125–128
Kommunikation 3, 6–7, 12–13, 20, 73–79, 90–92, 101, 105–112, 123–127, 131
Körper(lichkeit) 8–11, 20–23, 30, 43–53, 62–63, 66–68, 76–77, 82, 88, 96–99, 106–109, 121, 123, 127, 132–134

Leitmotiv 11, 30, 44, 45, 69, 79, 92–94, 102–104, 111, 117, 127, 133–134

Medialisierung 36, 39, 42, 46, 48, 84, 90
Mündlichkeit 3, 11, 19, 31, 34–35
– mündlich 13, 3–35, 69, 71, 123, 131

Performativität 6, 25, 31, 32
– performativ 3, 6, 8, 10, 14, 22, 25, 31, 35, 70, 87, 98, 118, 131, 134
Performanz 6, 8, 10, 14, 64

Realismus 4–8, 11, 13, 15–16, 25, 30, 36–37, 54, 56, 94, 96, 112, 127, 131–132
Reportage 19–21, 32, 65–66, 70, 83–85, 87–88, 94–95, 100, 102

Stimme(n) 7, 10, 13, 20, 22, 31, 33–35, 39, 42, 44, 57, 64, 68–71, 76, 80, 83, 86, 88, 94, 97, 99–103, 107–108, 111–114, 120–124, 134
Stolpern 62, 63, 68, 80
Stottern 7, 55, 62, 97
Subversion 22, 47, 77, 92
Szeno-Graphie 10, 16, 23, 60, 80, 83, 131–133
– Szene 9–10, 23, 27–28, 34, 40, 42, 46, 47, 55, 58, 61, 65, 86–87, 90, 101, 104–105, 126, 131
– Szenerie 53, 61
– Szenarium 19, 55, 66, 73, 10, 124

Wahrnehmung 2–5, 9–11, 24, 36, 41, 49, 53, 57, 68, 70, 74, 83, 88–90, 96, 99, 101, 105–106, 109, 115, 117–118, 128–129

www.ingramcontent.com/pod-product-compliance
Lightning Source LLC
Chambersburg PA
CBHW050909300426
44111CB00010B/1452